Ecce Romani

A Latin Reading Program
Revised Edition

5

Public Life and Private Lives

Longman

Ecce Romani Student's Book 5 Public Life and Private Lives

First Printing 1986
5 4 3 2 1

ISBN 0-582-36668-2

Cover illustration by Judy Hans Price. Photo research by Katherine Rangoon.

This edition of *Ecce Romani* is based on *Ecce Romani: A Latin Reading Course*, originally prepared by The Scottish Classics Group © copyright The Scottish Classics Group 1971, 1982, and published in the United Kingdom by Oliver and Boyd, a Division of Longman Group. This edition has been prepared by a team of American and Canadian educators:

Authors: Professor Carol Esler, The College of William and Mary, Williamsburg, VA
Ronald Palma, Holland Hall School, Tulsa, Oklahoma
Coordinator: Professor Gilbert Lawall, University of Massachusetts, Amherst, Massachusetts
Consultants: Professor Rudolph Masciantonio, Philadelphia Public Schools, Pennsylvania
Professor Edward Barnes, C. W. Jeffreys Secondary School, Downsview, Ontario
Shirley Lowe, Wayland Public Schools, Wayland, Massachusetts

Longman Inc.
95 Church Street
White Plains, N.Y. 10601

Associated companies:
Longman Group Ltd., London
Longman Cheshire Pty., Melbourne
Longman Paul Pty., Auckland
Copp Clark Pitman, Toronto
Pitman Publishing Inc., New York

Printed in the U.S.A.

CONTENTS

PART III: Warfare in the Late Republic 55

PART IV: Public Life and Imperial Administration in the Early Empire 81

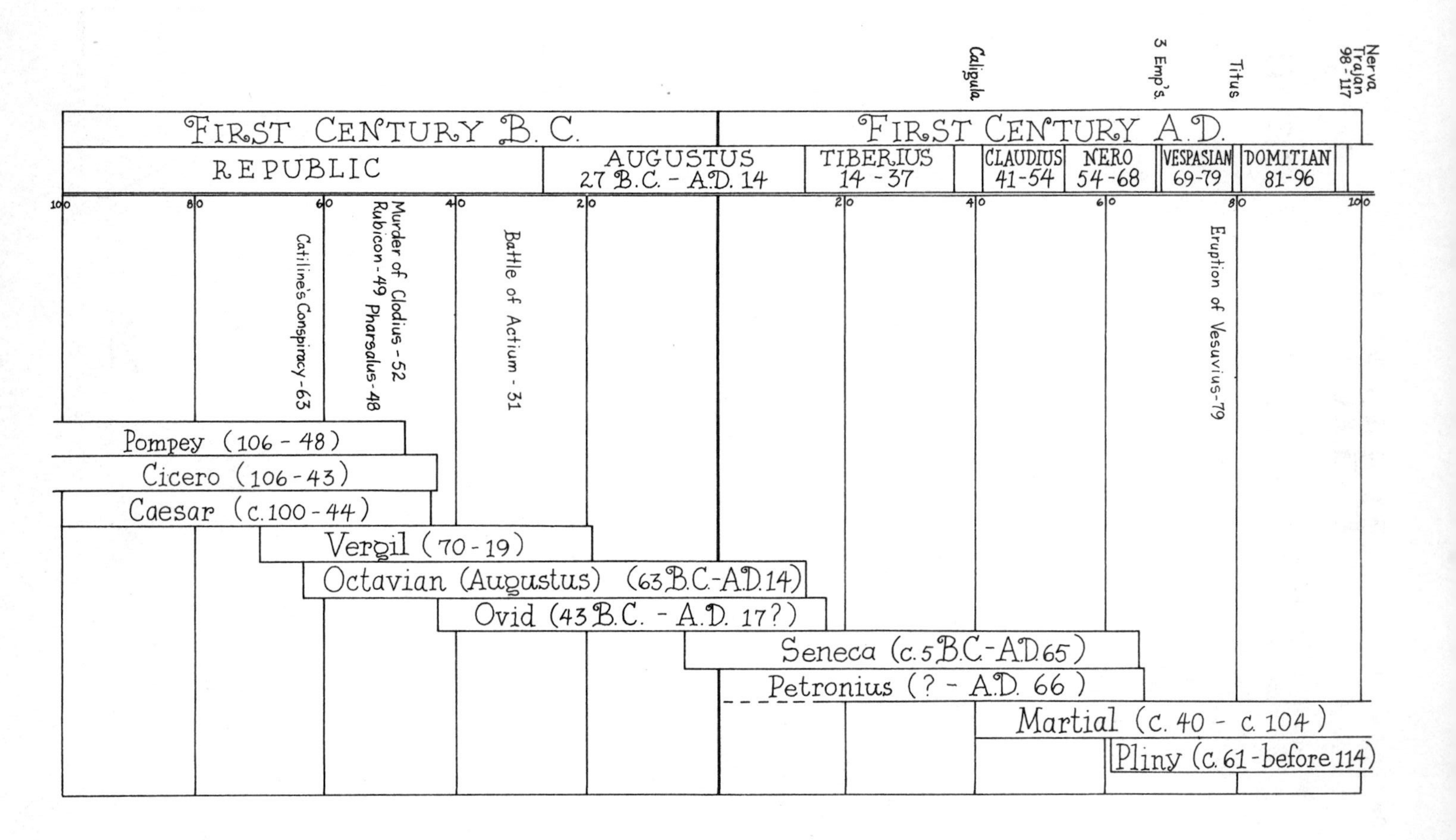

Caligula
3 Emp's.
Titus
Nerva
Trajan
98 - 117
FIRST CENTURY B.C.
FIRST CENTURY A.D.
REPUBLIC
AUGUSTUS 27 B.C. - A.D. 14
TIBERIUS 14 - 37
CLAUDIUS 41-54
NERO 54-68
VESPASIAN 69-79
DOMITIAN 81-96
100
80
60
40
20
20
40
60
80
100
Catiline's Conspiracy - 63
Murder of Clodius - 52
Rubicon - 49 Pharsalus - 48
Battle of Actium - 31
Eruption of Vesuvius-79
Pompey (106 - 48)
Cicero (106 - 43)
Caesar (c. 100 - 44)
Vergil (70 - 19)
Octavian (Augustus) (63 B.C.-A.D. 14)
Ovid (43 B.C. - A.D. 17?)
Seneca (c. 5 B.C.-A.D. 65)
Petronius (? - A.D. 66)
Martial (c. 40 - c. 104)
Pliny (c. 61 - before 114)

PART I
A Satirist's View of Life in the Early Empire

The readings for Chapters 54–56 are taken from a comic novel of the first century a.d. known as the *Satyricon*. Its author is usually identified with the C. Petronius described by Tacitus as a man who held a privileged but dangerous position as unofficial "Arbiter of Elegance" at the court of Nero. Yet as governor of Bithynia, and later consul, he showed himself a capable and energetic administrator. Eventually he aroused Nero's suspicions and died by suicide (a form of imperial execution), surrounded by friends who comforted him "not with philosophical doctrines but frivolous songs and light verse."

The longest and most famous of the surviving fragments of the *Satyricon* is the *Cena Trimalchionis* (*Banquet of Trimalchio*). It describes an elaborate dinner party given by the ex-slave and self-made millionaire Trimalchio. An army of slaves serves a vast array of dishes, most of them disguised as something other than what they are: glowing "coals" made of sliced damsons and pomegranates, a roast boar with sausages for entrails, a sow with pastry "piglets." From time to time the guests are entertained by musicians, actors, or singing waiters of various degrees of awfulness. But some of the most interesting and amusing passages of the *Cena* are those in which Petronius lets us eavesdrop on the conversations of Trimalchio and his guests. These conversations, from which our selections are taken, are unique in Latin literature for the vividness with which they portray the habits of speech and thought of ordinary people in the ancient Roman world.

The readings for this and the next chapter consist of monologues by two of Trimalchio's freedmen guests. Both are concerned with local politics, its relationship to the high cost of living, and the "bread and circuses" that were the Roman politician's key to popularity and re-election. Their philosophy is echoed by the Pompeian campaign posters shown below.

"SERVA ME, SERVABO TE" *"You take care of me, I'll take care of you."*

Sabīnum aed(īlem), Procule, fac et ille tē faciet. *Elect Sabinus aedile, Proculus, and he'll elect you.*

Popidium Secundum aed(īlem), Rufīne, favē et ille tē faciet. *Support Popidius Secundus for aedile, Rufinus, and he'll elect you.*

(Pompeian campaign posters)

1 **is**: the previous speaker, who has been gossiping about personal matters that Ganymedes regards as trivial and irrelevant (**nec . . . pertinet**).
quod: the antecedent is omitted: "He's talking about what. . . ."
2 **quid**: "how much."
mordet: we say the "pinch" of inflation. Why would **mordeat** be more correct?
4 **Aedīlēs . . . ēveniat**: more correctly, **aedīlibus** (dat.), "Damn the aediles!" (literally, "May it go badly for the aediles!").
5 **labōrat**: not just "work hard" but "suffer," "are oppressed."
maiōrēs māxillae: slang for "the greedy rich," "the fat cats"; **istī** used loosely for **istae** as if in apposition rather than agreement with the noun.
6 **habērēmus**: subjunctive expressing a wish, "if only we had. . . ."
leōnēs: i.e., bold and aggressive men, like Safinius in the next line.
7 **Asiā**: many Roman slaves came from the East, especially Asia Minor (Turkey).
8 **piper, nōn homō**: another slang expression, "(he wasn't) a man, he was a walking pepperbox," i.e., fiery-tempered.
10 **pilābat**: literally, "removed their hair," i.e., "gave them a scalping."
11 **schēmās**: "(fancy) figures of speech"; **schēma, schēmatis** (*n*) is here treated by an uneducated speaker as if it belonged to the 1st declension.
13 **nesciō quid Asiādis**: "something Asiatic (about him)"; to Ganymedes this is presumably a compliment, referring to Safinius' cool urbanity. **nesciō quid**: "something," often followed by a partitive genitive.
resalūtāre . . . reddere: infinitives loosely used to complete the meaning of **benīgnus**: "gracious in returning your greeting. . . ."
15 **prō lutō**: "equivalent to (i.e., as cheap as) mud," "dirt-cheap."
Asse: abl. of price, "for an **ās**," i.e., very cheaply.
ēmissēs: "you had bought."
16 **nōn potuissēs**: "you couldn't have."
17 **cōda** = **cauda**, reflecting colloquial pronunciation.
18 **trium cauniārum**: gen. of value, "worth three figs," i.e., worthless.
21 **Quod . . . attinet**: "as for (what concerns) me."
22 **pannōs . . . comēdī**: i.e., sold or pawned them to buy food.
23 **futūrum**: "going to happen."
colōniae: gen. object of **miserentur**.
24 **Ita . . . putō**: literally, "So may I enjoy my (family), as I think," or simply "So help me, I think. . . ."
diibus = **dīs**.
25 **pilī facit**: literally, "values at a hair" (gen. of value), i.e., "cares two cents for."
26 **opertīs oculīs**: Romans covered their heads during prayer; Ganymedes seems to suggest that his contemporaries hypocritically pretend to pray while in reality they are counting their cash.
27 **in clīvum**: "up the hill," i.e., the Capitoline in Rome, at the top of which stood the temple of Jupiter Capitolinus.
28 **urceātim**: "in pitchers" or "by the pitcherful," as we say "in buckets."
plovēbat = **pluēbat.**
29 **diī . . . habent**: the allusion is obscure, but it must mean the gods have turned away from, or been ignored by, the town because of its impiety.
30 **iacent**: i.e., unused, fallow; here Ganymedes is interrupted by the next speaker, whose speech forms the reading for the next chapter.

54
The Cost of Living

Ganymedes bemoans the sky-high price of food, the corruption of politicians, and the demise of the good old-fashioned virtues.

Dīxit Ganymēdēs: "Nārrat is quod nec ad caelum nec ad terram pertinet, cum interim nēmō cūrat, quid annōna mordet. Nōn mehercules hodiē buccam pānis invenīre potuī. Et quōmodo siccitās persevērat! Iam annum ēsurītiō fuit. Aedīlēs male ēveniat, quī cum pistōribus collūdunt: 'Servā mē, servābō tē.' Itaque populus minūtus labōrat; nam istī maiōrēs māxillae semper Sāturnālia agunt. Ō sī habērēmus illōs leōnēs, quōs ego hīc invēnī, cum prīmum ex Asiā vēnī! Illud erat vīvere. Sed meminī Safinium; tunc habitābat ad arcum veterem, mē puerō: piper, nōn homō. Is quācumque ībat, terram adūrēbat. Sed rēctus, sed certus, amīcus amīcō, cum quō audācter possēs in tenebrīs micāre. In cūriā autem quōmodo singulōs pilābat! Nec schēmās loquēbātur sed dīrēctum. Cum ageret porrō in forō, sīc illīus vōx crēscēbat tamquam tuba. Nec sūdāvit umquam nec expuit; putō eum nesciō quid Asiādis habuisse. Et quam benīgnus resalūtāre, nōmina omnium reddere, tamquam ūnus dē nōbīs!

"Itaque illō tempore annōna prō lutō erat. Asse pānem quem ēmissēs, nōn potuissēs cum alterō dēvorāre. Nunc oculum būblum vīdī maiōrem. Heu heu, cotīdiē pēius! Haec colōnia retrōversus crēscit tamquam cōda vitulī. Sed quārē nōs habēmus aedīlem trium cauniārum, quī sibi māvult assem quam vītam nostram? Itaque domī gaudet, plūs in diē nummōrum accipit quam alter patrimōnium habet. Iam sciō unde accēperit dēnāriōs mīlle aureōs. Sed populus est domī leōnēs, forās vulpēs. Quod ad mē attinet, iam pannōs meōs comēdī, et sī persevērat haec annōna, casulās meās vēndam. Quid enim futūrum est, sī nec diī nec hominēs eius colōniae miserentur? Ita meōs frūniscar, ut ego putō omnia illa ā diibus fierī. Nēmō enim caelum caelum putat, nēmō iēiūnium servat, nēmō Iovem pilī facit, sed omnēs opertīs oculīs bona sua computant. Anteā stolātae ībant nūdīs pedibus in clīvum, passīs capillīs, mentibus pūrīs, et Iovem aquam exōrābant. Itaque statim urceātim plovēbat, aut tunc aut numquam, et omnēs redībant ūdī tamquam mūrēs. Itaque diī pedēs lānātōs habent, quia nōs religiōsī nōn sumus. Agrī iacent—"

—Petronius, *Satyricon* 44

interim, meanwhile
annōna, -ae (*f*), (price of) grain
bucca, -ae (*f*), cheek, mouthful
siccitās, siccitātis (*f*), drought
ēsurītiō, ēsurītiōnis (*f*), famine
aedīlis, aedīlis (*m*), aedile

minūtus, -a, -um, little, minute
iste, ista, istud, this, that (of yours) (often disparaging)
māxilla, -ae (*f*), jaw
Sāturnālia, -ium (*n pl*), the Saturnalia, festival of Saturn; **Sāturnālia agere,** to celebrate the Saturnalia
tunc, then, at that time
piper, piperis (*n*), pepper
quācumque, wherever
audācter, boldly, with confidence
tenebrae, -ārum (*f pl*), darkness
singulī, -ae, -a, single, individual, each and every one
dīrēctum (*adverb*), directly, simply
porrō, then, furthermore
tamquam, like, as if
tuba, -ae (*f*), trumpet
sūdō (1), to sweat
benīgnus, -a, -um, kind, friendly
ās, assis (*m*), as, a small coin comparable to a penny
būb(u)lus, -a, -um, of or belonging to an ox
Heu! Alas! Ah me!
colōnia, -ae (*f*), colony, town
retrōversus (*adverb*), backwards
vitulus, -ī (*m*), calf
Quārē . . . ? Why . . . ?
nummus, -ī (*m*), coin, money
forās (*adverb*), out of doors
vulpēs, vulpis (*f*), fox
pannus, -ī (*m*), cloth, garment
casula, -ae (*f*), little house, hut
iēiūnium, -ī (*n*), a fast, fast-day
Iuppiter, Iovis (*m*), Jupiter, king of the gods
computō (1), to add up, count
stolāta, -ae (*f*), woman dressed in a stola (long robe)
passus, -a, -um, disheveled
mēns, mentis (*f*), mind, heart
exōrō (1), to pray for (implying that your prayer will be answered)
ūdus, -a, -um, wet
lānātus, -a, -um, bearing wool, wrapped in wool
quia, because

mordeō, mordēre (2), **momordī, morsum,** to bite
ēveniō, ēvenīre (4), **ēvēnī, ēventum,** to happen, turn out
collūdō, collūdere (3), **collūsī, collūsum,** to connive, be in cahoots
meminī, meminisse (perfect with present meaning), to remember
adūrō, adūrere (3), **adūssī, adūstum,** to set on fire, burn, scorch
crēscō, crēscere (3), **crēvī, crētum,** to rise, grow, swell
expuō, expuere (3), **expuī, expūtum,** to spit out, spit
attineō, attinēre (2), **attinuī,** to concern
comedō, comesse (3), **comēdī, comēsum,** to eat up, eat
misereor, miserērī (2), **miseritus sum** (+ *gen.*), to pity, take pity on
frūniscor, frūniscī (3), **frūnītus sum,** to enjoy

Exercise 54a

Answer the following questions in English, with reference to the specified lines of the reading passage.

1. What aspect of politics would you say is uppermost in Ganymedes' mind? (2–6, 15–16, 21–23)

2. Judging from Ganymedes' remarks, what did a Roman politician have to do to be popular with the common people? (6–9, 9–10, 10–12, 12–14)
3. Describe the style of political oratory preferred by Ganymedes. (10–12)
4. What does Ganymedes object to in present-day politicians? (4–6, 18–20)
5. How does Ganymedes describe his own condition? (2–3, 21–23)
6. What evidence do you find of a nostalgic view of the past on Ganymedes' part? (6–14, 15–17, 24–29)

Exercise 54b

1. Have you ever listened to a present-day conversation that reminded you of Ganymedes' speech? What would the similarities be? The differences?
2. Do you share Ganymedes' enthusiasm for Safinius? Why or why not?
3. Do Ganymedes' views on politicians seem to you similar to those of anyone you know or have read about? His views on religion?
4. In what senses is Ganymedes a "true Roman." In what senses is he not?

Building Up the Meaning IX

The Subjunctive in Subordinate Clauses

You have already met several types of subordinate clauses that use the subjunctive mood:

1. Indirect Questions:
   Pīrātae rogābant quī **essēmus**, unde **vēnissēmus**, quō iter **facerēmus**.
   The pirates kept asking who we were, where we had come from, and where we were traveling.
2. Circumstantial Clauses:
   Cum sē **exercuissent**, in tepidārium ingressī sunt.
   When they had exercised, they went into the warm room.
3. Causal Clauses:
   Grammaticus, cum Sextus ubi Hesperia esset **ignōrāret**, ferulam rapuit.
   Since Sextus didn't know where Hesperia was, the teacher snatched up his cane.
4. Result Clauses:
   Adeō perturbāta erat ut vix loquī **posset**.
   She was so confused that she could hardly speak.
5. Indirect Commands:
   Hī iānitōrem ōrant nē sē **dīmittat**.
   They keep begging the doorkeeper not to send them away.
6. Purpose Clauses:
   Auspex prōcēdit ut porcum **sacrificet.**
   The priest steps forward to sacrifice a pig.

Sequence of Tenses

As you learned in Chapter 49, all of these subjunctive clauses follow the sequence of tenses:

PRIMARY SEQUENCE

Verb of Main Clause	***Verb of Subordinate Clause***
present, future, or future perfect indicative	present subjunctive (for action going on at the *same time* as that of the main verb)

Nōn intellegō cūr servae mē **neglegant**.
I do not understand why the slave-girls **neglect** *me.*

perfect subjunctive (for action that took place *before* that of the main verb)

Nōn intellegō cūr servae mē **neglēxerint**.
I do not understand why the slave-girls **neglected** *me.*

SECONDARY SEQUENCE

Verb of Main Clause	***Verb of Subordinate Clause***
imperfect, perfect, or pluperfect indicative	imperfect subjunctive (for action going on at the *same time* as that of the main verb)

Nōn intellegēbam cūr servae mē **neglegerent**.
I did not understand why the slave-girls **were neglecting** *me.*

pluperfect subjunctive (for action that took place *before* that of the main verb)

Nōn intellegēbam cūr servae mē **neglēxissent**.
I did not understand why the slave-girls **had neglected** *me.*

Sequence of Tenses in Result Clauses

In result clauses there often occurs an apparent exception to the usual sequence of tenses. The perfect and pluperfect subjunctive are not used in the usual way, because a result cannot occur before the action that produces it. The *present subjunctive* is used in primary sequence, as you would expect. In secondary sequence, however the *perfect subjunctive* often replaces the expected imperfect. This use of the perfect emphasizes the finality or completeness of the result (**perfectum** = "completed").

Leō tantus et tam ferōx erat ut servus metū exanimātus **ceciderit**.
The lion was so big and so fierce that the slave **fell down** *paralyzed with fear.*

Exercise 54c

Select, read aloud, translate, and identify the type of subordinate clause in each sentence; pay careful attention to sequence of tenses.

1. Vōx Safiniī crēvit tamquam tuba cum in forō (ēgit, agat, ageret).
2. Safinius tam benīgnus erat ut omnibus grātissimus (fuit, esset, fuerit).
3. Nesciō quārē nōs (habēmus, habeāmus, habērēmus) aedīlem trium cauniārum.
4. Illī persuāsimus ut casulās suās (vēnderet, vēndidisset, vēndat).
5. Cum nēmō Iovem pilī (faciēbat, fēcit, faceret), diī huius colōniae nōn miseritī sunt.
6. Rōmānae Iovem tantum ōrāvērunt ut statim (pluerit, pluēbat, pluit).
7. Rogās cūr nōs religiōsī nōn (sumus, fuissēmus, sīmus).
8. Nēmō cūrābat quid annōna (mordēret, mordeat, momorderit).
9. Ille tam rēctus, tam certus est ut (potuerās, potueris, possīs) cum eō in tenebrīs micāre.
10. Safinius nōmina omnium reddēbat ut populō grātus (fuisset, esset, fuerit).

A Witch Story (Part One)

In addition to personal and political gossip, another kind of conversation enjoyed by Trimalchio and his dinner guests is the exchanging of spooky stories. You have already read Niceros' tale of the werewolf in Review XII. Trimalchio, never one to let himself be upstaged, replies to that story with one from his own experience.

Et ipse vōbīs rem horribilem nārrābō. Cum adhūc capillātus essem (nam ā puerō vītam Chīam gessī), ipsimī nostrī dēlicātus dēcessit, mehercules margarītum. Cum ergō illum māter misella plangeret et nōs tum plūrēs in trīstimōniō essēmus, subitō strīdēre strīgae coepērunt; putārēs canem le-

1 **capillātus:** "a long-haired boy"; handsome young slaves, such as Trimalchio was at the time of this story, were thought to be more attractive if their hair was worn long and curly.
2 **ā puerō:** "from childhood."
vītam Chīam: i.e., a life of luxury like that on the Greek island of Chios.
ipsimī: "master"; **ipsimus** is a shortened form of **ipsissimus**, superlative of **ipse**, "Himself," commonly used to designate the head of a household.
3 **misella:** "poor little"; colloquial speakers were fond of diminutives (see Word Study XI).
nōs . . . plūrēs: "several (of) us."
4 **trīstimōniō:** "sadness," "sorrow," another colloquial word, used instead of the classical **trīstitia**.
putārēs: "you would have thought."

porem persequī. Habēbāmus tunc hominem Cappadocem, longum, valdē audāculum et quī valēbat: poterat bovem īrātum tollere. Hic audācter strictō gladiō extrā ōstium prōcucurrit, involūtā sinistrā manū cūriōsē, et mulierem tamquam hōc locō (salvum sit, quod tangō!) mediam trāiēcit. Audīmus gemitum et (plānē nōn mentiar) ipsās nōn vīdimus. 5

—Petronius, *Satyricon* 63.2–6

(to be concluded in Chapter 55)

6 **audāculum:** from **audāx**; another diminutive form.

8 **tamquam hōc locō**: "just about here"; Trimalchio apparently points to his own abdomen as he speaks these words; this is implied by **salvum sit, quod tangō!**: "heaven preserve what I'm touching!"

dēlicātus, -ī (*m*), favorite, pet
margarītum, -ī (*n*), pearl
ergō, therefore, so
strīga, -ae (*f*), witch
Cappadox, Cappadocis, Cappadocian, of Cappadocia in Asia Minor
ōstium, -ī (*n*), door
cūriōsē, carefully
gemitus, -ūs (*m*), groan
plānē, wholly, absolutely

gerō, gerere (3), **gessī, gestum,** to live, spend (time)
plangō, plangere (3), **plānxī, planctum,** to beat (especially the breast or head, in grief), lament
strīdeō, strīdēre (2), **strīdī,** to shriek, howl
persequor, persequī (3), **persecūtus sum,** to pursue, chase
prōcurrō, prōcurrere (3), **prōcucurrī, prōcursum,** to run forth, rush out
involvō, involvere (3), **involvī, involūtum,** to wrap in, wrap up
tangō, tangere (3), **tetigī, tactum,** to touch
trāiciō, trāicere (3), **trāiēcī, trāiectum,** to stab through, pierce
mentior, mentīrī (4), **mentītus sum,** to lie, deceive

Exercise 54d

Using the witch story as a guide, give the Latin for:

1. Trimalchio says that he led a "Chian life" from childhood.
2. The poor little mother was lamenting (her) dead son.
3. The witches' shrieking (**strīdor**) was like (**similis** + *dat.*) the voice of a dog chasing a rabbit.
4. The Cappadocian was so strong that he could pick up an angry ox.
5. When he had drawn his sword and wrapped up his left hand, he rushed out the door.
6. He pierces the shrieking witch with his sword.
7. Trimalchio heard the witches' groans but did not see the women themselves.

55
Bread and Circuses

The gossip at Trimalchio's party is continued by another guest, a rag dealer named Echion. He emphasizes a different aspect of local politics: the gladiatorial shows and handouts of food or money that a Roman politician was expected to give his constituents. Echion's political attitudes were shared by real Romans, as is shown by these election posters from Pompeii:

C. IULIUM POLYBIUM AED(ILEM) O(RO) V(OS) F(ACIATIS): PANEM BONUM FERT!

I ask you to elect C. Julius Polybius aedile: he provides good bread!

M. CASELLIUM MARCELLUM AEDILEM BONUM ET MUNERARIUM MAGNUM.

M. Casellius Marcellus: a good aedile and a great show-sponsor!

Another aspect of Echion's attitude toward local officials is echoed by the following inscription in honor of a real-life politician who held office in the Campanian town of Minturnae in the middle of the third century A.D.:

> To Publius Baebius Justus, son of Publius, of the Terentine tribe. To this man the senate (of Minturnae) decreed that a statue be set up, because he had held every office in the city, because to each and every (citizen) he always showed equal respect, and because after holding the splendid office of duumvir, by popular request when his inaugural show was held, he willingly undertook a (second) gladiatorial show by imperial dispensation, consisting of three pairs (of gladiators) plus bears and herbivores. In consideration of the granting of the statue he gave each of the decurions three denarii. Land granted by decree of the decurions.
>
> He sponsored at Minturnae, in four days, eleven pairs (of gladiators): of these he killed eleven of Campania's finest gladiators; he also slaughtered ten bears, and cruelly. As you yourselves recall, excellent citizens, he killed all the herbivores on each of the four days.

"Dē Lucernā Equitēs"

1 **centōnārius**: a maker of patchwork, a rag dealer.
modo . . . sīc: "sometimes it's one way, sometimes another": i.e., life has its ups and downs. This is also the implication of the spotted pig (2).
3 **patria**: "town": this Campanian town, the setting of the *Cena*, is never named.
4 **habēret**: "if (only) it had."
5 **ubīque . . . est**: proverbial for "things are pretty much the same everywhere."
porcōs . . . ambulāre: i.e., an earthly paradise where life is effortless.
7 **in trīduō**: i.e., three days from now, "in three days"; **excellente** = **excellēns**.
familia . . . lanistīcia: "troupe (of gladiators) owned by a **lanista**," a manager-trainer. The gladiators provided by Titus are veterans freed (**lībertī**) as a reward for skillful fighting, and so presumably of better quality.
8 **Titus**: the current aedile, who is paying for the show.
magnum . . . caldicerebrius: "is generous and impulsive," spares no expense.
10 **miscix**: "mixed," i.e., diluted, wishy-washy; he doesn't do things by halves.
sine fugā: defeated gladiators will be killed, not dismissed to fight another day —an expensive policy for the sponsor, but popular with the fans.
11 **unde**: "(the funds) from which (to pay)," as we say "the wherewithal."
12 **trecentiēs**: this is the standard Roman way of expressing millions of sesterces: **sēstertiūm** (gen. pl. typical of nouns denoting coins), **centēna mīlia** understood, and a numerical adverb in **-iēs**; here 300 × 100,000 = 30,000,000.
male: probably implying premature rather than unnatural or painful death.
Ut: concessive, with subjunctive, "even if he should . . . ."
quadringenta: supply **mīlia sēstertiūm**.
14 **essedāriam**: "who fights from an **esseda**," a Celtic war-chariot.
15 **matella**: literally, "chamber-pot"; here, slang for "slut."
digna . . . iactāret: "deserved to be gored by a bull," rather than her lover.
16 **Quid . . . ?**: "Why . . . ?" or more freely, "What made him think . . . ?"
17 **filicem**: a weed that bothered farmers; metaphorically, a worthless person.
Ille: Hermogenes, the wife's father; **milvō volantī** is dative of interest, equivalent to a genitive; the phrase is proverbial for a sharp operator.
18 **colubra . . . parit**: another proverb, similar to "like father, like son."
19 **subolfaciō, quia**: "get a whiff (i.e., suspect) that . . . ."
epulum: here not a real dinner but a cash bonus, "two **dēnariī** per person."
20 **Quod sī**: "But if"; **Norbānō**: another local politician.
Sciās oportet: "You must know . . . ," "You better believe . . ."
21 **plēnīs vēlīs**: like a ship with favorable winds, easily, "hands down."
vincitūrum: Echion's illiterate attempt at the future participle of **vincō**.
22 **sēstertiāriōs**: "worth one **sēstertius**," as we say "two-bit."
sī sufflāssēs, cecidissent: "if you had . . . , they would have . . . ."
23 **Occīdit**: the subject is Norbanus; he did not literally kill the losers himself but authorized the **lanista** to have them killed rather than released.
dē lucernā equitēs: "knights off a lamp," i.e., puny, lifeless fighters.
gallōs . . . lōripēs: "barnyard roosters . . . a mere stick . . . a clubfoot."
24 **tertiārius**: a "third man" or substitute sent in to replace a dead fighter.
25 **quī . . . praecīsa**: he moved as if he were hamstrung.
quī . . . pugnāvit: "and even he fought by the rules," without imagination.
27 **'Adhibēte!'**: "(shouts of) 'Give it to 'em!' "
28 **plōdō** = **plaudō**, reflecting colloquial pronunciation.

Echion, the rag dealer, interrupts Ganymedes: "Look on the bright side of things," he says, "for example, the upcoming gladiatorial show."

"Ōrō tē," inquit Echion centōnārius, "melius loquere. 'Modo sīc, modo sīc,' inquit rūsticus: varium porcum perdiderat. Quod hodiē nōn est, crās erit: sīc vīta trūditur. Nōn mehercules patria melior dīcī potest, sī hominēs habēret. Sed labōrat hōc tempore, nec haec sōla. Nōn dēbēmus dēlicātī esse; ubīque medius caelus est. Tū sī aliubi fueris, dīcēs hīc porcōs coctōs 5 ambulāre.

"Et ecce habitūrī sumus mūnus excellente in trīduō diē festā; familia nōn lanistīcia, sed plūrimī lībertī. Et Titus noster magnum animum habet et est caldicerebrius; aut hoc aut illud erit, quid utique. Nam illī domesticus sum, nōn est miscix. Ferrum optimum datūrus est, sine fugā, carnārium 10 in mediō, ut amphitheāter videat. Et habet unde: relictum est illī sēstertiūm trecentiēs; dēcessit illīus pater male. Ut quadringenta impendat, nōn sentiet patrimōnium illīus, et sempiternō nōminābitur. Iam nannōs aliquot habet et mulierem essedāriam et dispēnsātōrem Glycōnis, quī dēprehēnsus est cum dominam suam dēlectārētur. Magis illa matella digna fuit quam taurus 15 iactāret. Sed quī asinum nōn potest, strātum caedit. Quid autem Glycō putābat Hermogenis filicem umquam bonum exitum factūram? Ille milvō volantī poterat unguēs resecāre; colubra restem nōn parit.

"Sed subolfaciō, quia nōbīs epulum datūrus est Mammaea, bīnōs dēnāriōs mihi et meīs. Quod sī hoc fēcerit, ēripiat Norbānō tōtum favōrem. Sciās 20 oportet plēnīs vēlīs hunc vincitūrum. Et rēvērā, quid ille nōbīs bonī fēcit? Dedit gladiātōrēs sēstertiāriōs iam dēcrepitōs, quōs sī sufflāssēs, cecidissent; iam meliōrēs bēstiāriōs vīdī. Occīdit dē lucernā equitēs; putārēs eōs gallōs gallīnāceōs: alter burdubasta, alter lōripēs, tertiārius mortuus prō mortuō, quī habēret nervia praecīsa. Ūnus alicuius flātūrae fuit Thraex, quī et ipse 25 ad dictāta pugnāvit. Ad summam, omnēs posteā sectī sunt; adeō dē magnā turbā 'Adhibēte!' accēperant: plānē fugae merae. 'Mūnus tamen,' inquit, 'tibi dedī': et ego tibi plōdō. Computā, et tibi plūs dō quam accēpī. Manus manum lavat."

—Petronius, *Satyricon* 45

modo . . . modo, now . . . now, sometimes . . . sometimes
dēlicātus, -a, -um, spoiled, fussy
ubīque, everywhere
aliubi, elsewhere, somewhere else
trīduum, -ī (*n*), three-day period
festus, -a, -um, festive, holiday
utique, at any rate, at least
domesticus, -a, -um, of the house or family, close, intimate
fuga, -ae (*f*), a fleeing, rout
carnārium, -ī (*n*), butcher-shop, slaughterhouse
sēstertius, -ī (*m*) (*gen. pl.* **sēstertiūm**), sestertius, a coin worth four **assēs**
trecentiēs (*adverb*), three hundred times
quadringentī, -ae, -a, four hundred
sempiternō, forever

nannus, -ī (*m*), dwarf
aliquot (*indeclinable*), some, a few
dispēnsātor, dispēnsātōris (*m*), steward, household manager
dēlector (1), to please, amuse
dignus, -a, -um, worthy, deserving
taurus, -ī (*m*), bull
asinus, -ī (*m*), ass, donkey
strātum, -ī (*n*), blanket, saddle-cloth, saddle
exitus, -ūs (*m*), outcome, end
volō (1), to fly
unguis, unguis (*m*), nail (of finger or toe), claw
colubra, -ae (*f*), snake
restis, restis (*f*), rope
epulum, -ī (*n*), banquet, feast
bīnī, -ae, -a, two each
favor, favōris (*m*), support
vēlum, -ī (*n*), sail
sufflō (1), to blow on
bēstiārius, -ī (*m*), animal-fighter (in the arena)
eques, equitis (*m*), horseman, knight
nervia, -ōrum (*n pl*), sinews, tendons
flātūra, -ae (*f*), breath, fighting spirit
Thraex, Thraecis (*m*), Thracian, native of Thrace in northern Greece; a gladiator with Thracian equipment
dictāta, -ōrum (*n pl*), things dictated, rules
ad summam, in sum, in short
merus, -a, -um, pure, nothing but

perdō, perdere (3), **perdidī, perditum,** to lose
trūdō, trūdere (3), **trūsī, trūsum,** to push, shove (along)
impendō, impendere (3), **impendī, impēnsum,** to spend
dēprehendō, dēprehendere (3), **dēprehendī, dēprehēnsum,** to seize, catch
caedō, caedere (3), **cecīdī, caesum,** to cut, beat
resecō, resecāre (1), **resecuī, resectum,** to cut off, clip
pariō, parere (3), **peperī, partum,** to bear, give birth to
praecīdō, praecīdere (3), **praecīdī, praecīsum,** to cut off, cut through
secō, secāre (1), **secuī, sectum,** to cut, beat, flog
plaudō, plaudere (3), **plausī, plausum,** to applaud, clap the hands

Exercise 55a

Answer the following questions in English with reference to the specified lines of the reading passage.

1. What qualities does Echion chiefly value in a politician? (8–11, 19–20)
2. Why does Echion think Mammaea is likely to beat Norbanus in the coming election? (19–21, 22–25)
3. Does Echion value anything in gladiatorial fighting besides pure bloodshed? (25–26)
4. What does Echion mean by "I'm giving you more than I got"? (28)
5. What similarities do you see between the fictional "Titus" and the historical Baebius of Minturnae? (8–13, and inscription, page 15)

Exercise 55b

1. How would you compare Echion's attitude toward violence in public entertainment with ours today?
2. Echion and Ganymedes are intended to represent the common man. But do you see anything in Petronius' portrayal of them that gives them individual personalities and distinguishes them from each other?
3. Do you find anything to admire in Echion or Ganymedes? Anything to dislike?

Conditional Sentences

A conditional sentence has two parts:

a subordinate clause (if-clause or *protasis*) introduced by **sī** (negative **nisi**) expressing a condition

a main clause (*apodosis*) describing the situation that results, or would result, if this condition is, or were, fulfilled; in English this clause may be introduced by "then" (for which there is no equivalent in Latin).

Different kinds of conditional sentences in Latin require different kinds of verbs:

1. **Simple or factual conditions:** the verb of both clauses is in the *indicative*, in the *present* or *past* (imperfect or perfect tense), e.g.:
   a. Sī id **dīcit, errat.**
      If (in fact) *he* **says** *that,* (then) *he* **is wrong.**
   b. Sī id **dīxit, errāvit.**
      If (in fact) *he* **said** *that,* (then) *he* **was wrong.**

This kind of condition should cause no difficulty, because the verbs can be translated directly into English in the usual way.

2. **Future more/less vivid:** in these conditions, the events described in both clauses have not yet occurred; the speaker is speculating about what will, or might, happen if a certain condition is, or should be, fulfilled in the future. Latin distinguishes between
   a. a future situation that seems likely ("more vivid" in the speaker's mind), and
   b. a future situation that seems less likely ("less vivid" in the speaker's mind).

   a. **Future more vivid:** in this kind of condition (which you first encountered in Chapter 25), the verb of both clauses is in the *future indicative* (the verb of the **sī**-clause often in the *future perfect indicative*), where

English rather illogically puts the verb of the if-clause into the *present*, ignoring the fact that the event referred to has not yet occurred:

Sī quadringenta **impendet**, nōn **sentiet** patrimōnium.

If he **spends** (*will spend*) *400,000, his inheritance* **will** *not* **feel** *it.*

Sī hoc **fēcerit, ēripiet** Norbānō tōtum favōrem.

If he **does** (*will have done*) *this, he* **will take away** *all support from Norbanus.*

b. **Future less vivid:** the verb of both clauses is in the *present subjunctive*; the subjunctive, as often in Latin, expresses the idea that something is less than certain or factual; the English equivalent is "should" or "were to" (if-clause) and "would" (main clause); these are often called *should-would conditions.*

Sī hoc **faciat, ēripiat** Norbānō tōtum favōrem.

If he **were to** (**should**) **do** *this, he* **would take away** *all support from Norbanus.*

Exercise 55c

Read aloud and translate. Pay particular attention to the tenses and moods of the verbs. Identify the type of condition in each sentence.

1. Sī dēprehēnsus erit, pūniētur.
2. Sī dēprehendātur, pūniātur.
3. Nisi gladiātōrēs bene pugnant, spectātōrēs "Adhibēte!" clāmant.
4. Sī gladiātōrēs bene pugnābunt, spectātōrēs "Optimē!" clāmābunt.
5. Sī gladiātōrēs dēcrepitōs dēs, nōn tibi plaudam.
6. Nisi gladiātōrēs meliōrēs dederis, nōn tibi plaudam.
7. Sī hōs gladiātōrēs sufflēs, cadant.
8. Norbānus, nisi bīnōs dēnāriōs nōbīs dabit, tōtum favōrem perdet.

Excercise 55d

Using the reading passage as a guide, give the Latin for:

1. If you were to go to another town (**patria**), you would say this one is better. (3–5)
2. If they were to spend four hundred (thousand sesterces), they could provide very good gladiators. (10, 12)
3. If his father should die, he would get thirty million. (11–12)
4. If that man's father dies, he will get thirty million. (11–12)
5. If you should do this, you would be talked about forever. (13)
6. If the aedile gives us a good dinner tomorrow, we will all be happy. (19)
7. Unless the aediles give a very good show, the people will be angry. (27–28)

A Witch Story (Part Two)

Bārō autem noster intrōversus sē prōiēcit in lect
līvidum habēbat quasi flagellīs caesus, quia scīlicet i
manus. Nōs clūsō ōstiō redīmus iterum ad officium, sed
plexāret corpus fīliī suī, tangit et videt manuciolum dē strām
Nōn cor habēbat, nōn intestīna, nōn quicquam: scīlicet iam pue
involāverant et supposuerant strāmenticium vavatōnem. Rogō vōs, et
crēdātis, sunt mulierēs plussciae, sunt nocturnae, et quod sūrsum est, deorsum faciunt. Cēterum bārō ille longus post hoc factum numquam colōris suī fuit, immō post paucōs diēs frenēticus periit.

—Petronius, *Satyricon* 63.7–10

bārō, bārōnis (*m*), lout
intrōversus (*adverb*), (once) indoors (again)
līvidus, -a, -um, black and blue (as by bruising)
flagellum, -ī (*n*), whip
scīlicet, of course, no doubt
mala manus, (a witch's) evil hand
clūsus, -a, -um, colloquial for **clausus**
amplexō (1), embrace
manuciolum, -ī (*n*), small bundle
strāmentum, -ī (*n*), straw
quisquam, quicquam, anyone, anything
involō (1), to fly at, attack, carry off
strāmenticius, -a, -um, of straw
vavatō, -ōnis (*m*), doll, puppet
oportet crēdātis, you must believe
plusscius, -a, -um, skilled in witchcraft (literally, who know more than others, from **plūs** + **sciō**)
nocturnae, -ārum (*f pl*), nocturnal ones, i.e., witches
sūrsum (*adverb*), up, high
deorsum (*adverb*), down, low
cēterum, but
colōris suī, himself (literally, of his proper color)
frenēticus, -a, -um, raving mad

prōiciō, prōicere (3), **prōiēcī, prōiectum,** to throw (forward, headlong)
suppōnō, suppōnere (3), **supposuī, suppositum,** to put in place of
pereō, perīre (*irreg.*), **periī, peritum,** to perish, die

Exercise 55e

Read aloud and translate each of the following sentences, then tell whether it is **Vērum** *or* **Falsum**; *if* **Falsum**, *give a correct Latin version.*

1. Corpus bārōnis līvidum erat quia flagellīs caesum erat.
2. Cum ōstium clausissēmus, prōiēcimus nōs in lectum.
3. Cum māter corpus fīliī tetigisset, vīdit strāmenticium vavatōnem.
4. Mulierēs plussciae puerum interfēcerant.
5. Bārō longus aliquot mēnsēs vīxit, deinde frenēticus periit.
6. Trimalchiō negat nocturnās esse.

...g Up the Meaning X

Indirect Statement

You have learned that Latin expresses indirect statement by means of an infinitive with its subject in the accusative. The most important thing to remember about this construction is that the tense of the verb (the infinitive) in the indirect statement is not absolute but *relative* to the tense of the main verb. The present infinitive expresses action at *the same time* as that of the main verb (whatever its tense), the perfect infinitive action *before*, and the future infinitive action *after* that of the main verb.

Main Vb.	***Inf.***	
Present	Pres.	Sciō vōs **esse** molestissimōs. *I know that you* **are** *very troublesome.*
	Perf.	Audīmus Caesarem amphitheātrum novum **aperuisse**. *We hear that Caesar* **has opened** (or **opened**) *a new amphitheater.*
	Fut.	Prō certō habeō nōs tē **vīsūrōs esse**. *I am sure that we* **will see** *you.*
Past	Pres.	Titus respondit sē domum redīre **nōlle**. *Titus replied that he* **was unwilling** *to return home.*
	Perf.	Sciēbāmus Marcum ad amphitheātrum **īvisse**. *We knew that Marcus* **had gone** *to the amphitheater.*
	Fut.	Prō certō habēbāmus Titum sērō **perventūrum esse.** *We were sure that Titus* **would arrive** *late.*

Another important point to remember: the perfect passive and future active infinitives usually consist of **esse** plus a participle, which must agree with the subject of the infinitive in gender, case, and number:

Putō **Aurēliam** eō nōn **itūram** esse.
I think that Aurelia **will not go** *there.*

Exercise 55f

Complete the Latin translations of the following sentences with indirect statements, paying particular attention to the tense of the verb.

1. We were hoping that Norbanus *would give* a better show.
   Spērābāmus Norbānum mūnus melius ____________________.
2. Do you know that that man *spent* four hundred (thousand sesterces)?
   Scīsne illum quadringenta ____________________?
3. They all believed that Norbanus *was making a mistake.* (**errō**)
   Omnēs crēdēbant Norbānum ____________________.
4. Nobody thought that the steward *had been* deservedly *punished.*
   Nēmō putāvit dispēnsātōrem meritō ____________________.
5. She was certain that *she was going to win.*
   Prō certō habēbat ____________________.

56
A Millionaire's Tomb

Ganymedes, Echion, and Trimalchio's other guests give us a vivid impression, unique in Latin literature, of the mentality and the speech of ordinary Romans. But the real heart of the *Cena* is the brilliant comic portrait of Trimalchio himself. Every aspect of the banquet reveals some facet of Trimalchio's life and personality: the culinary extravaganzas, the service and entertainment, and the guests' comments concerning their host, his career, and his fabulous wealth. But of all the ways in which Petronius brings to life this great comic figure, Trimalchio's own speeches are the most revealing. The following passage, in which he describes the preparations he has made for his own death, is an example of this kind of self-characterization. As you read it, try to share Petronius' double vision: on the one hand, the way Trimalchio sees himself (i.e., the image he thinks he is presenting to others) and on the other hand the way we the readers see him. It is in the gap between these two ways of looking at the same man that much of the humor and humanity of the *Cena* is to be found.

Relief from the tomb of Q. Haterius Tychicus, a rich building contractor of the late first century A.D. A tomb-temple is shown, every inch of its surface crammed with sculpture. A crane (operated by slaves on a treadwheel) symbolizes the owner's trade. The upper right-hand corner gives an interior view of the temple: Haterius himself reclines on a couch while his three children play on the floor and his old nurse lays a sacrifice on an altar. To their right is a shrine of Venus with ancestor-masks above.

1 **et servī**: "slaves, too"; Trimalchio has just invited his slaves to share the dining couches with his guests; as they scramble to accept this offer, the dining room is thrown into confusion; Trimalchio then defends his liberal gesture with bits of ill-digested "philosophy."

aequē: "equally," i.e., with us free men.

2 **lactem** = **lāc**: what is wrong here and in the following phrase **malus fātus**?

mē . . . gustābunt: a humorous confusion of two incompatible ideas, "(they'll be all right) as long as I'm around" and "they'll go free (when I die)."

3 **aquam . . . gustābunt**: "they will taste the water of freedom," a cliché.

4 **ideō**: anticipates **ut**; omit in translating.

6 **oblītus nūgārum**: "getting down to business" (literally, "forgetting trifles").

8 **Habinnam**: Habinnas, one of Trimalchio's friends, a stonemason.

11 **Petraitis**: genitive of **Petraites**, a real gladiator of the 1st century A.D.

12 **ut sint**: continuing the indirect command construction from **rogō** (10).

in fronte . . . in agrum: "frontage . . . deep"; such specifications for the size of a burial plot are common in Roman epitaphs.

13 **Omne genus . . . pōma**: "every kind *of* fruit tree"; the tombs of the wealthy were sometimes set in orchards or gardens.

sint: supply **ut.**

14 **vīneārum largiter**: "plenty of grapevines."

vīvō . . . esse: "for a living man to have"; **vīvō** is dative of possession, and the infinitives (**esse** and **cūrārī**) are the subjects of **est**.

15 **nōbīs habitandum est**: "we must live."

16 **Hoc . . . sequātur**: a formula often found in Roman epitaphs; it was intended to prevent sale or unauthorized use of the tomb by the heirs of the deceased: it did not "pass to" them (**sequātur**) with the rest of his possessions.

17 **nāvēs**: Trimalchio's vast fortune was founded on merchant shipping.

18 **tribūnālī**: in his epitaph (27) we learn that he was a **sēvir Augustālis**, one of the priests in charge of the worship of the emperor in the towns; a bordered toga, gold ring, and throne were symbols of the office.

19 **quod**: "that," introducing an indirect statement.

20 **Faciātur**: for **fīat**; singular either because Trimalchio mistakes **triclīnia** for a 1st declension noun, or because he is thinking in Greek, in which a neuter plural subject takes a singular verb; either way, his Latin is shaky.

21 **sibi suāviter facientem**: "enjoying themselves."

22 **cicarōnem**: "my little pet," probably his favorite slave.

23 **amphorās cōpiōsās gypsātās**: "large wine jars sealed with gypsum."

licet . . . sculpās: "you may carve."

24 **in mediō**: supply **sit,** "let there be."

25 **velit nōlit**: "whether he wants to or not."

26 **vidē . . . haec**: "consider carefully whether this (inscription) . . . ."

27 **sēvirātus**: "the office of **sēvir**"; see note on line 18 above.

absentī: with **huic**, "in his absence"; an additional honor, implying that he neither campaigned nor paid for the office.

28 **decuriīs**: the "boards" that formed the lower ranks of the Roman civil service.

29 **sēstertiūm . . . trecentiēs**: see note on 55:12.

30 **Valē. Et tū**: "Farewell (to you, passerby). And (to) you, (Trimalchio)." This and similar formulas are common in Roman epitaphs (see page 129).

Trimalchio describes the elaborate tomb he is having prepared for himself.

Trimalchiō, "Amīcī," inquit, "et servī hominēs sunt et aequē ūnum lactem bibērunt, etiam sī illōs malus fātus oppresserit. Tamen mē salvō, citō aquam līberam gustābunt. Ad summam, omnēs illōs in testāmentō meō manū mittō. Et haec ideō omnia pūblicō, ut familia mea iam nunc sīc mē amet tamquam mortuum." 5

Grātiās agere omnēs indulgentiae coeperant dominī, cum ille oblītus nūgārum exemplar testāmentī iussit afferrī et tōtum ā prīmō ad ultimum ingemēscente familiā recitāvit. Respiciēns deinde Habinnam, "Quid dīcis," inquit, "amīce cārissime? Aedificās monumentum meum, quemadmodum tē iussī? Valdē tē rogō, ut secundum pedēs statuae meae catellam pingās et 10 corōnās et unguenta et Petraitis omnēs pugnās, ut mihi contingat tuō beneficiō post mortem vīvere; praetereā ut sint in fronte pedēs centum, in agrum pedēs dūcentī. Omne genus enim pōma volō sint circā cinerēs meōs, et vīneārum largiter. Valdē enim falsum est vīvō quidem domōs cultās esse, nōn cūrārī eās, ubi diūtius nōbīs habitandum est. Et ideō ante omnia adicī 15 volō: 'Hoc monumentum hērēdem nōn sequātur.'

"Tē rogō ut nāvēs etiam in monumentō meō faciās plēnīs vēlīs euntēs, et mē in tribūnālī sedentem praetextātum cum ānulīs aureīs quīnque et nummōs in pūblicō dē sacculō effundentem; scīs enim, quod epulum dedī bīnōs dēnāriōs. Faciātur, sī tibi vidētur, et triclīnia. Faciēs et tōtum populum 20 sibi suāviter facientem. Ad dexteram meam pōnēs statuam Fortūnātae meae columbam tenentem, et catellam cingulō alligātam dūcat, et cicarōnem meum, et amphorās cōpiōsās gypsātās, nē effluant vīnum. Et urnam licet frāctam sculpās, et super eam puerum plōrantem. Hōrologium in mediō, ut quisquis hōrās īnspiciet, velit nōlit, nōmen meum legat. Īnscrīptiō quoque 25 vidē dīligenter sī haec satis idōnea tibi vidētur: 'C. Pompeius Trimalchiō Maecēnātiānus hīc requiēscit. Huic sēvirātus absentī dēcrētus est. Cum posset in omnibus decuriīs Rōmae esse, tamen nōluit. Pius, fortis, fidēlis, ex parvō crēvit, sēstertiūm relīquit trecentiēs, nec umquam philosophum audīvit. Valē. Et tū.' " Haec ut dīxit Trimalchiō, flēre coepit ūbertim. Flēbat 30 et Fortūnāta, flēbat et Habinnas, tōta dēnique familia, tamquam in fūnus rogāta, lāmentātiōne triclīnium implēvit. —Petronius, *Satyricon* 71

lāc, lactis (*n*), milk
fātum, -ī (*n*), fate, destiny
citō, quickly, soon
līber, -era, -erum, free
gustō (1), to taste
ideō, for this reason, therefore
pūblicō (1), to make public
nūgae, -ārum (*f pl*), jokes, trifles
exemplar, exemplāris (*n*), copy
quemadmodum, in what way, as
secundum (+ *acc.*), by, beside
catella, -ae (*f*), puppy
beneficium, -ī (*n*), kindness
dūcentī, -ae, -a, two hundred
pōmum, -ī (*n*), fruit tree
circā (+ *acc.*), around
cinis, cineris (*m*), ashes
vīvus, -a, -um, alive, living

cultus, -a, -um, cultivated, elegant
diūtius (*adverb*), longer
tribūnal, tribūnālis (*n*), magistrates' raised platform, tribunal
sacculus, -ī (*m*), little sack
columba, -ae (*f*), dove
cingulum, -ī (*n*), belt, leash
alligō (1), to tie
super (+ *acc.*), over, above
plōrō (1), to weep
hōrologium, -ī (*n*), clock, sundial
quisquis, quicquid, whoever, whatever
idōneus, -a, -um, suitable
pius, -a, -um, dutiful, conscientious
ūbertim, copiously, abundantly
dēnique, at last, finally

oblīvīscor, oblīvīscī (3), **oblītus sum** (+ *gen.*), to forget
ingemēscō, ingemēscere (3), to groan
pingō, pingere (3), **pinxī, pictum,** to paint, portray, represent
contingō, contingere (3), **contigī, contāctum,** to befall, happen to
adiciō, adicere (3), **adiēcī, adiectum,** to add
effundō, effundere (3), **effūdī, effūsum,** to pour out
effluō, effluere (3), **effluxī,** to flow out, to spill
sculpō, sculpere (3), **sculpsī, sculptum,** to sculpt, carve
requiēscō, requiēscere (3), **requiēvī, requiētum,** to rest
dēcernō, dēcernere (3), **dēcrēvī, dēcrētum,** to decide, decree
fleō, flēre (2), **flēvī, flētum,** to weep
impleō, implēre (2), **implēvī, implētum,** to fill

EPITAPH FOR A SON

Lagge fīlī, bene quiēscās, māter tua rogat tē ut mē ad tē recipiās. Valē. P(edēs) q(uadrātī) XV. *Laggus my son, may you rest well; (I) your mother ask that you take me to you. Farewell. 15 square feet.*

Exercise 56a

1. What does Trimalchio intend his guests to think about his will? His tomb?
2. What is his guests' actual reaction to them? What is yours?
3. Would you describe Trimalchio as hypocritical? Generous? Altruistic? Humanitarian? Self-centered? How would he describe himself?
4. Is Trimalchio afraid of death?
5. Is it true that Trimalchio "never listened to a philosopher"? What words suggest that he has somehow picked up a smattering of philosophy? Why does he make this claim? As part of an epitaph, what is the effect of the remark?
6. Explain what is humorous about the following phrases: "**ut familia . . . tamquam mortuum**" (4–5); "**ingemēscente familiā**" (8); "**corōnās et unguenta . . . pugnās**" (11); "**nē effluant vīnum**" (23); "**velit nōlit**" (25).

Jussive and Hortatory Subjunctives

You have studied several kinds of subordinate clauses that require subjunctive verbs: circumstantial and causal clauses introduced by **cum**, result and purpose clauses introduced by **ut**, and indirect questions (see Chapter 54, page 11, "The Subjunctive in Subordinate Clauses").

The *present* subjunctive can also be used in a *main* or *independent* clause to give a command. It is found mainly in the 1st and 3rd persons; for the 2nd person the imperative mood is used. The negative is **nē**. Several examples in the 3rd person occur in the reading:

Hoc monumentum hērēdem nōn (*more correctly*, nē) **sequātur**.
Let *this tomb not* **pass** *to (my) heir.*

Faciātur (*more correctly*, **fiat**) et triclīnia.
Let *a dining room* **be made** *also.*

Catellam cingulō alligātam **dūcat**.
Let her be leading *a puppy tied with a leash.*

In line 24 the subjunctive of **esse** is not expressed but has to be supplied:

Hōrologium in mediō [**sit**].
[**Let there be**] *a clock in the middle.*

When the subjunctive is used this way in the 3rd person, it is called *jussive* (from **iubeō, iubēre**, 2, **iussī, iussum,** *to command*).

When this kind of subjunctive occurs in the 1st person plural, it is called *hortatory* (from **hortor, hortārī**, 1, **hortātus sum,** *to urge*). Some famous examples of the hortatory subjunctive are:

Vīvāmus, mea Lesbia, atque **amēmus**!
Let us live, *my Lesbia, and* **let us love**!

Gaudeāmus igitur, iuvenēs dum sumus.
Let us rejoice *then, while we are young.*

Exercise 56b

Read aloud and translate:

1. "Testāmentum meum," inquit Trimalchiō, "afferātur."
2. Gustēmus omnēs aquam līberam!
3. Omnēs servōs manū mittant dominī.
4. Statua Fortūnātae in monumentō pōnātur.
5. Nē philosophōs audiāmus!
6. Amīcīs cārissimīs grātiās agāmus omnēs!
7. Nē iniūriam accipiat hoc monumentum.
8. Rēs gestae et nōmen Trimalchiōnis ab omnibus legantur.
9. Īnscrīptiōnem idōneam in monumentō meō habeam.
10. Requiēscat in pāce C. Pompēius Trimalchiō Maecēnātiānus.

Exercise 56c

The following is a love charm laid on a woman named Vettia by a man named Felix; it was found in Tunisia, scratched on a lead tablet. Read it aloud, translate it, and identify nine examples of the jussive subjunctive.

Faciat quodcumque dēsīderō Vettia quam peperit Optāta; amōris meī causā, nē dormiat neque cibum accipere possit. Amet mē, Fēlīcem quem peperit Frūcta; oblīvīscātur patris et mātris et propinquōrum suōrum et amīcōrum omnium et aliōrum virōrum. Sōlum mē in mente habeat, dormiēns vigilāns ūrātur frīgeat ardeat Vettia amōris et dēsīderī meī causā. 5

quīcumque, quaecumque, quodcumque, whoever, whatever

dēsīderium, -ī (*n*), desire

ūrō, ūrere (3), **ūssī, ūstum,** to burn
frīgeō, frīgēre (2), to freeze, be cold

Building Up the Meaning XI

Commands

You have now studied three ways of expressing a command or request in Latin:

A. Directly, by using the imperative (Chapter 10):

"**Tacēte**, omnēs!" magnā vōce clāmat. "**Audīte** mē!"
"**Be quiet,** *everyone!" he cries in a loud voice.* "**Listen** *to me*!"

The usual negative is **Nōlī/Nōlīte** + infinitive:

Nōlīte cistam **iacere**, servi!
Don't throw *the trunk, slaves!*

Nē + 2nd person of the present or perfect subjunctive can also express a negative command:

Nē discēdās! *Don't go away!*

The *passive* imperative (found mostly in deponents) ends in **-re** (sing.) or **-minī** (pl.) (Chapter 35):

"Amīcī," inquit, "**ingrediminī** domum meam!"
"Friends," he said, "**come** *into my house!"*

B. Indirectly, by using an **ut**-clause with the subjunctive (negative **nē**) (Chapter 50):

Tē rogō, ut nāvēs in monumentō meō **faciās**.
I ask you **to make** *some ships on my monument.*

C. By using the jussive or hortatory subjunctive (negative **nē**) (Chapter 56):

Catellam cingulō alligātam **dūcat**.
Let her be leading *a puppy tied with a leash.*

Vīvāmus, mea Lesbia, atque **amēmus**!
Let us live, *my Lesbia, and* **let us love!**

Exercise 56d

Select, read aloud, and translate.

1. Trimalchiō praecēpit servīs ut exemplar testāmentī (afferunt / afferrent/ afferant).
2. "Amīce," inquit, "(affer / afferant / afferrent) testāmentum meum!"
3. Trimalchiō dīxit, "(Afferāmus / Afferrent / Afferant) servī testāmentum meum."
4. Amīcī, (sequiminī / sequātur / sequī) mē omnēs!
5. (Adiciāmur / adiciātur / adicerētur) H.M.H.N.S. monumentō meō.
6. "(Nōlīte / Nōlit / Nōlī) flēre, Fortūnāta," inquit Trimalchiō.
7. Fortūnātae autem nōn persuāsit nē (flēret / flet / flēre).
8. Monēbat convīvās nē philosophōs (audiant / audīrentur / audīrent).
9. "Nōs," inquit, "nē philosophōs (audiant / audiāmus / audīrēmus)."

The Millionaire's Autobiography: Ex Parvo Crevit

Having regaled his guests with a detailed account of his preparations for death, Trimalchio next treats them to the story of his life, a classic of the rags-to-riches genre.

"Ad hanc mē fortūnam frūgālitās mea perdūxit. Tam magnus ex Asiā vēnī, quam hic candēlābrus est. Cēterum, quemadmodum dī volunt, dominus in domō factus sum et ecce cēpī ipsimī cerebellum. Quid multa? Cohērēdem mē Caesarī fēcit, et accēpī patrimōnium lāticlāvium. Nēminī tamen nihil satis est. Concupīvī negōtiārī. Nē multīs vōs morer, quīnque 5
nāvēs aedificāvī, onerāvī vīnum—et tunc erat contrā aurum—mīsī Rōmam. Putārēs mē hoc iussisse: omnēs nāvēs naufragāvērunt. Factum, nōn fābula. Alterās fēcī maiōrēs et meliōrēs et fēlīciōrēs. Citō fit quod dī volunt. Ūnō cursū centiēs sēstertiūm corrotundāvī. Quicquid tangēbam, crēscēbat tamquam favus. Postquam coepī plūs habēre quam tōta patria mea habet, manum dē 10
tabulā: sustulī mē dē negōtiātiōne. Crēdite mihi: assem habeās, assem valeās. Sīc amīcus vester, quī fuit rāna, nunc est rēx."

—Petronius, *Satyricon* 75–77 (excerpts)

candēlābrum, -ī (*n*), lampstand
cerebellum, -ī (*n*), brain, heart
Quid multa? to make a long story short, to put it briefly
lāticlāvius, -a, -um, fit for a senator, princely
Nē . . . morer, to cut a long story short
onerō (1), to load
contrā (+ *acc.*), worth its weight in . . .
putārēs, you would think
naufragō (1), to be wrecked
cursus, -ūs (*m*), run, voyage
corrotundō (1), to round off, "clear"
favus, -ī (*m*), honeycomb

manum dē tabulā, hand(s) off (the tablet, or painting, or gaming-board—exact meaning disputed)
negōtiātiō, -ōnis (*f*), business
assem . . . valeās, (if you) have an **as,** an **as** is what you're worth
amīcus vester, yours truly
rāna, -ae (*f*), frog; metaphorically, a nobody

concupīscō, concupīscere (3), **concupīvī, concupītum,** to long for
negōtior, negōtiārī (1), **negōtiātus sum,** to go into business

Word Study XIV

Romance Derivatives: Survival of the Simplest

Many Romance words derive from colloquial, rather than literary ("classical") Latin. Some common literary words were short, irregular, and/or easily confused with other words; ordinary speakers of Latin preferred synonyms that were easier to recognize and to inflect. Hence:

1. **Ōs, ōris** (*n*,), "mouth," was a very short word and liable to be confused with **os, ossis** (*n*), "bone"; it lost out, in popular speech, to **bucca, -ae** (*f*), "cheek," from which derive It. *bocca*, Sp. *boca*, and Fr. *bouche*.
2. **Rēs, reī** (*f*), "thing," another short word and a member of the relatively rare 5th declension, was replaced by **causa**, which eventually produced It. and Sp. *cosa* and Fr. *chose*.
3. Where a classical verb had an alternative form in the 1st conjugation, the latter tended to survive, as being easier to conjugate; hence the Romance verbs for "to sing" derive not from **canere** but from the frequentative form **cantāre**: It. *cantare*, Sp. *cantar*, Fr. *chanter*.
4. Some short words were easier to remember and inflect in their diminutive form: classical **auris, -is** (*f*), "ear" (not to be confused with **aura**, "breeze," or **aurum**, "gold") gave way to its diminutive form **auricula**, from which derive Sp. *oreja* and Fr. *oreille*.
5. Some of the commonest classical words seem to have been rejected by ordinary people as being too literary or "fancy." To them, **equus** sounded something like "steed," and you don't hitch a "steed" to a plow or a wagon; they called the beast a **caballus** ("nag"); hence It. *cavallo*, Sp. *caballo*, and Fr. *cheval*. An amusing illustration of the ordinary person's preference for the slang word over the literary word is the Italian noun *testa* (Fr. *tête*), "head." These words come from **testa, -ae** (*f*), whose literal meaning was "a ceramic pot," but which was used jokingly of the human head until it eventually supplanted the classical **caput** altogether.

These modern Romance words bear eloquent witness to the difficulties and frustrations ordinary Romans experienced in handling their language. Like us, they found look-alike words confusing, they liked simplicity and regularity, and they bypassed "fancy" or "poetic" words.

PART II
Public Life, Government, and Politics in the Late Republic

Thus far, you have been reading about the time of the imperial period of Roman history in the 1st century A.D. We now turn to an earlier time, the time of the Republic (509–27 B.C.), which began after the period of the kings (753–509 B.C.). The early Republic saw the extension of Roman power throughout the Italian peninsula and the subsequent expansion of Roman influence throughout the Mediterranean world after the Punic Wars with Carthage (264–146 B.C.). Politically, the period of the Republic was a time of struggle between the noble or senatorial class, which held control of the government, and the middle or equestrian class, which wanted more political control. The last century B.C., known as the late Republic, was a turbulent time of transition between the political orders of Republican and Imperial Rome (27 B.C.–A.D. 476).

At the center of the events of the late Republic was Marcus Tullius Cicero, orator and statesman, philosopher and writer. Always a political idealist, Cicero was often confused by the perplexities of Republican politics and became a pawn of men with more powerful ambitions: first Caesar and Pompey, and then Antony and Octavian. During the final two decades of the Republic, the struggles of these men for control of Rome led to two civil wars, the first between Caesar and Pompey (49–45 B.C.) and the second between Antony and Octavian (44–31 B.C.). These wars led to the final dissolution of the Republic.

The events of 53–52 B.C. serve to illustrate the political forces and public personalities of the late Republic. During the previous decade, political bands, led by P. Clodius Pulcher, agent of Caesar, and T. Annius Milo, henchman of the senatorial faction, opposed each other and disrupted the normal constitutional processes of state. Milo and Clodius themselves became political candidates for the elections of 53; the subsequent postponement of elections due to violence eventually led to the murder of Clodius by Milo. During this crisis, the Senate turned to Pompey while Caesar was fighting in Gaul, and this set up a confrontation between Pompey and Caesar that was to lead to civil war. In 52 B.C., Cicero delivered a courtroom speech of defense on behalf of his friend Milo, a speech which has been preserved and is titled *Pro Milone* (*For Milo*). The commentary on this speech by Q. Asconius Pedianus, a scholar of the 1st century A.D., who consulted official records of the trial, gives us a unique perspective on Cicero's courtroom pyrotechnics and on the volatile politics of the late Republic.

3 **Milōnī . . . erant inimīcitiae:** the dative with **esse** shows possession; literally, "There were to Milo and Clodius. . . ." A smoother English translation would be "Milo and Clodius had. . . ."

inimīcitiae: literally, "hostility," but here a technical term meaning "political rivalry." Cf. **amīcissimus** (4).

4 **in redūcendōque eō:** Milo had helped to recall Cicero from exile five years earlier, in 57 B.C. Clodius had been responsible for his exile in 58 B.C.

tribūnus plēbis: this officer, one of 10, protected the rights of the plebs, or common people, by interposing his veto when an act, decree, or law proved detrimental to the interests of the plebeians.

8 **erant uterque: uterque** refers to both Clodius and Milo, considered separately, and therefore the verb is plural.

audāciā: ablative of respect, designating the specific way or respect in which Clodius and Milo were equal.

prō meliōribus partibus: these were the Optimates or "best people," that faction of the Senate interested in maintaining senatorial dominance in government. Their rivals were the Populares or those from the middle class who sought the support of the poor in opposition to the control of the Senate.

9 **quam dēbilem futūram cōnsule Milōne:** the praetorship was subordinate to the consulship in status and authority, so Milo would have a political advantage over Clodius.

10 **futūram:** = **futūram esse,** future infinitive of **esse**.

11 **eius:** i.e., Milo's.

12 **T. Munātius Plancus:** tribune of 52 B.C. and archenemy of Cicero, Plancus was later accused by him and condemned for public violence.

referrī ad senātum: technical term, "(that a motion) be put before (referred to) the Senate."

patriciīs: patricians were members of the Roman nobility, whose ancestors had been advisors to the kings during the period of the monarchy. The patricians had originally appointed an **interrēx** to exercise provisional authority upon the death of the king. During the Republic, the patrician members of the Senate would select an **interrēx** as an emergency measure from among their number to serve for five-day periods in the absence of consuls.

13 **quī interrēgem prōderent:** here, as often, the relative pronoun **quī** is equivalent to **ut** in introducing a purpose clause; it links the purpose directly to a particular word, in this case the antecedent **patriciīs**, and introduces a *relative clause of purpose*.

14 **aliī ex aliīs:** "one after another."

16 **senātūs cōnsultum ultimum:** "final decree of the Senate," often abbreviated S.C.U., was passed in times of emergency and granted martial powers to magistrates. Asconius provides the traditional formula of the grant, **ut vidērent nē quid dētrīmentī rēs pūblica caperet**, that the magistrates "see to it that the State should come to no harm." The S.C.U. was invoked 10 times during the final 45 years of the Republic.

57
Government in Crisis

Milo and Clodius, deadly political enemies, are both seeking office for the same year, 52 B.C. Milo is a candidate for the consulship, Clodius for a judicial office known as the praetorship. Asconius's vivid account of how the elections were postponed and of the final outcome gives the reader a ringside seat in this political arena.

T. Annius Milō et P. Plautius Hypsaeus et Q. Metellus Scīpiō cōnsulātum petīvērunt, nōn sōlum largītiōne palam profūsā sed etiam factiōnibus armātōrum succinctī. Milōnī et Clōdiō summae erant inimīcitiae, quod Milō Cicerōnis erat amīcissimus, in redūcendōque eō ēnixē operam tribūnus plēbis dederat; et P. Clōdius restitūtō quoque Cicerōnī erat īnfestissimus, 5 ideōque summē studēbat Hypsaeō et Scīpiōnī contrā Milōnem. Ac saepe inter sē Milō et Clōdius cum suīs factiōnibus Rōmae dēpugnāvērunt: et erant uterque audāciā pārēs, sed Milō prō meliōribus partibus stābat. Praetereā eōdem annō cōnsulātum Milō, Clōdius praetūram petēbat, quam dēbilem futūram cōnsule Milōne intellegēbat. 10

Asconius goes on to explain that the elections had to be postponed due to the violence of the candidates. Milo, however, was confident of election for he enjoyed the support of the Optimates, who opposed Clodius, and the favor of the people, whose votes he solicited through lavish expenditures on games and shows.

Competītōrēs eius trahere diem volēbant, ideōque Pompēius gener Scīpiōnis et T. Munātius Plancus tribūnus plēbis referrī ad senātum dē patriciīs convocandīs, quī interrēgem prōderent, nōn sunt passī, cum interrēgem prōdere ob statum rērum opus esset. Fiēbant tandem aliī ex aliīs interrēgēs, quia comitia cōnsulāria propter eōsdem candidatōrum tumultūs et eāsdem 15 manūs armātās habērī nōn poterant. Itaque prīmō factum est senātūs cōnsultum ultimum ut interrēx et tribūnī plēbis et Pompēius, quī prō cōnsule ad urbem erat, vidērent nē quid dētrīmentī rēs pūblica caperet atque dīlectūs autem Pompēius tōtā Italiā habēret.

Inter haec cum crēbrēsceret rūmor Cn. Pompēium creārī dictātōrem 20 oportēre neque aliter mala cīvitātis sēdārī posse, vīsum est optimātibus tūtius esse cōnsulem sine collēgā creārī, et cum tractāta ea rēs esset in senātū, factō in M. Bibulī sententiam senātūs cōnsultō, Pompēius ab interrēge Serviō Sulpiciō cōnsul creātus est statimque cōnsulātum iniit.

—Asconius, *Commentary on Cicero's Speech for Milo* (excerpts)

17 **prō cōnsule ad urbem erat:** a magistrate acting **prō cōnsule**, more commonly known as a **prōcōnsul**, was a former consul who retained military authority as governor of a province. Pompey, although nominally serving as proconsul of Spain, had remained near Rome to protect his political interests.

19 **tōtā Italiā:** = **ā tōtā Italiā,** ablative of place from which.

20 **cum crēbrēsceret rūmor:** "although the rumor grew stronger. . . ."; **cum** here means "although," and the clause with the subjunctive is called a *concessive clause,* because it grants or concedes the truth of what is being maintained.

Cn. Pompēium: Pompey the Great, an earlier political ally of Caesar and the Populares, was now supported by senatorial extremists who wanted him to intercede in the riots provoked by Caesar's henchman Clodius.

21 **oportēre . . . posse:** infinitives after **rūmor crēbrēsceret**, in an indirect statement. **Creārī** and **sēdārī** complement the meanings of these infinitives.

vīsum est: "it seemed (best). . . ." = "they decided. . . ."

22 **cōnsulem sine collēgā:** consuls, regular chief magistrates of state, were usually two in number. Pompey's sole consulship would be sure to hasten his inevitable confrontation with Caesar, since both aspired to the leadership of Rome. Caesar was fighting in Gaul at the time.

23 **in M. Bibulī sententiam:** "on the motion of Bibulus," a technical idiom.

nōn sōlum . . . sed etiam, not only, but also
largītiō, largītiōnis (*f*), bribery
palam, openly, publicly
factiō, factiōnis (*f*), gang, political partisans
inimīcitia, -ae (*f*), political rivalry
in redūcendō eō, in bringing him back
ēnixē, eagerly
operam dare, to give attention to, work hard to
tribūnus plēbis, tribune or representative of the common people
īnfestus, -a, -um, hostile to (+ *dat.*)
studeō (2) (+ *dat.*), to support, be eager for
pār, paris, equal
prō (+ *abl.*), for, on behalf of
praetūra, -ae (*f*), praetorship, office of praetor, one of eight judges
dēbilis, -is, -e, feeble, powerless
gener, generī (*m*), son-in-law
dē patriciīs convocandīs, about assembling the patricians
cum (+ *subjunctive*), although
interrēx, interrēgis (*m*), interrex, temporary chief magistrate
status, -ūs (*m*), condition, state
opus est, it is necessary, there is need to
comitia cōnsulāria, assembly to elect consuls and praetors
manus, -ūs (*f*), band, gang
senātūs cōnsultum, decree of the Senate
prō cōnsule, with consular power
dīlectus, -ūs (*m*), draft of troops, levy
dictātor, dictātōris (*m*), dictator, magistrate with absolute power in emergencies
aliter, otherwise
cīvitās, cīvitātis (*f*), state, body of citizens
sēdō (1), to settle, calm
tūtus, -a, -um, safe
collēga, -ae (*m*), colleague, partner
creō (1), to elect
tractō (1), to discuss, handle
sententia, -ae (*f*), feeling, opinion

profundō, profundere (3), **profūdī, profūsum,** to pour forth
succingō, succingere (3), **succinxī, succinctum,** to equip
restituō, restituere (3), **restituī, restitūtum,** to restore, reinstate
prōdō, prōdere (3), **prōdidī, prōditum,** to appoint
crēbrēscō, crēbrēscere (3), **crēbuī,** to increase, gather strength

Exercise 57a

Answer the following questions in English, with reference to the specified lines of the reading passage. Questions 4 and 5 refer to the English following line 10.

1. By what means did the consular candidates secure votes during their election campaigns? (2–3)
2. What offices did Clodius and Milo each seek? (1–2, 9–10)
3. What role did Cicero play in the rivalry between the candidates? (3–5)
4. What immediate consequences did the behavior of the candidates have for the election?
5. For what reasons did Milo feel confident about winning?
6. What further measures did Milo's rivals take? (11–14)
7. What were the provisions of the **senātūs cōnsultum ultimum**? (17–19)
8. How was the crisis temporarily resolved? (20–24)

Exercise 57b

1. Was Roman society classless? What indications do we have in this passage that it was not? What were the political positions of these classes?
2. What is meant by the term "republic"? What evidence is there in this reading passage that Rome was a republic at this time?
3. To what extent was Rome a government of laws? To what extent was it a government of men? What features of Roman politics and government seem familiar to you? What features seem strange?

Virtūs, probitās, integritās in candidātō, nōn linguae volūbilitās, nōn ars, nōn scientia requīrī solet. *Moral courage, honesty, and integrity are usually sought in candidates, not a glib tongue, skill, or knowledge.* (Cicero, *For Plancius*, 62)

Politics in the Late Republic

A candidate for political office, when canvassing for votes in the Forum, an activity termed **ambitiō**, wore a toga of bright white rubbed with chalk (**toga candida**) as a symbol of his purity and fitness for office. The candidate was accompanied by a slave (**nōmenclātor**), who reminded him of voters' names, and by a crowd of partisans (**sectātōrēs**), mostly freedmen clients, whose task it was to secure votes through promises and even bribery.

In 64 B.C., Cicero's brother Quintus wrote a campaign handbook titled *On Being a Candidate for the Consulship*, to assist his elder brother's election bid for the consulship of 63. This political pamphlet lists some things for a candidate to consider during a campaign:

> Take care to have followers at your heels daily, of every kind, class, and age; because from their number people can figure out how much power and support you are going to have at the polls.
>
> You particularly need to use flattery. No matter how vicious and vile it is on the other days of a man's life, when he runs for office it is indispensable.
>
> Getting votes among the rank and file requires calling everyone by his name. Make it clear you know people's names; practice, get better at it day to day. Nothing seems to me better for popularity and gaining favor.
>
> If you make a promise, the matter is not fixed. It's for a future day, and it affects only a few people. But if you say no, you are sure to alienate people right away, and a lot of them.

But, of all the forces at work in determining the outcome of an election, it was usually the character of the candidate himself which was the most influential factor.

> When Scipio Nasica was seeking the office of curule aedile and, in the custom of a campaigner, had firmly grasped the hand of a certain man worn leathery with farm work, to get a laugh he asked the man whether or not he usually walked on his hands. This comment, when heard by bystanders and passed around, was the source of Scipio's downfall: for all the country voters thought that he was laughing at poverty.
>
> Valerius Maximus, VII.5.2

Cōnsul: chief officer of state

Praetor: presided over courts

Aedilis: oversaw public works and games

Quaestor: managed state finances

CURSUS HONORUM

VERBS: The Gerundive or Future Passive Participle

Look at these examples from the reading passage:

Milō . . . in **redūcendō** . . . eō ēnixē operam . . . dederat. . . . (4–5)
Milo had given serious attention to **bringing** *him* **back***. . . .*
Pompēius . . . et . . . Plancus . . . referrī ad senātum dē patriciīs **convocandīs** nōn sunt passī. . . . (11–13)
Pompey and Plancus did not allow the Senate to be consulted about **assembling** *the patricians. . . .*

As future passive participles, the gerundives **redūcendō** and **convocandīs** are future and passive: "about to be brought back," "about to be assembled." They are also adjectives, agreeing with the pronoun **eō** and the noun **patriciīs**, respectively. The literal future passive meaning of the gerundive is present in such English words as *agenda*, "things about to be done," but in translating the Latin gerundive into idiomatic English, often a verbal noun ending in *-ing* will be used, as in the examples above: "bringing . . . back" and "assembling."

Here are some examples of how gerundives are used in Latin and translated into English. Note how the gerundive and the noun it modifies can serve any of the usual constructions of nouns in the various cases.

1. The gerundive and its noun in the *genitive case* are used with **causā** or **grātiā**, "for the sake of," to express purpose, e.g.:
   Cōnsul creātus est reī pūblicae **gubernandae causā.**
   The consul was elected for the sake of governing the state (literally, *for the sake of the state about to be governed*).
2. The gerundive and its noun in the *genitive case* are also used with special adjectives, e.g.:
   Cōnsul erat **cupidus** reī pūblicae **gubernandae.**
   The consul was desirous of governing the state.
3. The *dative case* of the gerundive and its noun is used when the gerundive phrase serves as the indirect object, e.g.:
   Cōnsul multum tempus reī pūblicae **gubernandae** dedit.
   The consul gave much time to governing the state.
4. The gerundive and its noun are also used in the *dative case* with special adjectives, e.g.:
   Cōnsul erat **idōneus** reī pūblicae **gubernandae**.
   The consul was suitable for governing the state.
5. The gerundive and its noun are found in the *accusative case* with **ad**, showing purpose, e.g.:
   Cōnsul creātus est **ad** rem pūblicam **gubernandam**.
   The consul was elected for the purpose of governing (i.e., to govern) the state.

6. The *ablative case* of the gerundive and its noun is used in prepositional phrases with **dē**, **ex**, and **in**, e.g.:
   Cōnsul cōnsilia capiēbat **dē** rē pūblicā **gubernandā**.
   The consul made plans concerning governing the state.
7. The *ablative case* of the gerundive and its noun may also serve as an ablative of means, e.g.:
   Cōnsul rem pūblicam gubernāvit cōnsiliīs **capiendīs**.
   The consul governed the state by making plans.

Remember that in form and function the *gerundive* is an *adjective*, which means that it will modify a noun.

1st Conj.	parand***us, -a, -um***
2nd Conj.	habend***us, -a, -um***
3rd Conj.	mittend***us, -a, -um***
	iaciend***us, -a, -um***
4th Conj.	audiend***us, -a, -um***

Salūs populī suprēma lēx est. *The safety of the people is the supreme law.* (Cicero, *On Laws*, III.8)

Exercise 57c

Read aloud and translate the following sentences.

1. Patriciī propter candidātōrum tumultūs ad interrēgēs prōdendōs convocābantur.
2. Comitia cōnsulāria cōnsulum praetōrumque creandōrum causā habita sunt.
3. Multī crēdēbant Pompēium virum Caesarī auctoritāte pārem esse idōneumque reī pūblicae gubernandae.
4. Senātōrēs Caesare necandō rem pūblicam restituere cōnātī sunt.
5. Cicerō cupidus bonae ōrātiōnis audiendae semper erat.
6. Senātūs cōnsultum ultimum ad conservandam rem pūblicam factum est.
7. Tribūnus plēbis referrī ad senātum dē lēgibus ferendīs quae factiōnibus resisterent nōn passus est.
8. Itaque Cicerōnī rogantī cūr ipse cōnsul factus esset, Cn. Pompēius respondit, "Reī pūblicae conservandae grātiā."
9. Milō operam dedit redūcendō Cicerōnī.
10. Senātōrēs saepe convocātī sunt rērum tractandārum causā.

auctoritās, auctoritātis (*f*), influence
gubernō (1), to govern, rule
cupidus, -a, -um (+ *gen.*), desirous
lēgem ferre, to pass a law
grātiā (+ *gen.*), for the sake of

Building Up the Meaning XII

Expressions of Purpose

You have now learned several different ways to express the idea of purpose in Latin. Observe how the following sentence may be rendered in Latin:

The Senate makes laws to govern the people.

Purpose Clause: Senātus lēgēs fert **ut** populum Rōmānum **gubernent**.
Relative Clause of Purpose: Senātus lēgēs fert **quae** populum Rōmānum **gubernent**.
Gerundive with **ad**: Senātus lēgēs fert **ad** populum Rōmānum **gubernandum**.
Gerundive with **causā**: Senātus lēgēs fert populī Rōmānī **gubernandī causā**.
Gerundive with **grātiā**: Senātus lēgēs fert populī Rōmānī **gubernandī grātiā**.

Note: the gerundive usually precedes **causā** and **grātiā**.

Word Study XV

Participles in the Romance Languages

In later Latin, the gerundive with the ablative singular ending came to be used as the equivalent of the present participle and, in fact, was adopted as such by Italian. Spanish preserved the function of the Latin gerundive and called it the *gerundio*. Compare the French present participle, which derives from the present participle in **-nt-**, in the chart below:

Latin *Gerundive (abl. sing.)*	*Italian* *Pres. Part.*	*Spanish* Gerundio	*French* *Pres. Part.*
amandō	amando	amando	aimant
tenendō	tenendo	teniendo	tenant
vīvendō	vivendo	viviendo	vivant

Exercise 57d

Construct the Latin gerundive equivalents of the following Italian and Spanish forms. The French is given for comparison.

Italian *Pres. Part.*	*Spanish* Gerundio	*Latin* *Gerundive (abl. sing.)*	*French* *Pres. Part.*
desiderando	desiendo	______________	désirant
facendo	haciendo	______________	faisant
preparando	preparando	______________	préparant
scrivendo	escribiendo	______________	écrivant
videndo	viendo	______________	voyant

1 **A.D. XV Kal. Febr.**: fifteen days before the Kalends of February = January 18.

2 **dictātor:** Milo was chief magistrate, or dictator, of Lanuvium, a small town in the Alban hills south of Rome. He was visiting for the purpose of appointing a priest, most likely for the city's famous cult of Juno Sospita.

3 **Bovillās . . . Arīciā:** Bovillae was a small but ancient town some 12 miles (7 1/2 kilometers) south of Rome. Aricia, about 4 miles (2 1/2 kilometers) further south, was the first way station on the Appian Way; Horace stopped there en route to Brundisium. See the map on page 90.

6 **ūnus, duo dē plēbe nōtī hominēs:** note the asyndeton or lack of conjunction. The verb **erant** is to be understood (an example of ellipsis).

7 **L. Sullae dictātōris:** L. Cornelius Sulla, some thirty years before this, had been the first military dictator of the late Republic. His victory in a civil war left him master of Rome and champion of the Optimate cause. Note the methodical presentation of facts throughout this first paragraph, almost as if Asconius were presenting a transcript of the trial. Notice, also, the interplay of the historical perfect tense with the imperfect.

10 **in ultimō agmine:** "at the rear of the column." The two parties were passing one another, going in opposite directions.

euntēs: present participle of the irregular verb **eō.**

rixam commīsērunt: this phrase makes it clear that Asconius believed the responsibility for initiating hostilities lay with Milo's men. **Rixa** is a skirmish, **pugna** (12), a pitched battle.

14 **Milō . . . exturbārī tabernam iussit:** this complex sentence may reveal the difficulty in Milo's mind of making the decision to do away with Clodius. It contrasts with the previous rather terse, simple sentences, which had given momentum to the narration.

vulnerātum: another example of ellipsis, **esse** being omitted.

15 **cum . . . intellegeret:** a **cum** causal clause, as is (**cum**) . . . **esset habitūrus** (15–16).

vīvō eō . . . occīsō (eō): ablative absolutes; **eō = Clōdiō.**

futūrum: again, ellipsis of **esse;** the subject of the infinitive is **illud,** referring to the wounding of Clodius.

16 **etiamsī subeunda esset poena:** "even if he had to undergo punishment. . . ."; **esset** is subjunctive in a conditional clause.

17 **multīsque vulneribus cōnfectus:** ellipsis of **est** after **cōnfectus;** the connective **-que** binds together **extractus est** and **cōnfectus (est).**

18 **Cadāver in viā relictum: cadāver** is the object of **sustulit** and **iussit.**

21 **ante . . . hōram:** before the end of the first hour of the night, about 7 p.m.

23 **factī invidiam:** "anger at the deed. . . ."; the objective genitive **factī** denotes the object of the anger, the killing of Clodius.

26 **Eīsque hortantibus:** ablative absolute.

vulgus imperītum: note **vulgus,** a rare 2nd declension neuter noun in **-us.**

27 **in rostrīs posuit:** the speaker's platform (**rostra,** literally "beaks of ships," which decorated the platform and gave it its name) was not in the same place at Asconius's writing as it was in the time of the events narrated. It was moved by Julius Caesar from just in front of the Curia to an adjacent site.

58
A Political Murder

The political struggles of 53 B.C. reached a climax in January of 52, when a brawl on the Appian Way between Clodius and Milo led to Clodius's death. This homicide triggered mob riots and the subsequent burning of the Senate House in Rome.

A.d. XV Kal. Febr. Milō Lānuvium, ex quō erat mūnicipiō et ubi tum dictātor, profectus est ad flāminem prōdendum posterā diē. Occurrit eī circā hōram nōnam Clōdius paulō ultrā Bovillās, rediēns Arīciā, ubi decuriōnēs erat allocūtus. Vehēbātur Clōdius equō; servī XXX ferē expedītī, ut illō tempore mōs erat iter facientibus, gladiīs cinctī sequēbantur. Erant cum 5 Clōdiō praetereā trēs comitēs eius, ex quibus eques Rōmānus ūnus, duo dē plēbe nōtī hominēs. Milō raedā vehēbātur cum uxōre Faustā, fīliā L. Sullae dictātōris, et M. Fufiō familiāre suō. Sequēbātur eōs magnum servōrum agmen, inter quōs gladiātōrēs quoque erant, ex quibus duo nōtī, Eudamus et Birria. Eī in ultimō agmine tardius euntēs cum servīs P. Clōdiī rixam 10 commīsērunt. Ad quem tumultum cum respexisset Clōdius minitābundus, umerum eius Birria rumpiā trāiēcit. Inde cum orta esset pugna, plūrēs causā adiuvandī ad Milōnem accurrērunt. Clōdius vulnerātus in tabernam proximam in Bovillānō agrō dēlātus est. Milō, cum cognōvit vulnerātum Clōdium, cum sibi perīculōsius illud vīvō eō futūrum intellegeret, occīsō autem 15 magnum sōlācium esset habitūrus etiamsī subeunda esset poena, exturbārī tabernam iussit. Atque ita Clōdius latēns extractus est multīsque vulneribus cōnfectus. Cadāver in viā relictum, quia servī Clōdiī aut occīsī erant aut graviter sauciī latēbant, Sex. Teidius senātor, quī forte rūre in urbem revertēbātur, sustulit et lectīcā suā Rōmam ferrī iussit. 20

Perlātum est corpus Clōdiī ante prīmam noctis hōram, īnfimaeque plēbis et servōrum maxima multitūdō magnō luctū corpus in ātriō domūs positum circumstetit. Augēbat autem factī invidiam uxor Clōdiī Fulvia, quae cum effūsā lamentātiōne vulnera eius ostendēbat. Maior posterā diē lūce prīmā multitūdō eiusdem generis cōnflūxit, complūrēsque nōtī hominēs vīsī sunt. 25 Eīsque hortantibus vulgus imperītum corpus nūdum ac lutātum, ut vulnera vidērī possent, in Forum dētulit et in rostrīs posuit. Ibi prō contiōne T. Munātius Plancus, quī competītōribus studēbat, invidiam in Milōnem invehendō fēcit. Populus, duce Sex. Clōdiō scrība, corpus in Cūriam intulit cremāvitque subselliīs et tribūnālibus et mēnsīs et cōdicibus librāriōrum; 30 quō igne et ipsa quoque Cūria flagrāvit et item Porcia Basilica, quae erat eī iūncta, ambusta est.

—Asconius, *Commentary on Cicero's Speech for Milo* (excerpts)

prō contiōne: contiō is a technical political term meaning an open meeting of the people to discuss the issues involved in an upcoming vote for a law or magistrate. Such meetings, usually held in the Forum, were rowdy and boisterous and often resulted in violence during the late Republic.

T. Munātius Plancus: Plancus had supported Milo's political opponents and had interfered with the election of an **interrēx** in 52 B.C. (see 57:12–14).

29 **duce Sex. Clōdiō scrībā:** an agent and probably freedman of P. Clodius.

31 **quō igne:** ablative of cause, approximating **propter** or **ob** + acc.

Porcia Basilica: this basilica, the earliest in Rome, was built in 184 B.C.

mūnicipium, -ī (*n*), town
flāmen, flāminis (*m*), priest
ultrā (+ *acc.*), beyond
decuriō, decuriōnis (*m*), town councilman
expedītus, -a, -um, lightly equipped
eques, equitis (*m*), knight, member of the equestrian order
agmen, agminis (*n*), column, band
minitābundus, -a, -um, menacing
umerus, -ī (*m*), upper arm
rumpia, -ae (*f*), pike, spear
causā adiuvandī, for the sake of helping
proximus, -a, -um, nearest
solācium, -ī (*n*), relief
etiamsī, even if, although
exturbō (1), to take by storm
cadāver, cadāveris (*n*), corpse, body
saucius, -a, -um, wounded, hurt
rūre, from the country
īnfimus, -a, -um, lowest, most vile
luctus, -ūs (*m*), mourning
invidia, -ae (*f*), ill will
vulgus, -ī (*n*), mob, rabble
imperītus, -a, -um, ignorant
lutō (1), to make grimy, soil
rostra, -ōrum (*n pl*), Rostra, speaker's platform in the Forum
prō (+ *abl.*), in front of, before
contiō, contiōnis (*f*), public meeting
in (+ *acc.*), against
invehendō, by assaulting with words
dux, ducis (*m*), leader
scrība, -ae (*m*), scribe, clerk
cremō (1), to burn
subsellium, -ī (*n*), bench
cōdex, cōdicis (*m*), ledger, tablet
librārius, -ī (*m*), copier, secretary
ignis, ignis (*m*), fire
flagrō (1), to blaze up, burn
item, likewise, also
Porcius, -a, -um, Porcian, of M. Porcius Cato, famous Roman censor
basilica, -ae (*f*), basilica, public courthall

vehō, vehere (3), **vexī, vectum,** to carry, convey
cingō, cingere (3), **cīnxī, cinctum,** to gird, equip
dēferō, dēferre (*irreg.*), **dētulī, dēlātum,** to bring down
subeō, subīre (*irreg.*), **subiī, subitum,** to undergo, endure
cōnficiō, cōnficere (3), **cōnfēcī, cōnfectum,** to finish off
revertor, revertī (3), **reversus sum,** to turn back, return
perferō, perferre (*irreg.*), **pertulī, perlātum,** to deliver, bring
cōnfluō, cōnfluere (3), **cōnflūxī, cōnfluctum,** to flow together
invehō, invehere (3), **invexī, invectum,** to speak out against
ambūrō, ambūrere (3), **ambussī, ambustum,** to scorch, burn

Exercise 58a

Answer the following questions in English, with reference to the specified lines of the reading passage.

1. When and where did the events of the narrative take place? (1–3)
2. Why was Milo on the Appian Way? Why was Clodius? (2–4)
3. Describe the respective traveling styles of Clodius and Milo. (4–10)
4. Who began the ruckus? Describe what happened to Clodius. (10–11 and 11–12)
5. Describe how the body came to Rome and its reception on arrival. (19–21 and 22–25)
6. How did the mob come to bring the body into the Forum? What was its appearance? (26–27)
7. What finally happened to the body of Clodius and what consequences did this act have? (29–30 and 31–32)

Exercise 58b

1. Why did Milo decide to kill Clodius? Can you think of other examples of violent acts perpetrated for political reasons?
2. Explain how Asconius's account of the events on the Appian Way makes Milo's plea of self-defense untenable.
3. What are the characteristics of Asconius's prose style? Is the narrative simple and straightforward or embroidered with supposition and personal opinion? Does the style fit the content?

Exercise 58c

Imagine that you were traveling in Milo's party along the Appian Way. Write a descriptive and dramatic account of the events of January 18 as you witnessed them. Include a map showing the relative locations of the places referred to in the reading and the positions of Clodius and Milo.

VERBS: The Gerund or Verbal Noun

Look at these examples from the reading:

Inde cum orta esset pugna, plūrēs causā **adiuvandī** ad Milōnem accurrērunt. (12–13)

Then, when an all-out battle had begun, more (slaves) ran toward Milo for the sake of **helping out**.

Ibi prō cōntione T. Munātius Plancus . . . invidiam in Milōnem **invehendō** fēcit. (27–29)

There, before a public gathering, T. Munatius Plancus raised hatred against Milo **by assaulting him with words**.

In these examples, **adiuvandī** and **invehendō** are genitive and ablative forms, respectively, of the *gerund*, or verbal noun, corresponding to the English verbal noun in *-ing*. The Latin gerund is active in meaning: "helping," "assaulting." It has the same forms as the neuter singular of the gerundive, except that the nominative is replaced by the present active infinitive. Similarly, in English we can say either *Writing well is an art* (gerund) or *To write well is an art* (infinitive). Here are the forms of the gerund:

Nom.	(parāre)	preparing
Gen.	habend*ī*	of having
Dat.	mittend*ō*	for sending
Acc.	iaciend***um***	throwing
Abl.	audiend*ō*	by listening

The Gerundive	*The Gerund*
is a verbal adjective; is passive in its literal sense; agrees with a noun or pronoun; and has all the case forms of the adjective **magnus, -a, -um**.	is a verbal noun; is active in sense; is equivalent to the English verbal noun in -ing; has all the case forms of the neuter singular gerundive, except the nominative; and uses the present active infinitive for the nominative case.

The Romans preferred a gerundive to a gerund when the thought required a direct object. For example, the sentence "The boy is becoming more desirous of hearing the speech" could be translated with a gerund in the genitive case ("of hearing") and a direct object of the verbal idea contained in the gerund:

Puer **ōrātiōnem audiendī** cupidior fit.
The boy is becoming more desirous of hearing the speech.

The Romans, however, preferred to put the direct object of the gerund (i.e., **ōrātiōnem**) into the genitive case, dependent on "more desirous (of)," and to modify it with a gerundive:

Puer **ōrātiōnis audiendae** cupidior fit.
(literally) *The boy is becoming more desirous of the speech about to be heard.*

The following sentence from Cicero (*On the State*, III.35) shows both a gerund and a gerundive construction:

> Nam extrā **ulcīscendī** aut **prōpulsandōrum hostium** causam, bellum gerī iūstum nūllum potest.
>
> *For no war can be waged justly except for the sake of avenging (a wrong)* (**ulcīscendī**: gerund) *or repelling an enemy* (**prōpulsandōrum hostium**: gerundive).

Exercise 58d

Read each of the following sentences aloud and determine whether a gerund or gerundive is being used. Then translate.

1. Praedōnibus īnsidiae sunt modus operandī.
2. Tribūnī in Milōnem dīcendō invidiam īnfimae plēbis augēre cōnātī sunt.
3. Servī praedōnum repellendōrum causā viātōrēs comitantur.
4. Gladiātōribus vīsīs, servī Clōdiī ācriōrēs ad pugnandum factī sunt.
5. Ad corpus Clōdiī cremandum scelestī hominēs Cūriam flagrāvērunt.
6. Cicerō, arbiter bibendī creātus, "Bene Clōdiō" iterum iterumque dīcēbat. Causā iocī?
7. Senātōrī Rōmānō nūllum tempus ad revertendum Rōmam erat.
8. Milō iter faciēbat Lānuvium flāminis prōdendī grātiā.
9. Complūrēs servī adiuvandī causā ad Milōnem accurrērunt.
10. Fuitne Cūria idōneus locus cremandō corporī Clōdiī?

īnsidiae, -ārum (*f pl*), ambush

ācer, ācris, ācre, fierce

Exercise 58e

Complete the thoughts of the following authors with the correct form of the gerund. The infinitive of each verb is given in parentheses.

1. Homō ad duās rēs, ad ____________, et ad ____________est nātus. (intellegere) (agere)
   Man is born for two purposes, for thinking and for doing. (Cicero)
2. ____________, ____________, bene ____________prospera omnia cēdunt. (vigilāre) (agere) (cōnsulere)
   All success comes from vigilance, energy, planning. (Sallust)
3. Studium ____________voluntāte, quae cōgī nōn potest, cōnstat. (discere)
   The eagerness of learning depends on willingness, which cannot be secured by force. (Quintilian)
4. Hae vicissitūdinēs fortūnae, etsī nōbīs iūcundae in ____________nōn fuērunt, in ____________tamen erunt iūcundae. (experīrī) (legere)
   These changes of fortune, even though they have not been pleasant for us in the experiencing, nevertheless will be pleasant in the reading. (Cicero)

Political Hooliganism

Here Cicero writes in a letter to his brother Quintus about what had happened in a public meeting in the Forum, prior to a trial of Milo in 56 B.C. Charges of public violence had been brought by the tribune Clodius. As you read aloud and translate, try to identify the ways in which Cicero makes his narrative more vivid and more personal. We begin **in mediās rēs**, right in the middle of things.

Milō adfuit. Dīxit Marcellus, ā mē rogātus. Eī Pompēius advocātus dīxit, sīve voluit; nam, ut surrēxit, operae Clōdiānae clāmōrem sustulērunt; idque eī perpetuā ōrātiōne contigit, nōn modo ut acclāmātiōne, sed ut convīciō et maledictīs impedīrētur.

Quī ut perōrāvit, surrēxit Clōdius. Eī tantus clāmor ā nostrīs (placuerat 5
enim referre grātiam), ut neque mente neque linguā neque ōre cōnsisteret. Ea rēs ācta est, cum hōrā sextā vix Pompēius perōrāsset, usque ad hōram octāvam, cum omnia maledicta, versūs etiam obscēnissimī in Clōdium et Clōdiam dīcerentur. Hōrā ferē nōnā, quasī signō datō, Clōdiānī nostrōs cōnspūtāre coepērunt. Exarsit dolor. Urgērunt illī, ut ē locō nōs movērent. 10
Factus est ā nostrīs impetus; fuga operārum. Ēiectus dē rostrīs Clōdius; ac nōs quoque tum fūgimus, nē quid turbā.

—Cicero, *Letters to His Brother Quintus*, II.3

advocātus, -ī (*m*), supporter
sīve, or rather
opera, -ae (*f*), hooligan, ruffian
eī . . . contigit, it befell him, happened to him
ut . . . impedīrētur, result clause dependent upon **contigit**
convīcium, -ī (*n*), insult
perōrō (1), to complete a speech
referre grātiam, to return the favor (said with sarcasm)
mēns, mentis (*f*), mental faculties
cōnsisteret, he could continue
ea rēs ācta est, this went on
hōrā sextā, at noon
cum, during which time
Clōdia, Clodius's notorious sister
cōnspūtō (1), to spit on in contempt
urgeō (2), to press hard, push
fuga operārum, supply **fuit**
ēiectus = **ēiectus est**
nē quid = **nē aliquid accideret**, so that nothing might happen
turbā = **in turbā**

Oratory in Republican Politics

Skill in public speaking, or rhetoric, was a requirement for political success in Rome, for all public offices required speechmaking and the ability to persuade. By Cicero's time, the final stage in the education of a Roman youth was contact with a **rhētor**, an instructor in public speaking who taught skills in debate and in advocating a particular course of action. The preparation of a speech included gathering of material and its proper arrangement, selection of appropriate language, memorization, and delivery. A good speech had a certain desirable structure to it, including a beginning (**exordium**), designed to win the favorable attention of the audience; the body (consisting of **partītiō**, "outline"; **cōnfirmātiō**, "positive arguments"; and **refūtātio**, "rebuttal"); and the conclusion (**perōrātiō**), designed to summarize and appeal to emotion. In *On the Orator*, Cicero wrote:

> Eloquence requires many things: a wide knowledge of very many subjects (verbal fluency without this being worthless and even ridiculous), a style, too, carefully formed not merely by selection, but by arrangement of words, and a thorough familiarity with all the feelings which nature has given to men, because the whole force and art of the orator must be put forth in allaying or exciting the emotions of his audience.

These figures represent typical oratorical gestures and postures of the 1st centuries B.C. and A.D. The **āctiō**, or delivery of a speech, involved theatrics such as running about, the stamping of feet, getting on one's knees, waving of arms, and a wide range of voices and expressions to play on the audience's emotions.

1 **Nisi Clōdius . . . occīsus esset, ille . . . fēcisset:** "If Clodius had not been killed, would he have done? . . ." This is a *past contrary to fact condition*, where **nisi . . . occīsus esset** is the if-clause, and **ille . . . fēcisset** the main clause. Such conditions, using the pluperfect subjunctive, refer to events which could have happened in the past but, in fact, did not. Cicero uses this construction to play on the imagined fears of the jury by creating a "What if?" scenario.
Nisi . . . incenderit?: this, and the questions which follow, are called rhetorical questions, that is, they have no answer or the answer is assumed as obvious.
ille praetor. . . .: "would he as praetor. . . ."

2 **quī . . . incenderit:** "the type of person who burned . . . ."; this is a *relative clause of characteristic*, describing the general type of person who would do a particular thing. The thought is: what could be expected from Clodius, if he were elected, when even as a dead man he caused such destruction?
ūnō . . . duce: ablative absolute. Sextus Clodius was the henchman of P. Clodius who instigated the burning of his corpse. See 58:29.

3 **Quō:** ablative of comparison with **miserius, acerbius**, and **luctuōsius**. The antecedent is the burning of the Senate House. Note the singsong rhythm of the adjectives and the punching repetition, or anaphora, of **quid**.

4 **Templum sanctitātis . . . ūnī ordinī:** Cicero refers to the Senate House, in all its dimensions, as the sanctuary of the senatorial order (**ūnī ordinī**) and the symbol of the Republic. This part of the conclusion is called the **indignātiō**, an emotional outburst designed to arouse the audience against the opponent.

6 **īnflammārī, exscindī, fūnestārī, . . . fierī:** these infinitives follow **vīdimus** (4), in indirect statement. "What have we seen more appalling . . . than that this precinct of holiness . . . was torched. . . ." Note the asyndeton.

7 **imperītā:** Asconius also used this word to describe the mob, in Chapter 58:26.
quamquam esset miserum id ipsum: "although that itself would have been tragic enough. . . ."; **quamquam** is found with the subjunctive when introducing an act as conceived but not achieved.

8 **Cum . . . ausus sit:** a **cum** circumstantial or causal clause with the perfect subjunctive. Translate "when he dared" or "since he dared." **Audēre** is a semi-deponent verb, that is, its present system is in the active and its perfect system in the passive.
ustor . . . signifer: Sextus Clodius is characterized as a corpse burner, an attendant or assistant to the undertaker who cremated the dead, and as a soldier who carried the insignia of his unit, leading the charge.
quid signifer prō vīvō nōn esset ausus: "what would he not have dared as a standard-bearer for the living (Clodius)?" Note the balance between **ausus sit ustor prō mortuō** and **signifer prō vīvō nōn esset ausus**.

9 **sunt quī . . . querantur:** "there are those who . . . ," a relative clause of characteristic. So also (**quī**) **taceant** and **quī . . . putent** (9–10).
querantur, (quī) taceant: supply a connecting word, such as "but" or "yet." Cicero expresses indignation here about the alleged hypocrisy of those who complain about Milo's deed on the Appian Way, yet keep silent about such a monstrous deed as the arson of the Senate House.

59
Cicero Defends Milo

In this selection from the **perōrātiō** of the speech *Pro Milone*, Cicero completes his defensive strategy—to depict Clodius as a would-be tyrant and to celebrate Milo as a tyrannicide and patriot. Note the attempts to win the sympathy of the jury by appealing to god and country and by emotional reference to the Curia as symbol of the Republic.

Nisi Clōdius pestis occīsus esset, ille praetor, ille vērō cōnsul, ille dēnique vīvus malī nihil fēcisset, quī mortuus ūnō ex suīs satellitibus Sex. Clōdiō duce Cūriam incenderit? Quō quid miserius, quid acerbius, quid luctuōsius vīdimus? Templum sanctitātis, amplitūdinis, mentis, cōnsiliī pūblicī, caput urbis, āram sociōrum, portum omnium gentium, sēdem ab ūniversō populō 5
concessam ūnī ordinī—īnflammārī, exscindī, fūnestārī, neque id fierī ā multitūdine imperītā, quamquam esset miserum id ipsum, sed ab ūnō? Cum tantum ausus sit ustor prō mortuō, quid signifer prō vīvō nōn esset ausus? Et sunt quī dē viā Appiā querantur, taceant dē Cūriā! Et quī ab eō spīrante Forum putent potuisse defendī, cuius nōn restiterit cadāverī Cūria! 10
Excitāte, excitāte ipsum, sī potestis, ā mortuīs: frangētis impetum vīvī, cuius vix sustinētis furiās īnsepultī?

Sed obstābat eī nēmō praeter Milōnem; Milō ūnus urgēbat. Haec tanta virtūs, iūdicēs, ex hāc urbe expellētur, exterminābitur, prōiciētur? Ō mē miserum! Ō mē īnfēlīcem! Revocāre tū mē in patriam, Milō, potuistī, ego 15
tē in patriā retinēre nōn poterō? Utinam dī immortālēs fēcissent—pāce tuā, patria, dīxerim—utinam P. Clōdius nōn modo vīveret, sed etiam praetor, cōnsul, dictātor esset potius quam hoc spectāculum vidērem! Ō dī immortālēs! Fortem et ā vōbīs, iūdicēs, cōnservandum virum! "Minimē, minimē," inquit, "immō vērō poenās ille dēbitās luerit: nōs subeāmus, sī ita necesse 20
est, nōn dēbitās." Hicine vir patriae nātus usquam nisi in patriā moriētur, aut, sī forte, prō patriā? Huius vōs animī monumenta retinēbitis, corporis in Italiā nūllum sepulcrum esse patiēminī? Hunc suā quisquam sententiā ex hāc urbe expellet, quem omnēs urbēs expulsum ā vōbīs ad sē vocābunt? Ō terram illam beātam, quae hunc virum excēperit, hanc ingrātam, sī 25
ēiēcerit, miseram, sī āmīserit!

—Cicero, *Pro Milone*, 90, 101–105 (excerpts)

(The verdict in Milo's trial appears on p. 54)

10. **cadāverī:** dative with **restiterit**. Subordinate clauses (here, **cuius . . . Cūria**) that follow a subjunctive clause (here, **quī . . . putent**) are sometimes attracted into the subjunctive mood themselves when they contribute to the main thought; so **restiterit** here. The antecedent of **cuius** is **eō**, Clodius.

12 **īnsepultī:** Cicero's continual comments on the power of Clodius dead as well as alive (2, 8, 9–12) reinforce in the jurors' minds what kind of man Clodius was and, therefore, the magnitude of Milo's "service" to Rome.

13 **Sed obstābat:** here begins the **conquestiō** or appeal to the jury for sympathy.

15 **tū mē in patriam . . . ego tē in patriā:** reference to Milo's assistance in Cicero's recall from exile. See 57:4. Note the balance of words here.

16 **Utinam . . . fēcissent:** "If only the gods had brought it about that. . . ."; **utinam** with a past subjunctive regularly expresses a wish incapable of fulfillment. Here, the pluperfect tense expresses a wish unfulfilled in the past.

pacē tuā . . . dīxerim: "I say this with your permission," an example of the *potential* subjunctive, expressing a possibility. The perfect tense may be translated as present.

17 **utinam . . . vīveret . . . esset . . . vidērem:** the imperfect subjunctive is used to indicate a wish unfulfilled in present time. "If only Clodius were alive now (but he is not). . . ."

19 **Fortem . . . virum:** exclamatory accusatives. The gerundive **cōnservandum** here expresses obligation or necessity, "a man who must be preserved."

Minimē . . . nōn dēbitās: Cicero uses this imaginary remark spoken by Milo to dramatize the latter's self-sacrifice. What happened to Clodius (**ille**) was his due (**dēbitās**); Milo (**nōs**) is prepared to face what might happen, however unjust (**nōn dēbitās**).

21 **Hicine . . . Huius . . . Hunc:** note the interplay of question and exclamation in this final paragraph, and compare this with the questions and exclamations following **ille . . . ille . . . ille** (1) in the preceding paragraph.

vir patriae nātus: "a man born for his country. . . ."; **patriae** is dative of purpose.

patriae . . . patriā . . . patriā: the emphasis here is on the fact that it is the jury's patriotic duty to reward Milo, as a tyrannicide, with freedom.

22 **Huius . . . animī monumenta:** the memorial to Milo is Rome's freedom from Clodius.

24 **expulsum ā vōbīs:** the traditional worst penalty for guilty members of the senatorial order was exile, here depicted as a fate worse than death (as Cicero himself well knew!) for a man as "patriotic" as Milo.

25 **Ō terram illam beātam . . . hanc ingrātam . . . miseram:** exclamatory accusatives. Note how the successively abbreviated accusative phrases bring things to a final halt. The interspersed future more vivid conditions suggest that the consequences for Rome in banishing Milo will be real ones.

pestis, pestis (*f*), plague, disease
satellēs, satellitis (*m/f*), accomplice
acerbus, -a, -um, hideous, appalling
luctuōsus, -a, -um, heartbreaking
sanctitās, sanctitātis (*f*), holiness
amplitūdō, amplitūdinis (*f*), grandeur, majesty
socius, -ī (*m*), ally
portus, -ūs (*m*), harbor, haven
sēdēs, sēdis (*f*), site, abode
ordō, ordinis (*m*), order, rank, class

inflammō (1), to kindle, set aflame
fūnestō (1), to defile or pollute with a corpse
ustor, ustōris (*m*), corpse-burner
signifer, -ī (*m*), standard-bearer, leader
spīrō (1), to breathe, be alive
sustineō (2), to withstand, check
furia, -ae (*f*), frenzy, madness
īnsepultus, -a, -um, unburied
iūdex, iūdicis (*m*), judge, juror
exterminō (1), to drive out, banish
Utinam . . . ! Would that . . . !, I wish that . . . !
pāce tuā, pardon me, by your leave
cōnservandum, to be preserved
poenās luere, to pay the price
hicine, emphatic form of **hic** + **-ne**
usquam, anywhere
monumentum, -ī (*n*), memorial
beātus, -a, -um, happy
ingrātus, -a, -um, ungrateful

concēdō, concēdere (3), **concessī, concessum,** to grant
exscindō, exscindere (3), **exscidī, exscissum,** to destroy utterly
queror, querī (3), **questus sum,** to moan, whine, complain
obstō, obstāre (1), **obstitī** (+ *dat.*), to stand against, oppose
āmittō, āmittere (3), **āmīsī, āmissum,** to lose

Exercise 59a

Answer in English the following questions on the reading passage.

1. How does Cicero characterize Clodius in this passage? Milo? What words, images, and rhetorical techniques bring out the contrast?
2. Cicero suggests that Milo deserves acquittal for protecting Rome against Clodius. Is this a valid defense? Can illegal acts justly be defended in the interest of national security?
3. How does Cicero manipulate the fears of the jury regarding political violence? Given the facts of the case as presented by Asconius, was this a safe strategy?
4. Find examples of the following techniques of Cicero's forensic oratory. Do you think that theatrics should have a place in the courtroom?
   exaggeration emotional appeal suggestion invective
   rhetorical question exclamation sarcasm

Exercise 59b

Contrast Cicero's rhetoric with Asconius's careful description of Milo's shrewd political calculations prior to his decision to murder Clodius (58:14–17). Compare Asconius's version of Milo's motives with Cicero's picture of Milo as a noble, self-sacrificing patriot and savior of his country. Then choose one of these positions and prepare arguments for class debate on the question of Milo's guilt or innocence.

VERBS: Contrary to Fact Conditions

In Chapter 55 you learned three general types of conditional sentences in Latin: simple, future more vivid, and future less vivid. There is a fourth, general type, called *contrary to fact*. Look at the following sentences:

Sī Clōdius cōnsul **esset**, rem pūblicam **dēlēret**.
If Clodius **were** *consul (now in the present, which he is not),* **he would** *(now, in the present)* **destroy** *the state.*
Sī Clōdius cōnsul **fuisset**, rem pūblicam **dēlēvisset**.
If Clodius **had been** *consul (in the past, which he was not),* **he would have** *(sometime in the past)* **destroyed** *the state.*

As do other conditions, the *contrary to fact*, or *unreal*, condition contains an if-clause introduced by **sī** or **nisi**, and a main clause or conclusion. The difference between contrary to fact and other conditions is that the former uses past subjunctives in both the if- and main clauses, the imperfect referring to the present and the pluperfect to past time. In meaning, contrary to fact conditions refer to hypothetical events or situations which could have or might have happened but, in fact, did not happen.

Exercise 59c

Read aloud and translate the following sentences.

1. Sī Clōdius vīveret, omnēs Rōmānī facta eius timērent.
2. Sex. Clōdius sī Clōdiō mortuō Cūriam flammāre ausus esset, quid eō vīvō fēcisset?
3. Rēs pūblica dēlērētur, nisi lēgēs firmae essent.
4. Timērētisne Clōdium, iudicēs, sī vīvus esset?
5. Sī Milō per viam Appiam occīsus esset, Clōdius praetor factus esset.
6. Nisi factiōnēs perīculōsae removērentur, nūllī candidātī salvī essent.
7. Sī Milō suōs servōs Clōdium occīdisse negāvisset, errāvisset.
8. Sī tū Rōmānus essēs, peterēsne cōnsulātum?
9. Nōnne rēs pūblica conservāta esset, sī Milō cōnsul creātus esset?
10. Sī Milō līberātus esset, Plancus laetus nōn fuisset.

negō (1), to deny

Utinam populus Rōmānus ūnam cervīcem habēret! *If only the Roman people had but one neck!* Quoting the emperor Caligula as he raged against popular opposition to his wishes. (Suetonius, *Caligula*, XXX.2)

Utinam lēx esset eadem quae uxōrī est virō. *I wish that the same rules applied to both man and wife.* (Plautus, *The Merchant*, 821)

Building Up the Meaning XIII

Distinguishing Conditional Sentences

You have now met the four main types of conditional sentences in Latin, each characterized by a dependent if-clause introduced by **sī** or **nisi**, and a main clause or conclusion.

1. **Simple** or **factual**: corresponding indicative tenses in each clause.
   a. Sī tē **videō**, laetus **sum**. — *If I see you, I am happy.*
   b. Sī tē **vidēbam**, laetus **eram**. — *If I saw you, I was happy.*
2. **Future more vivid**: future indicative in each clause.
   a. Sī tē **vidēbō**, laetus **erō**. — *If I see (will see) you, I will be happy.*
   b. Sī tē **vīderō**, laetus **erō**. — *If I see (will have seen) you, I will be happy.*
3. **Future less vivid** or **should-would**: present subjunctive in each clause.
   a. Sī tē **videam**, laetus **sim**. — *If I should see you (and I may), I would be happy.*
4. **Contrary to fact**: imperfect or pluperfect subjunctive in each clause.
   a. **Present**: imperfect subjunctive in each clause.
      Sī tē **vidērem**, laetus **essem**. — *If I were seeing you (but I'm not), I would be happy.*
   b. **Past**: pluperfect subjunctive in each clause.
      Sī tē **vīdissem**, laetus **fuissem**. — *If I had seen you (but I didn't), I would have been happy.*

Here are several things to remember when dealing with conditional sentences:

1. Simple and future more vivid conditions are real or factual and thus are found with the indicative mood. Future less vivid and contrary to fact conditions are unreal or hypothetical and are found with the subjunctive.
2. When translating future more vivid conditions, attention should be paid to translating the future or future perfect indicative as an English present indicative. The future perfect indicative, which the Romans often preferred to the simple future, appears when the action of the if-clause is seen as completed before that of the main clause, which itself is future:

   Sī Rōmam **vēnerimus**, laetī **erimus**. — *If we come (shall have come) to Rome, we will be happy.*

3. The tenses of the if- and main clauses in conditionals may be mixed as the sense requires:
   Sī tē heri **vīdissem**, laetus hodiē **essem**. — *If I had seen you yesterday, today I would be happy.*

Exercise 59d

Categorize each of the following conditions as simple, future more vivid, future less vivid, present contrary to fact, past contrary to fact, or mixed, and then translate.

1. Miser sum, nisi tē videō.
2. Miser essem, nisi tē vīdissem.
3. Miser eram, nisi tē vidēbam.
4. Miser sim, nisi tē videam.
5. Miser fuissem, nisi tē vīdissem.
6. Miser fuī, nisi tē vīdī.
7. Miser erō, nisi tē vīderō.
8. Miser erō, nisi tē vidēbō.
9. Miser essem, nisi tē vidērem.

Exercise 59e

Repeat the previous exercise, substituting **audīre** *for* **vidēre**. *Read each conditional sentence aloud with the correct verb form before translating.*

The Verdict

During the first day of Milo's four-day trial, some 81 potential jurors had been selected by Pompey. After the summations and before the vote was taken on the final day, both prosecution and defense rejected five jurors from each of the three classes, 30 in all, leaving 51 to decide the verdict. Each juror erased one of the letters on his voting tablet, one side of which was marked **A** (**absolvō**) and the other **C** (**condemnō**). Here is the decision.

Senātōrēs condemnāvērunt XII, absolvērunt VI; equitēs condemnāvērunt XIII, absolvērunt IIII; tribūnī aerāriī condemnāvērunt XIII, absolvērunt III. Vidēbantur nōn ignōrāvisse iūdicēs īnsciō Milōne initiō vulnerātum esse Clōdium, sed compererant, postquam vulnerātus esset, iussū Milōnis occīsum. Milō in exsilium Massiliam intrā paucissimōs diēs profectus est. 5
Bona eius propter aeris aliēnī magnitūdinem sēmiunciā vēniērunt.

—Asconius, *Commentary on Cicero's Speech for Milo* (excerpt)

Massilia, -ae (*f*), a city in Gaul
initium, -ī (*n*), beginning
aes aliēnum, debt
sēmiuncia, -ae (*f*), 1/24th (the value)

comperiō, comperīre (4), **comperī, compertum,** to find out for certain
vēneō, vēnīre (4), **vēniī, vēnitum,** to be sold

PART III
Warfare in the Late Republic

The supreme man of war during the late Republic was C. Julius Caesar. He fought a continuous war (58–51 B.C.) against the barbarians of Gaul, ostensibly to protect the northern frontier of Rome but in reality to win allies, increase his war chest, and build up an army personally loyal to him as commander. His achievements, which included the conquest of all Gaul, its addition to the Roman Empire, and Rome's first official contact with the far-flung shores of Britain, were chronicled in his famous *Commentarii de bello Gallico* (*Commentaries on the Gallic War*). Caesar's Gallic achievements and Pompey's rise to the sole consulship of Rome precipitated a confrontation between the two generals, which erupted in 49 B.C. when Caesar led his troops out of his province of Gaul and across the Rubicon River into Italy. What followed was four years of bloody civil war between the Pompeians, representing the Republic and the interests of the Senate, and the Caesarians, who favored radical political change and the transfer of power to the middle class. Pompey, along with many senators, fled to Greece. Caesar, postponing a march on Rome itself, first protected his flank by reducing Pompeian forces in Spain and then met Pompey in Greece at the decisive battle of Pharsalus.

In his *Commentaries on the Civil War*, Caesar provides memoirs or reports of the events of 49–48 B.C., in which he attempts to present himself and his cause in the best possible light. Cicero's letters to his friends and family during this period provide a personal counterpoint to the propaganda of Caesar's writing. Upon the outbreak of hostilities, Cicero found himself caught in a dilemma: should he support Pompey, who had helped in his recall from exile and now represented the cause of the Republic, or should he support Caesar to insure his own safety and that of his family?

C. Iulius Caesar

M. Tullius Cicero

Cn. Pompeius Magnus

2 **S.P.D.: Salūtem plūrimam dīcit.** Note the special warmth of Cicero's greeting.

4 **quid sit vōbīs faciendum:** "what you must do."

ille: Caesar, after crossing the Rubicon on the night of January 11, had postponed his entry into Rome (**urbem,** 5) to pursue Pompey to the south.

5 **dīripiendam:** "to be plundered."

6 **vereor ut . . . possit:** "I am afraid that he will not be able."

Dolābella: P. Cornelius Dolabella was husband of Cicero's daughter Tullia and a supporter of Julius Caesar.

metuō nē. . . .: "I fear that. . . ."

7 **ut . . . nōn liceat:** a result clause.

8 **vestrī similēs:** "like you"; **vestrī** is genitive plural of the personal pronoun **vōs.** Cicero often prefers the genitive to the dative with **similis** when referring to people.

sintne: "whether or not there are. . . ."

9 **videndum est ut . . . possītis:** "you must consider whether. . . ."; **ut** sometimes means "how" or "whether" in an indirect question.

Quōmodo quidem nunc sē rēs habet: "As things stand now," literally, "How the situation holds itself now."

10 **modo . . . nōbīs . . . liceat: modo** with the subjunctive means "provided that. . . ."

haec . . . loca: that is, the area of Campania, centering on Capua, where Cicero was in charge.

11 **in nostrīs praediīs:** several days after this letter was written, Cicero's family left Rome for their villa at Formiae.

verendum est, nē. . . .: "there should be concern that. . . ."

12 **famēs in urbe:** the dislocation and anxiety following the evacuation of the Republicans from Rome and the impending arrival of Caesar's army is described elsewhere by Cicero as **plēna timōris et errōris omnia.**

velim . . . consīderētis: "I would like you to make plans. . . ."; **velim,** when followed by a verb in the present subjunctive, introduces a wish referring to the future.

Pompōniō . . . Camillō: T. Pomponius Atticus was Cicero's literary advisor and confidant, to whom he addressed over 400 letters. Camillus was a friend and fellow lawyer.

13 **animō fortī:** "stout-hearted"; an ablative noun followed by an adjective is used to describe a personal quality or characteristic.

17 **Pedem:** one **pēs** or Roman foot = .97 English feet, or .29 meters.

istīus: Caesar; **iste** is frequently used to show contempt. By the time of this letter, Pompey had fled to Greece, leaving all of Italy in Caesar's hands.

18 **exceptum īrī:** "going to be captured," the rare future passive infinitive.

19 **quid agam?:** "what should I do?" This use of the subjunctive expresses doubt or uncertainty in the form of an unanswered question; similarly, **persequar** (19) and **trādam** (20).

20 **Fac (mē) posse (trādere) tūtō:** "Suppose that I could do so (surrender to Caesar) safely. . . ."

60
An Eyewitness to Civil War

These four selections from Cicero's correspondence date from the early months of the Civil War and reveal his personal and political fears and anxieties, as he witnessed what were to become the death throes of the Republic.

A. Cicero is writing en route to Capua on January 22, 49 B.C., in reply to a letter from his wife Terentia. At Pompey's request, he had taken charge of levying troops in Campania, leaving Rome and family behind.

TULLIUS TERENTIAE ET PATER TULLIOLAE DUABUS ANIMIS SUIS ET CICERO MATRI OPTIMAE, SUAVISS. SORORI S. P. D.

Sī vōs valētis, nōs valēmus. Vestrum iam cōnsilium est, nōn sōlum meum, quid sit vōbīs faciendum. Sī ille Rōmam modestē ventūrus est, rēctē in praesentiā domī esse potestis; sīn homō āmēns dīripiendam urbem datūrus 5
est, vereor ut Dolābella ipse satis nōbīs prōdesse possit. Etiam illud metuō nē iam interclūdāmur, ut, cum velītis, exīre nōn liceat. Reliquum est, quod ipsae optimē cōnsīderābitis, vestrī similēs fēminae sintne Rōmae. Sī enim nōn sunt, videndum est ut honestē vōs esse possītis. Quōmodo quidem nunc sē rēs habet, modo ut haec nōbīs loca tenēre liceat, bellissimē vel mēcum 10
vel in nostrīs praediīs esse poteritis. Etiam illud verendum est, nē brevī tempore famēs in urbe sit. Hīs dē rēbus velim cum Pompōniō, cum Camillō, cum quibus vōbīs vidēbitur, consīderētis, ad summam, animō fortī sītis. Vōs, meae cārissimae animae, quam saepissimē ad mē scrībite et vōs quid agātis et quid istīc agātur. Valēte. 15

—Cicero, *Letters to His Friends*, XIV.14

B. The following letter to Atticus clearly reveals Cicero's indecision about whether to align himself with Caesar or Pompey in the war.

CICERO ATTICO SAL.

Pedem in Italiā videō nūllum esse, quī nōn in istīus potestāte sit. Dē Pompēiō sciō nihil, eumque, nisi in nāvem sē contulerit, exceptum īrī putō. Ego quid agam? Quā aut terrā aut marī persequar eum, quī ubi sit, nesciō? Trādam igitur istī mē? Fac posse tūtō (multī enim hortantur), num etiam 20
honestē? Nūllō modō. Equidem ā tē petam cōnsilium, ut soleō. Explicārī rēs nōn potest.

—Cicero, *Letters to Atticus*, VII.22 (excerpt)

23 **CN. MAGNUS:** Pompey was called Magnus after 81 B.C. because of victories in Italy, Sicily, and Africa.

24 **S.V.B.: Sī valēs, bene (est).**

Tuās litterās: this letter is in reply to one received from Cicero several days earlier, asking whether Cicero should stay in Capua or join Pompey.

25 **Āpūliā:** Apulia is still the name of a region of southeastern Italy.

27 **commūnī cōnsiliō:** despite his reservations about Pompey's strategy against Caesar, Cicero was personally in his debt, owing to Pompey's influence in gaining his recall from exile nine years previously. Pompey also now represented the cause of the Republic and, thus, of Cicero himself.

31 **legiōnibus:** the strength of a **legiō**, the largest fighting unit of the Roman army, varied from 4000–6000 men. Although Caesar had commanded 10 legions in Gaul, he was seriously undermanned during the Civil War.

32 **nōn dubitāvī quīn:** "I did not hesitate to. . . ."; **quīn** introduces the subjunctive in a clause of doubt.

33 **saepius . . . videor:** Caesar here subtly suggests that Cicero will come over to him (but he is wrong!). Note the confident tone.

Ita dē mē merēris: "You deserve this from me," **ita** referring to Caesar's claim in the previous sentence (**saepius mihi factūrus videor**) that he will remain in Cicero's debt. After refusing an invitation to join the Triumvirate, Cicero had been forced to reconcile himself to the control of Pompey, Caesar, and Crassus in 56 B.C.

Exercise 60a

Answer the following questions on the reading selections.

1. In what ways does Cicero reveal his affection for his family in letter A?
2. What are Cicero's fears for his family as war breaks out? Why do you suppose he left his family in Rome?
3. Under what conditions might Cicero's family leave Rome now?
4. What specific features of language reveal Cicero's sense of urgency and anxiety in this letter?
5. In B, what seems to be Cicero's attitude toward Pompey's strategy against Caesar? Who seems to have the upper hand, early in the war?
6. Discuss Cicero's options as he expresses them to Atticus. What technique of expression does he use? Does Cicero seem to be a decisive person?
7. Compare the letters of Pompey and Caesar (C and D) to Cicero. How are the content, tone, and language similar? How are they different?
8. What does each general hope to gain from Cicero? On what does each base his appeal?
9. What do letters C and D reveal about the personalities of the opponents?
10. What do all four letters tell us about Cicero as a private citizen? As a man of public affairs?

C. Pompey addresses the following letter to Cicero while retreating south to Brundisium, a port of embarkation to Greece. Cicero is greeted as a victorious general (**imperātor**) by virtue of his conquest of native bandits while governing Cilicia the previous year. Pompey is governor (**prōcōnsul**) of Spain.

CN. MAGNUS PROCOS. S. D. M. CICERONI IMP.

S.V.B. Tuās litterās libenter lēgī. Recognōvī enim tuam pristinam virtūtem etiam in salūte commūnī. Cōnsulēs ad eum exercitum, quem in Āpūliā 25 habuī, vēnērunt. Magnōpere tē hortor prō tuō singulārī perpetuōque studiō in rem pūblicam, ut tē ad nōs cōnferās, ut commūnī cōnsiliō reī pūblicae adflictae opem atque auxilium ferāmus. Cēnseō ut viā Appiā iter faciās et celeriter Brundisium veniās.

—Cicero, *Letters to Atticus,* VIII.11c

D. Caesar, who wrote the following letter while on the march against Pompey, apologizes for his necessary brevity. He is attempting to woo Cicero as an ally.

CAESAR IMP. S. D. CICERONI IMP. 30

Cum properārem atque essem in itinere, praemissīs iam legiōnibus, tamen nōn dubitāvī quīn et scrīberem ad tē et grātiās tibi agerem, etsi hoc et fēcī saepe et saepius mihi factūrus videor. Ita dē mē merēris. In prīmīs ā tē petō, quoniam cōnfīdō mē celeriter ad urbem ventūrum, ut tē ibi videam, ut tuō cōnsiliō, grātiā, dignitāte, ope omnium rērum ūtī possim. Festīnātiōnī meae 35 brevitātīque litterārum ignōscēs.

—Cicero, *Letters to Atticus,* IX.6a (excerpt)

anima, -ae (*f*), darling, heart, soul
modestē, under control, with restraint
in praesentiā, present
sīn, but if, on the other hand
āmēns, āmentis, mad, insane
honestē, respectably, with honor
bellissimē, in great comfort, elegance
praedium, -ī (*n*), estate, property
famēs, famis (*f*), hunger
ad summam, above all
istīc, over there
pedem, a foot (length of measure)
potestās, potestātis (*f*), power, control
sē cōnferre, to take oneself, flee
tūtō, safely
equidem, certainly, surely
pristinus, -a, -um, previous, former
salūs, salūtis (*f*), safety
exercitus, -ūs (*m*), army
singulāris, -is, -e, extraordinary, unique
ops, opis (*f*), aid, help
properō (1), to hurry, hasten
legiō, legiōnis (*f*), legion, military unit
dubitō (1), to hesitate, be in doubt
etsi, even if, although
dignitās, dignitātis (*f*), reputation

dīripiō, dīripere (3), **dīripuī, dīreptum,** to lay waste, plunder
prōsum, prōdesse (*irreg.*), **prōfuī** (+ *dat.*), to be useful, benefit, help
metuō, metuere (3), **metuī, metūtum,** to fear, be afraid of
interclūdō, interclūdere (3), **interclūsī, interclūsum,** to shut off
excipiō, excipere (3), **excēpī, exceptum,** to catch, capture
adflīgō, adflīgere (3), **adflīxī, adflīctum,** to strike down
cēnseō, cēnsēre (2), **cēnsuī, cēnsum,** to be of the opinion
mereor, merērī (2), **meritus sum,** to deserve, earn
ūtor, ūtī (3), **ūsus sum** (+ *abl.*), to use, take advantage of
ignōscō, ignōscere (3), **ignōvī, ignōtum** (+ *dat.*), to pardon, forgive

VERBS: Clauses of Fearing

Thus far, you have learned that **ut** (or negative **nē**) introduces several different types of subjunctive clauses: indirect command, purpose, and result (negative **ut nōn**). A fourth type, clauses of *fearing*, is illustrated by the following sentences taken from the reading:

. . . vereor **ut** Dolābella ipse satis nōbīs prōdesse **possit**. (6)
I fear that Dolabella himself cannot be of sufficient help to us.
. . . metuō **nē** iam **interclūdāmur**. . . . (6–7)
I am afraid that we may be cut off already. . . .

You will note that a clause of fearing is introduced by a word of fearing and uses **ut** or **nē** and a verb in the subjunctive (usually present or imperfect), following the regular rules for sequence of tenses. The word of fearing is usually a verb such as **metuō, timeō,** or **vereor,** but it can be a noun such as **metus, timor,** or **perīculum**. Note in the examples above that in clauses of fearing, unlike other **ut** or **nē** clauses, **ut** is translated *that . . . not,* and **nē** is translated *that.*

As an alternative to a subjunctive clause of fearing, the verb **timeō** may be accompanied by an infinitive:

Cicerō Terentiam **relinquere** timēbat. *Cicero was afraid to leave Terentia behind.*

Exercise 60b

Read aloud and translate these sentences containing clauses of fearing.

1. Pompēius veritus est nē Caesar tōtam Italiam in eius potestāte iam habēret.
2. Terentia atque Tullia Rōmae diūtius manēre timēbant.
3. Equidem Caesar nōn verēbātur ut Pompēium vinceret.
4. Cicerō verērī vidētur nē Caesar cīvibus Rōmānīs noceat.
5. Cicerō timet ut Terentia litterās heri scrīpserit.
6. Atticus semper metuēbat nē Caesar dictātor fierī vellet.

7. "Metuō et timeō nē hoc bellum cīvīle tandem fiat," inquit Cicerō.
8. Nē Cicerō ā Terentiā iam interclūsus esset summum perīculum fuit.
9. Rōmānī numquam veritī sunt nē bellō vincerentur.
10. Metuitne Pompēius ut omnēs legiōnēs suae essent fidēlēs?

Building Up the Meaning XIV

Uses of the Independent Subjunctive

In this and recent chapters, you have seen several uses of the independent subjunctive, that is, subjunctive verbs that are found in main (not subordinate) clauses. These uses may be summarized as follows:

1. **Jussive** and **hortatory** were both introduced in Chapter 56. Jussive subjunctives are found in the 3rd person, hortatory in the 1st person.

Discēdat.	*Let him leave.*	(jussive)
Exeāmus Rōmā.	*Let us leave Rome.*	(hortatory)

2. **Deliberative** (the formal term derives from **dēlīberāre**, "to mull over" or "weigh carefully"). This subjunctive expresses doubt or uncertainty and is usually found in the 1st person singular or plural only. Deliberative questions may be introduced by a question word such as an interrogative pronoun.

Discēdāmus?	*Should we go?*
Quid facerem?	*What was I to do?*

The negative is **nōn**:

Nōn discēdāmus?	*Should we not go?*

3. **Optative** (the formal term derives from **optāre**, "to wish for"). Wishes are usually introduced by **Utinam . . .** , followed by the subjunctive. The present tense is used when the wish may be fulfilled in the future:

Utinam discēdāmus.	*I wish we would go (and we might).*

The imperfect tense refers to an unfulfilled wish in the present:

Utinam discēderēmus.	*I wish we were going (but we're not).*

The pluperfect tense refers to an unfulfilled wish in past time.

Utinam discessissēmus.	*I wish we had gone (but we hadn't).*

The negative of an optative subjunctive is **nē**:

Utinam nē discēdāmus.	*I wish we wouldn't go.*

Velim, nōlim, or **mālim** may replace **Utinam . . .** in introducing a wish with the present subjunctive referring to future time:

Velim discēdāmus.	*I would like us to go.*

This is a roundabout or polite form of command, as in the following example from the reading:

. . . **velim . . . consīderētis.** . . . *I would like you to make plans. . . .* (12–13)

Exercise 60c

Identify the type of subjunctive construction (jussive, hortatory, deliberative, or optative) in each sentence, and read aloud and translate.

1. Velim mihi ignōscās.
2. Spērēmus quae volumus, sed quod acciderit ferāmus.
3. Quō Pompēiānī fugere possint?
4. Quid dīcerem?
5. Utinam nē mē vīdissēs.
6. "Omnia vincit amor et nōs cēdāmus amōrī," scrīpsit Vergilius poēta.
7. Palmam quī meruit, ferat.
8. Quī beneficium dedit, taceat; narret quī accēpit.
9. "Quid agam, iūdicēs?" rogāvit Cicerō. "Ēloquar an sileam?"
10. Velim tibi persuādeās.
11. Utinam Cicerō mihi epistulam scrīpsisset!
12. Iuvenālis scrīpsit, "Quid Rōmae faciam? Mentīrī nesciō."
13. Utinam facile vēra invenīre possēmus.
14. "Cēdant arma togae" significat "lēx magis quam vīs."
15. Mīlitēs Caesaris Rōmā quam celerrimē discēdant.

palma, -ae (*f*), palm branch of victory

Iuvenālis, -is (*m*), Juvenal, a Roman poet

cēdō, cēdere (3), **cessī, cessum,** to yield, to submit to

Word Study XVI

Salutations

The salutations used by the Romans in letters reflected those used in familiar conversational speech. Epistles began with **S.V.B.E. (Sī valēs, bene est)** or **S.V.B.E.E.V. (Sī valēs, bene est, ego valeō)** and ended with **Valē** or **Avē**. **Avē** was often used as a morning salutation and **Valē** in the evening, whereas **Salvē** was used interchangeably. Although these words were not adopted into Romance speech for familiar salutations, Latin has had an important effect on the way people have greeted each other over the centuries.

	Good Day!	*Good Evening!*	*Good Night!*	*Good-bye!*
Latin	**Bona diēs!**	**Bonum serum!**	**Bona nox! (noct-)**	**Ad deum!**
Italian	Buon giorno!	Buona sera!	Buona notte!	Addio!
French	Bonjour!	Bonsoir!	Bonne nuit!	Adieu!
Spanish	¡Buenos días!	¡Buenas tardes!	¡Buenas noches!	¡Adiós!

Although *jour* and *giorno* might not be obvious derivatives from **diēs**, they arrive through the intermediary Latin word **diūrnus, -a, -um**, which itself came into English as *journal* and *diary*. The Latin adjective **sērus, -a, -um**, adverb **sērō**, and noun **sērum, -ī**, all mean *late in the day*, and it is easy to see the relevance of the Spanish *tardes*. The phrase **Ad deum**, *To God*, and its Romance derivatives may be compared to the English *Good-bye*, which is a contraction of the phrase *God be with you*, the word *good* being substituted for the word *God*.

Roman Siege Warfare

Through a combination of discipline, practical ingenuity, and technology, the Romans excelled in the art of taking walled cities and strongholds. If a city seemed vulnerable, it was surrounded by holding troops who drove the defenders from the walls using slingstones, arrows, and missile engines, such as the "wild ass" (**onager**), for hurling stones, or the various **tormenta,** such as the "hurlers" (**ballista, catapulta**), for throwing stones and darts. Roman artillery was capable of throwing a 60 pound (27 kilogram) stone or a 12 foot (3.6 meter) pike over half a mile (1 kilometer). The remaining troops attempted to scale the walls with ladders or to break open the gates using the "tortoise" (**testūdō**), a formation of soldiers with shields locked overhead in tortoiseshell fashion. If storming the walls proved unproductive or impractical, then the army began a more formal siege (**oppugnātiō**). With the legionaries working under the protection of various kinds of sheds and shelters, such as the "little mouse" (**musculus**) and "vineyard" (**vīnea**) and under the covering fire of the various siege engines, an earthen ramp (**agger**) was built up to the point of attack on the wall. When the ramp reached the wall, movable towers (**turrēs**) were dragged to the top, from which soldiers could assault the city with siege engines, pull down the walls with large hooks on poles, breach the wall with a battering ram, or go under it with "rabbit tunnels" (**cunīculī**).

1 **illō**: Caesar promotes objectivity by referring to himself in the 3rd person. He was engaging Pompey's western forces in Spain while Trebonius was in Gaul.
geruntur: the historic present is used for vividness.

2 **Massiliae**: Massilia, modern Marseilles, was an important seaport in southern Gaul, founded by the Greeks (see the map on p. 90). This area had been Romanized in the 2nd century B.C.; Caesar pacified the remainder of Gaul in 58–51 B.C.

4 **prōvinciā**: Massilia was situated in Gallia Narbonensis, an area of Transalpine Gaul referred to by the Romans as "The Province." The French still call this area in southern France "Provence."

5 **vīmina māteriamque**: wicker, covered with raw hides to protect against fire, was used in the construction of **vīneae** and other sheds designed for siege.

7 **castrīs**: a Roman camp was a small, self-sustaining city, fortified by a ditch (**fossa**), an earthen wall (**agger**), and a log rampart (**vallum**).
prōspicere . . . ut: "to see how. . . ."; an implied indirect question, governing **tenderent, adīrent,** and **exposcerent**. The direct question in its simplest form would have been, "What's going on down there?"

8 **omnis iuventūs**: the abstract noun **iuventūs,** "youth," is used here for the concrete noun **iuvenēs,** "young men." These ranged in age from 20–45.

9 **superiōris aetātis**: the genitive, modified by an adjective, can be used to describe or characterize.

11 **Neque . . . quīn . . . exīstimāret**: "There was no one who did not think. . . ."; **quīn** (**quī** + **nē**) introduces a (negative) *relative clause of characteristic* with the subjunctive, describing a general type of person.

13 **honestī ex iuventūte**: "the best of the young men"; a part of the whole can be indicated either by **ex** + abl., as here, or by the partitive genitive, as **cuiusque aetātis amplissimī,** following.

15 **ad virtūtem: ad** + acc. indicates purpose or respect.
hōc animō: = **tantō animō,** introducing the result clause **ut . . . vidērentur**.

17 **nostrīs . . . nāvibus**: the Roman fleet consisted of 12 warships (**nāvēs longae**), hastily constructed nearby and manned by legionaries commanded by Decimus Brutus. The Massiliote and Pompeian fleet consisted of over 30 ships.
artificiō . . . et mōbilitātī: datives with **locus dabātur.**

18 **ferreīs manibus iniectīs**: these "iron hands," or grappling hooks, enabled naval warfare to be turned into land fighting.

21 **īnferēbant: īnferre** can mean "to inflict something" (acc.) "on someone" (dat.). Note how the prefixes **im-, im-, im-** emphasize the unexpected resistance.

22 **trirēmēs**: three banks of oars (**trēs rēmī**) were used to power these war galleys to ramming speed. Tactics required maneuvering an enemy vessel into a position of disadvantage, then ramming it with the **rōstrum** or bronze beak which projected from the ship's prow.

25 **graviter . . . vehementissimē**: these adverbs and the emphatic verb prefixes heighten the action and contribute to the drama of Brutus's escape.
utraque: singular, with **nāvis** understood. The verb is plural because two ships are involved, albeit individually.

61
The Siege of Massilia

In this selection from his Civil War, Caesar has left the land and naval siege of Massilia, a Gallic city loyal to Pompey, in the hands of a subordinate officer, C. Trebonius.

Dum haec in Hispāniā ab illō geruntur, C. Trebōnius lēgātus, quī ad oppugnātiōnem Massiliae relictus erat, duābus ex partibus aggerem, vīneās turrēsque ad oppidum agere īnstituit. Ad ea perficienda opera C. Trebōnius magnam iūmentōrum atque hominum multitūdinem ex omnī prōvinciā vocat; vīmina māteriamque comportārī iubet. Quibus comparātīs rēbus, 5 aggerem in altitūdinem pedum LXXX exstruit.

After briefly describing the preparations for the land siege, Caesar praises the enemy's courage and then turns to the fight at sea.

Facile erat ē castrīs C. Trebōnī atque omnibus superiōribus locīs prōspicere in urbem, ut omnis iuventus quae in oppidō remānserat omnēsque superiōris aetātis cum līberīs atque uxōribus aut in mūrō ad caelum manūs tenderent aut templa deōrum immortālium adīrent et ante simulācra prōiectī 10 victōriam ā dīs exposcerent. Neque erat quisquam omnium quīn in eius diēī cāsū suārum omnium fortūnārum ēventum cōnsistere exīstimāret. Nam et honestī ex iuventūte et cuiusque aetātis amplissimī nōminātim ēvocātī atque obsecrātī nāvēs cōnscenderant. Commissō proeliō nāvālī, Massiliēnsibus rēs nūlla ad virtūtem dēfuit; hōc animō dēcertābant ut nūllum aliud 15 tempus ad cōnandum habitūrī vidērentur.

Dīductīsque nostrīs paulātim nāvibus et artificiō gubernātōrum et mōbilitātī nāvium locus dabātur et sī quandō nostrī facultātem nactī ferreīs manibus iniectīs nāvem religāverant, undique suīs labōrantibus succurrēbant. Simul ex minōribus nāvibus magna vīs ēminus missa tēlōrum multa 20 nostrīs dē imprōvīsō imprūdentibus atque impedītīs vulnera īnferēbant. Cōnspicātaeque nāvēs trirēmēs duae nāvem D. Brūtī, quae ex īnsignī facile agnōscī poterat, duābus ex partibus sēsē in eam incitāvērunt. Sed tantum, rē prōvīsā, Brūtus celeritāte nāvis ēnīsus est ut parvō mōmentō antecēderet. Illae adeō graviter inter sē incitātae cōnflīxērunt ut vehementissimē utraque 25 ex concursū labōrārent, altera vērō praefractō rōstrō tōta conlabefieret. Quā rē animadversā, quae proximae eī locō ex Brūtī classe nāvēs erant in eās impedītās impetum faciunt celeriterque ambās dēprimunt.

The Caesarians routed the Massiliote fleet, sinking five ships and capturing four, while driving off the ships of Pompey.

—Caesar, *Commentaries on the Civil War,* II.1–6 (excerpts)

lēgātus, -ī (*m*), 2nd in command, lieutenant
opera, operum (*n pl*), siege-works
iūmentum, -ī (*n*), work animal
vīmen, vīminis (*n*), wicker, reed
castra, -ōrum (*n pl*), camp
iuventūs, iuventūtis (*f*), youth, young men
aetās, aetātis (*f*), age, time of life
simulācrum, -ī (*n*), image, statue
cāsus, -ūs (*m*), outcome, happening
ēventus, -ūs (*m*), consequence, result
exīstimō (1), to think
honestus, -a, -um, respected, best
cuiusque, of every
amplus, -a, -um, eminent, important
nōminātim ēvocātī, mustered or called out by name
proelium, -ī (*n*), battle
dēcertō (1), to fight to the finish
gubernātor, gubernātōris (*m*), helmsman
mōbilitās, mōbilitātis (*f*), maneuverability
sī quandō, whenever
facultās, facultātis (*f*), opportunity
ferreus, -a, -um, made of iron
ēminus, from a distance
tēlum, -ī (*n*), weapon
dē imprōvīsō, unexpectedly
īnsigne, īnsignis (*n*), insignia, colors
parvō mōmentō, a little way
concursus, -ūs (*m*), collision
classis, classis (*f*), fleet

perficiō, perficere (3), **perfēcī, perfectum,** to complete, accomplish
tendō, tendere (3), **tetendī, tēntum,** to stretch, extend
cōnscendō, cōnscendere (3), **cōnscendī, cōnscēnsum,** to board ship
dēsum, dēesse (*irreg.*), **dēfuī** (+ *dat.*), to be lacking
dīdūcō, dīdūcere (3), **dīdūxī, dīductum,** to separate, draw apart
nanciscor, nanciscī (3), **nactus sum,** to obtain
succurrō, succurrere (3), **succurrī, succursum** (+ *dat.*), to help, aid
cōnspicor, cōnspicārī (1), **cōnspicātus sum,** to catch sight of
ēnītor, ēnītī (3), **ēnīsus sum,** to strive, make an effort
antecēdō, antecēdere (3), **antecessī, antecessum,** to get ahead of, precede
cōnflīgō, cōnflīgere (3), **cōnflixī, cōnflictum,** to collide
conlabefīō, conlabefierī (*irreg.*), **conlabefactus sum,** to fall, collapse, break up
dēprimō, dēprimere (3), **dēpressī, dēpressum,** to sink, press down

Exercise 61a

Answer the following questions in English, with reference to the specified lines of the reading passage.

1. Describe the siege preparations of the Romans. (1–6)
2. Pompey was in Greece at this time. Why do you suppose Caesar was attacking a city in southern Gaul? (see Section introduction)
3. As seen from the Roman camp, what was the scene inside the walls of Massilia? (7–11)
4. What was so special to the Massiliotes about this particular day? (11–12)
5. How would you characterize the people of Massilia? What Latin phrase brings out Caesar's respect for the enemy's courage? (15)

6. For what reason did the sailors on board the Massiliote ships fight with special determination on this day? (15–16)
7. What advantages did the enemy enjoy over the Romans and why? What enemy tactics caused the Romans special problems? (17–19 and 20–21)

Exercise 61b

You are a crewman aboard one of Brutus's ships and you have just witnessed the battle. Write a letter in English to your family or a friend and describe the battle and its outcome.

Review of Interrogative and Relative Pronouns

Remember that the function of a relative pronoun in its own clause determines its case, e.g., **Ego sum vir *quem* heri vīdistī.** The interrogative adjective has the same form as the relative pronoun.

Exercise 61c

In each of the following sentences, fill in the blank with the correct Latin form corresponding to the English cue, and then read the sentence aloud and translate.

1. Trirēmēs incitāvērunt nāvem Brūtī, ____________ ex īnsignī facile agnōscī poterat. (which)
2. Massiliēnsibus victīs, ____________ Caesar nunc proelium committet? (with whom, pl.)
3. Omnēs Massiliēnsēs ____________ templa deōrum adiērunt eō diē spem habuērunt. (who)
4. Tēla, ____________ ad Rōmānōs repellendōs nactī erāmus, ferrea erant. (which)
5. ____________ rēbus comparātīs, mīlitēs aggerem exstruere coepērunt. (Which)
6. Utinam lēgātus ____________ oppugnātiō Massiliae cōnfīsa erat nē dēficiat. (to whom)
7. Omnēs rogābant ____________ nautae optimī essent. (whose, sing.)
8. ____________ cīvēs exīstimāvērunt deōs victōriam sibi datūrōs esse? (Which)
9. ____________ opus iūmentum in castrīs Rōmānīs perficit? (What)
10. Vultne Caesar, ____________ dictātor esse māvult quam cōnsul, rēx fierī? (who)

Indefinite Pronouns and Adjectives

In this and recent chapters, you have seen several pronouns and adjectives related to **quis** and **quī**. These are known as *indefinites*, because they designate some person or thing without specifying which one. Observe the following:

> Neque erat **quisquam** . . . quīn . . . exīstimāret. (11–12)
> *And there was not* **anyone** *(i.e., no one) who did not think. . . .*
> Nam et honestī ex iuventūte et **cuiusque** aetātis amplissimī. . . . (12–13)
> *For the best of the youth and the worthiest of* **every** *age. . . .*

In the first example, **quisquam** is an indefinite pronoun; in the second, **cuiusque** is an indefinite adjective. Both are compound forms of the word **quis**. Some of these words, such as **quīdam** and **aliquis** and their other forms, will be familiar, since you have seen them frequently in readings. Observe the following sets of indefinite pronouns and adjectives:

Servus **aliquid** portat.	*The slave is carrying* **something**.
Servus **aliquās** epistulās portat.	*The slave is carrying* **some** *letters.*
Exīstimō **quōsdam** bonōs nātūrā esse.	*I think that* **certain** *people are naturally good.*
Quīdam milēs fratrem suum necāvit.	A **certain** *soldier slew his brother.*
Quisque sē optimum esse exīstimat.	**Everyone** *thinks that he is the best.*
Mercātor **cuique** nautae pecūniam dedit.	*The merchant gave* **each** *sailor money.*
Iūstitia numquam nocet **cuiquam.**	*Justice never harms* **anyone.**

The adjective form of **quisquam** is rarely found.

Here is a summary of indefinite pronouns and adjectives; for a complete list of these forms, refer to the charts at the end of this book. Remember that it is only the **quis** or **quī** part of the word that changes.

Pronoun	*Adjective*
m f n	**m f n**
ali**quis**, ali**quis**, ali**quid** (*someone, something*)	ali**quī**, ali**qua**, ali**quod** (*some, any*)
quīdam, **quae**dam, **quid**dam (*a certain one*)	**quī**dam, **quae**dam, **quod**dam (*a certain*)
quisque, **quis**que, **quid**que (*each, every one*)	**quis**que, **quae**que, **quod**que (*each, every*)
quisquam, **quis**quam, **quid**quam (*anyone, anything*)	same as pronoun but rarely found (*any*)

Notes

1. The feminine singular form of the adjective **aliquī** is **aliqua,** rather than **aliquae.** This is also true of the neuter nominative and accusative plural.

2. The neuter singular form of the pronoun **quīdam** is **quiddam,** of the adjective, **quoddam.**

3. Due to pronunciation, the **-m** in the accusative singular and genitive plural forms of **quīdam** changes to **-n: quendam, quandam, quōrundam, quārundam.**

4. The nominative singular masculine form of the adjective corresponding to the pronoun **quisque** is **quisque,** not **quīque.**

5. The forms of **quisquam** occur mostly with a negative, expressed or implied, as in the example above: **neque . . . quisquam.**

6. **Quidquam** has an alternative spelling, **quicquam.**

Cum dēbēre carnufex cuiquam quicquam quemquam, quemque quisque conveniat, neget. *Since the rascal denies that anyone owes anything to anyone, let whoever sue whomever.* (Ennius, fragment of a comedy)

Exercise 61d

Read aloud and translate the following sentences.

1. Sī aliquis illud dīcit, mentītur.
2. Quīdam ē mīlitibus dīxit sē glande vulnerātum esse.
3. "Estne aliquis domī?" clāmāvit praedō.
4. Quot hominēs, tot sententiae: suus cuique mōs.
5. Iūstitia numquam nocet cuiquam.
6. Alicui rogantī melius quam iubentī parēmus.
7. Exemplum deī quisque est in imāgine parvā.
8. Nūlla causa iūsta cuiquam esse potest contrā patriam arma capiendī.
9. Aliquid bonī semper bonīs.
10. Videō quōsdam adesse quī Massiliae pugnāverint.
11. Quaedam ē mulieribus cogitābant suōs virōs eō diē nōn reditūrōs esse.
12. Neque est quisquam quī sine aliquō metū in proelium introeat.

iūstitia, -ae (*f*), justice

At tuba terribilī sonitū taratantara dīxit. *But the war trumpet spoke its frightening call:* **"Taratantara."** (Ennius, *Annals*, II)

Roman Bullets

Lead shots were the projectiles used by slingers (**funditōrēs**), auxiliary soldiers who provided protection for troops during battle or construction of siege-works. The bullets, which the Romans called "acorns" (**glandēs**), were pointed ovals inscribed with the name of the commanding general, the corps of slingers, or the maker of the bullet. Often the inscription contained curses or insults directed at the enemy. The bullet with this inscription was used against Caesar in the Civil War:

Cn. Mag(nus) Imp(erātor)

In 91 B.C. Pompeius Strabo, father of Pompey the Great, laid a two-year siege against Asculum, an allied Italian city which had revolted against Roman domination. Here are inscriptions from several bullets found there:

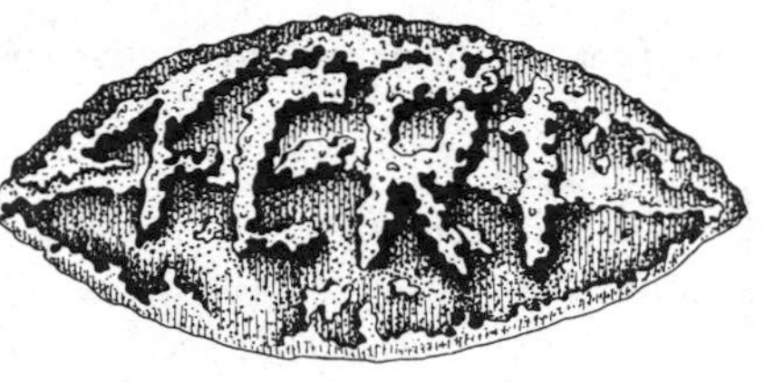

feriō, ferīre (4), to strike

Ferī (side 1) **Pomp(ēium)** (side 2)
Asclānīs (d)ōn(um).
Fugitīvī peristis.
Em tibi malum malō.

Massilia Falls

Given the difficulties of besieging Massilia on land and the courage of its inhabitants, the Romans were forced to build a brickwork tower (**turris laterīcia**) up against their siege wall. They then constructed a 60 foot (18 meter) covered gallery (**mūsculus**) extending from the tower to the enemy's wall. Find out what finally happened by reading Caesar's narrative.

Interim sub mūsculō mīlitēs vectibus īnfima saxa turris hostium quibus fundāmenta continēbantur convellunt. Musculus ē turrī laterīciā ā nostrīs tēlīs tormentīsque dēfenditur; hostēs ē mūrō ac turribus summoventur; nōn datur lībera mūrī dēfendendī facultās. Complūribus iam lapidibus ex illīs quae suberant turrī subductīs, repentīnā ruīnā pars eius turris concidit, pars 5
reliqua cōnsequēns prōcumbēbat, cum hostēs urbis dīreptiōne perterritī inermēs cum īnfulīs sē portīs forās ūniversī praecipitant, ad lēgātōs atque exercitum supplicēs manūs tendunt.

—Caesar, *Commentaries on the Civil War*, II.11 (excerpts)

vectis, vectis (*m*), lever, crowbar
saxum, -ī (*n*), rock, stone
fundāmentum, -ī (*n*), foundation
repentīnus, -a, -um, sudden
dīreptiō, dīreptiōnis (*f*), breach
inermis, -is, -e, unarmed
īnfula, -ae (*f*), heavy wool band worn by suppliants
ūniversus, -a, -um, all together
supplex, supplicis (*m/f*), suppliant

convellō, convellere (3), **convellī, convulsum,** to tear away, weaken
prōcumbō, prōcumbere (3), **prōcubuī, prōcubitum,** to keel over

A Casualty of War

This epitaph, commemorating a soldier who fell in battle, was inscribed on a cenotaph, that is, a tomb with no remains. Use a classical dictionary or other reference work on Roman history to investigate the circumstances of his death, and then write his biography, incorporating the information contained in the epitaph.

M CAELIO T F LEM BON
O LEG XIIX ANN LIII S
CECIDIT BELLO VARIANO OSSA
INFERRE LICEBIT P CAELIVS T F
LEM FRATER FECIT

M(arcō) Caeliō T(itī) f(īliō), Lem(ōniā) (tribū), (domō) Bon(ōniā),
c(enturiōnī) Leg(iōnis) XIIX, ann(ōrum) LIII s(ēmissis);
cecidit bellō Vāriānō. Ossa
īnferre licēbit. P(ūblius) Caelius T(itī) f(īlius),
Lem(ōniā) (tribū), frāter fēcit.

tribus, -ūs (*f*), tribe
Lemōnia, one of 16 rustic tribes near Rome

O = centum, for **centuriō**
XIIX = XVIII
sēmis, sēmissis (*m*), one-half

1 **equitēs ab sinistrō . . . cornū:** these **equitēs** are cavalry, which consisted of non-Roman allies from Gaul and Spain. Pompey hoped to win the day with superior cavalry, with which he had a 7 to 1 advantage. Fighting at Pharsalus took place only on Caesar's right wing, as the left wing was protected by the Enipeus River. For the location of Pharsalus, see the map on p. 90.

2 **sagittariōrum:** the auxiliary forces, called **auxilia,** consisted of archers and slingers drawn from the Romanized areas of the empire and were stationed on the wings as support artillery.

4 **turmātim: turmae** were squadrons of 30 men, ten of which made an **āla,** or cavalry wing.

6 **quartae aciēī, quam īnstituerat ex cohortium numerō:** Caesar's favorite battle formation was the **triplex aciēs**, consisting of three battle lines, one line behind the other with the legions side by side. Caesar's main force numbered 80 cohorts of 22,000, Pompey's 110 cohorts of 45,000 men. Caesar had formed a fourth line from the cohorts of the third to face Pompey's superior cavalry.

dedit signum: signals in the field were given by warhorns, **cornua** and **tubae.**

7 **īnfestīs . . . signīs:** "with unit colors in battle array."

11 **pugnantibus . . . Pompēiānīs:** "of those Pompeians fighting . . ."; the dative of reference is used here where a genitive would be expected in English.

17 **Caesar . . . oppugnārent:** Pompey's army routed, Caesar turns to attack his camp, behind the lines. Caesar, who wore a red cloak (**palūdāmentum**) in battle, was often in the thick of the fighting.

vallum: a wooden palisade and earthen embankment fortified a Roman camp.

18 **cohortātus est:** do not confuse **cohortor** with **cohors.**

beneficiō . . . ūterentur: ūtor takes an ablative object.

21 **animō perterritī:** "broken in spirit"; **animō** is ablative of respect.

22 **signīsque mīlitāribus:** for a legion to lose its insignia or eagle (**aquila**) in battle was a disgrace and could lead to the disbandment of the unit.

25 **centuriōnibus tribūnīsque mīlitum:** centurions were the backbone of the army and usually were grizzled veterans. **Tribūnī mīlitum,** of which there were six per legion, each commanded the unit for two months of the year.

28 **quae . . . , quī . . . , cui . . . :** these relative pronouns introduce subjunctive clauses of characteristic, denoting a general type. In a previous, and perhaps biased, chapter, Caesar tells us that before the battle, Pompey's men were squabbling openly among themselves about rewards and priesthoods and were assigning consulships for years to come, while some were claiming the houses and property of the soldiers in Caesar's camp.

30 **miserrimō ac patientissimō:** this description may be exaggerated and somewhat propagandistic, although Caesar was, no doubt, short of supplies.

33 **decumānā portā:** the gate of the Roman camp farthest from the enemy, so called because the 10th cohort of each legion was stationed there.

34 **Lārīsam:** Larisa was a town in Thessaly, near Pharsalus. Pompey fled to Egypt, where he was stabbed to death by agents of King Ptolemy.

62
The Battle of Pharsalus

Caesar met Pompey on the Greek plain of Pharsalus on August 9, 48 B.C. We pick up the narrative here after the initial engagement, which, in the tactics of the time, required the legionaries of the army to throw their javelins from formation and then draw their swords and charge into hand-to-hand combat.

Eōdem tempore equitēs ab sinistrō Pompēī cornū, ut erat imperātum, ūniversī prōcucurrērunt, omnisque multitūdō sagittāriōrum sē prōfūdit. Quōrum impetum noster equitātus nōn tulit sed paulātim ē locō mōtus cessit, equitēsque Pompēī hōc ācrius īnstāre et sē turmātim explicāre aciemque nostram ā latere apertō circumīre coepērunt. Quod ubi Caesar 5 animadvertit, quārtae aciēī, quam īnstituerat ex cohortium numerō, dedit signum. Illae celeriter prōcucurrērunt īnfestīsque signīs tantā vī in Pompēī equitēs impetum fēcērunt ut eōrum nēmō cōnsisteret omnēsque conversī nōn sōlum locō excēderent, sed prōtinus incitātī fugā montēs altissimōs peterent. Quibus summōtīs omnēs sagittāriī funditōrēsque dēstitūtī inermēs 10 sine praesidiō interfectī sunt. Eōdem impetū cohortēs sinistrum cornū pugnantibus etiam tum ac resistentibus in aciē Pompēiānīs circumiērunt eōsque ā tergō sunt adortae. Eōdem tempore tertiam aciem Caesar, quae quiēta fuerat et sē ad id tempus locō tenuerat, prōcurrere iussit. Ita cum recentēs atque integrī dēfessīs successissent, aliī autem ā tergō adorīrentur, sustinēre 15 Pompēiāni nōn potuērunt atque ūniversī terga vertērunt.

Caesar Pompēiānīs ex fugā intrā vallum compulsīs nūllum spatium perterritīs darī oportēre exīstimāns mīlitēs cohortātus est ut beneficiō fortunae ūterentur castraque oppugnārent. Castra ā cohortibus quae ibi praesidiō erant relictae industriē dēfendēbantur, multō etiam ācrius ā Thrācibus bar- 20 barīsque auxiliīs. Nam quī ab aciē refūgerant mīlitēs, et animō perterritī et lassitūdine cōnfectī, missīs plērīque armīs signīsque mīlitāribus magis dē reliquā fugā quam dē castrōrum dēfēnsiōne cōgitābant. Neque vērō diūtius quī in vāllō cōnstiterant multitūdinem tēlōrum sustinēre potuērunt sed cōnfectī vulneribus locum relīquērunt, prōtinusque omnēs ducibus ūsī cen- 25 turiōnibus tribūnīsque mīlitum in altissimōs montēs, quī ad castra pertinēbant, cōnfūgērunt.

In castrīs Pompēī vidēre licuit multa quae nimiam luxuriam et victōriae fīdūciam dēsignārent, ut facile exīstimārī posset nihil eōs dē ēventū eius diēī timuisse, quī nōn necessāriās conquīrerent voluptātēs. At hī miserrimō 30 ac patientissimō exercituī Caesaris luxuriam obiciēbant, cui semper omnia ad necessārium ūsum dēfuissent. Pompēīus, iam cum intrā vāllum nostrī versārentur, equum nactus dētrāctīs īnsignibus imperātōris decumānā portā sē ex castrīs ēiēcit prōtinusque equō citātō Lārīsam contendit.

—Caesar, *Commentaries on the Civil War,* III.93–96 (excerpts)

cornū, -ūs (*n*), end of a battle line, wing
sagittārius, -ī (*m*), archer
equitātus, -ūs (*m*), cavalry
turmātim, in squadrons
explicō (1), to extend ranks
aciēs, aciēī (*f*), battle line
latus, lateris (*n*), side, flank
cohors, cohortis (*f*), cohort, 1/10th of a legion of troops
signum, -ī (*n*), unit ensign or colors, used for battle signals
prōtinus, immediately
funditor, funditōris (*m*), slinger
praesidium, -ī (*n*), defense, protection
etiam tum, even then
integer, -gra, -grum, whole, fresh
spatium, -ī (*n*), space
industriē, with energy
lassitūdō, lassitūdinis (*f*), exhaustion
plērīque, plēraeque, plēraque, very many
centuriō, centuriōnis (*m*), centurion, leader of 100 men
tribūnus mīlitum, military tribune, legionary officer
pertineō (2), to extend to, reach
nimius, -a, -um, too much, excessive
fidūcia, -ae (*f*), confidence
voluptās, voluptātis (*f*), pleasure
citō (1), to spur on, rouse up

īnstō, īnstāre (1), **īnstitī,** to pursue eagerly
summoveō, summovēre (2), **summōvī, summōtum,** to drive off
dēstituō, dēstituere (3), **dēstituī, dēstitūtum,** to desert, abandon
interficiō, interficere (3), **interfēcī, interfectum,** to kill
succēdō, succēdere (3), **successī, successum** (+ *dat.*), to relieve, reinforce
conquīrō, conquīrere (3), **conquīsīvī, conquīsītum,** to procure, obtain
obiciō, obicere (3), **obiēcī, obiectum,** to throw in one's face, taunt
versor, versārī (1), **versātus sum,** to stay, be situated in
contendō, contendere (3), **contendī, contentum,** to hurry, try to reach

Exercise 62a

Answer the following questions in English, with reference to the specified lines of the reading passage.

1. What initiative does Pompey take at the beginning of the passage? (1–2)
2. What advantage does he hope to exploit with this tactic? (1–5)
3. What unusual tactic does Caesar use to counter this maneuver? (5–7)
4. Describe how Caesar gained the upper hand in the engagement. (7–10)
5. What was the fate of Pompey's auxiliaries? How did Caesar exploit this? (10–11)

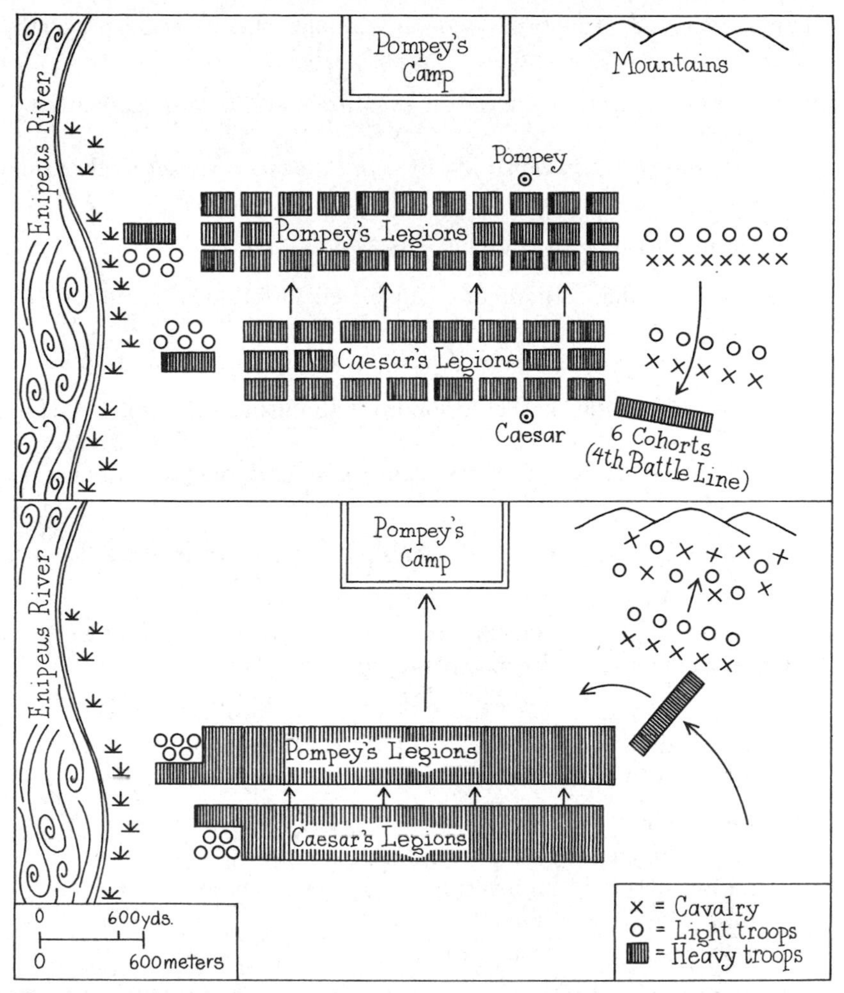

The Battle of Pharsalus 48 B.C.

6. What was Caesar's final, crushing blow? What happened to Pompey's men? (13–16)
7. Describe the resistance of the Pompeians at the camp. (19–21)
8. How did the refugees from the battle behave? What were the reasons? (21–27)
9. What did Caesar find in Pompey's camp? Why should he have derived special satisfaction from this discovery? (28–32)
10. From the last sentence, what do we learn about Pompey? (32–34)

VERBS: Ablative with Special Verbs

Several deponent verbs and their compounds are used with the ablative case: **fruor, fungor, potior, ūtor,** and **vescor,** of which **ūtor** is the most commonly found. You met **vescor** in *Pastimes and Ceremonies*, Chapter 47:

> Trēs annōs ego et leō in eādem spēluncā habitābāmus, **eōdem cibō** vescentēs.
>
> *For three years, the lion and I lived in the same cave, eating* **the same food.**

In the current passage we have:

> Caesar . . . mīlitēs cohortātus est ut **beneficiō** fortunae ūterentur. . . . (17–19)
>
> *Caesar encouraged his men to take advantage of fortune's* **favor**. . . .
>
> . . . omnēs **ducibus** ūsī **centuriōnibus tribūnīsque mīlitum.** . . . (25–26)
>
> *all having made use of* **the centurions and military tribunes as leaders.** . . .

These ablatives serve as ablatives of means, as illustrated by the following:

Ūtitur **gladiō**.	*He makes use of his sword.* (literally, *He benefits himself* **by his sword**.)
Castrīs potītus est.	*He took possession of the camp.* (literally, *He made himself powerful* **by the camp**.)

Be sure you know the principal parts and meanings of these special verbs that are used with the ablative case:

fruor, fruī (3), **fructus sum,** to enjoy, have benefit of
fungor, fungī (3), **functus sum,** to perform, discharge
potior, potīrī (4), **potītus sum,** to get possession of, obtain
ūtor, ūtī (3), **ūsus sum,** to use, make use of
vescor, vescī (3), to eat, feed on

Quō usque tandem abūtēre, Catilīna, patientiā nostrā? *For how long will you abuse our patience, Catiline?* (Cicero, *First Oration Against Catiline*, 1)

Exercise 62b

Complete the following sentences with the correct forms of the words in parentheses, then read aloud and translate. The singular or plural nominative is provided.

1. Fruimur atque ūtimur ______________. (plūrimae maritimae rēs)
2. Leō ex manū hominis ______________ vescēbātur. (cibus)
3. Nē audeat Caesar ūtī ______________ rēgis nisi iussū populī. (insignia, -ium)

4. Ita nōbīs ______________ perfruī liceat. (salva rēs pūblica)
5. Velim ē patre obtineās pecūniam ______________ ūtāmur. (quae)
6. Cum ______________ perfunctī essent, centuriōnēs ā Caesare laudātī sunt. (maximī labōrēs)
7. Pompēiānī ______________ perfruī vīsī sunt. (voluptās)
8. In proeliō Pharsālī, Caesar quattuor ______________ ūtēbātur. (aciēs)
9. Plūrimī mīlitēs ______________ ūtī possunt. (gladius)
10. Diū cum esset pugnātum, ______________ ______________-que nostrī potītī sunt. (impedīmenta) (castra)

Building Up the Meaning XV

Genitive and Dative with Special Verbs

In addition to the verbs found with the ablative, you have met other special verbs, those with objects in the genitive or dative case.

1. Genitive with Special Verbs
   Oblīvīscor, meminī, and **misereor** all take the *genitive case,* **meminī** being found most often with these genitive forms of the personal pronoun:

Singular	**meī**	*of me*	**tuī**	*of you*
Plural	**nostrī**	*of us*	**vestrī**	*of you*

   Thus,
   Meminit **nostrī.** *He remembers us. He is mindful of us.*
   Oblīvīscor and **meminī** may also be found with the accusative, with the same sense.
   Oblīvīscor **nōmina** or **nōminum.** *I forget names. I am forgetful of names.*

2. Dative with Special Verbs
   These verbs fall into two main groups:
   a. Certain intransitive verbs may be found with the *dative of the indirect object*. These verbs have no direct object, as in English.

Caesar **nēminī** cēdit.	*Caesar yields* **to no one.**
Bonīs nocet quī **malīs** parcit.	*He does harm* **to the good** *who is sparing* **to the bad.**

   Among the most important of these verbs which you have seen are:

appropinquāre, to approach	**licēre,** to be allowed	**parēre,** to obey
crēdere, to believe	**nocēre,** to harm	**persuādēre,** to persuade
favēre, to favor	**nūbere,** to marry	**placēre,** to please
ignōscere, to pardon	**occurrere,** to meet	**resistere,** to resist
imperāre, to order	**parcere,** to spare	

b. The second group consists of verbs which are compounded with prepositions.

Mīles **vulnerātō amīcō** *successit.*	The soldier *aided* **his wounded comrade.**
Aliquandō ducēs **virtūtī** *dēsunt.*	Sometimes leaders *lack* **courage.**

You have seen:

dēesse, to be lacking
praecipere, to instruct
prōdesse, to benefit
succēdere, to relieve
succurrere, to help

In addition, **praeficiō** and **praesum** are commonly used with the dative:

Caesar Trebōnium **oppugnātiōnī** *praefēcit.*	Caesar *placed* Trebonius *in command of* **the siege.**
Antonius **sinistrō cornū** *praefuit.*	Antony *was in charge of* **the left wing.**

Be sure you know the principal parts and meanings of these verbs:

praeficiō, praeficere (3), **praefēcī, praefectum,** to put in charge of
praesum, praeesse (*irreg.*), **praefuī,** to be in charge of

Exercise 62c

Complete each sentence with the proper form of the word in parentheses, and then read aloud and translate. The nominative singular or plural is given.

1. Meminit ____________, sed oblīvīscitur ____________. (ego) (tū)
2. ____________ imperābātur ut signum dārent. (Tubicinēs)
3. Centuriōnēs semper pārent ____________. (imperātor)
4. Caesar praefēcit Marcum Antōnium ____________. (cornū sinistrum)
5. Miserēminī ____________ quī in proeliō mortuī sunt. (mīlitēs)
6. Pompēius imperāvit ____________ ut ____________ pārērent. (omnēs suī) (tribūnī)
7. Potestne Caesar meminisse ____________ cuiusque omnium centuriōnum? (nōmen)
8. Cum Pompēiānī acerrimē pugnāvissent, Caesariānī ____________ parcere voluērunt. (eī)
9. Labiēnus exīstimāvit frātrem suum ____________ praefutūrum esse. (sagittāriī)
10. ____________ nōn licet oblīvīscī ____________. (Nōs) (Caesar)

The Ides of March

On March 15, 44 B.C., Julius Caesar was murdered by a faction of the senatorial nobility because, as dictator, he threatened senatorial control of the government of the Republic. Of the events that took place on the Ides of March, no eyewitness accounts survive. Nicolaus of Damascus came to Rome sometime during Augustus's reign and had the opportunity to interview those who may have witnessed the murder.

> The Senate rose in respect for his position when they saw him entering. Those who were to have a part in the plot stood near him. Right next to him went Tullius Cimber, whose brother had been exiled by Caesar. Under pretext of a humble request on behalf of his brother, Cimber approached and grasped the mantle of his toga, seeming to want to make a more positive move with his hands upon Caesar. Caesar wanted to get up and use his hands, but was prevented by Cimber and became exceedingly annoyed. That was the moment for the men to set to work. All quickly unsheathed their daggers and rushed at him. Caesar rose to defend himself. They were just like men doing battle against him. Under the mass of wounds, he fell at the foot of Pompey's statue. Everyone wanted to seem to have had some part in the murder, and there was not one of them who failed to strike his body as it lay there, until, wounded thirty-five times, he breathed his last.
>
> Nicolaus of Damascus, *Historici Graeci Minores*, para. 24

Denarius of Greek mint, 42 B.C. This face shows the cap of liberty (**pilleus**), between two daggers, and the legend: **EID(ibus), MAR(tiīs)**.

Exercise 62d

The following hasty note of congratulations to Basilus is thought to have been written by Cicero on the day of the assassination, in reply to a report received from Basilus. L. Minucius Basilus was an officer in Gaul under Caesar and was one of his assassins. Translate Cicero's message.

CICERO BASILO SAL.

Tibi grātulor, mihi gaudeō; tē amō, tua tueor; ā tē amārī et quid agās quidque agātur certior fierī volō.

—Cicero, *Letters to His Friends*, VI.15

tueor, tuērī (2), **tuitus sum,** to look out for, protect
certior fierī, to be informed

The Death of Pompey

Pompey met his end on September 28, 48 B.C. as he landed in Egypt, seeking asylum after his disastrous loss at Pharsalus.

It was some distance from the trireme to (the shore of Alexandria) and Pompey, seeing that none of the company addressed a single friendly word to him, turned his eyes toward Septimius (who had been one of Pompey's officers) and said: "Surely I am not mistaken. You and I have been comrades-in-arms together." Septimius merely nodded his head, saying nothing and giving no sign of friendly feeling. Deep silence fell again, and Pompey took a small notebook in which he had written down in Greek the speech which he proposed to use in addressing King Ptolemy, and began to look through it. As they drew near the shore his wife Cornelia and his friends watched from the trireme to see what would happen. Cornelia was in a state of terrible anxiety, but she began to take heart when she saw great numbers of the King's people gathering together at the landing place, apparently to give him an honorable reception. But just then, as Pompey took Philip's hand so as to rise up more easily to his feet, Septimius ran him through the body with his sword from behind; then Salvius and then Achillas drew their daggers and stabbed him. And Pompey, drawing his toga down over his face with both hands, endured their blows; he neither said nor did anything unworthy of himself, only groaned a little, and so ended his life in his sixtieth year and only one day after his birthday.

Plutarch, *Pompey*

The Death of Cicero

On December 7, 43 B.C., Cicero bravely faced death at the hands of assassins sent by Mark Antony, who sought to succeed Caesar as dictator of Rome.

Cicero, realizing that he could not be rescued from the hands of Antony, first made for his estate at Tusculum and, from there, by traveling crossways across the peninsula, he set out for Formiae to board a ship leaving Gaeta. There, weariness of both flight and life itself seized him, for, having set out to sea several times, contrary winds had brought him back and then the tossing of the ship had become unendurable. On returning to his villa, he exclaimed, "I will now die in the land I have so often served." It is a fact that he ordered his slaves, willing to fight bravely and loyally to the finish, to put down his litter and to endure without resistance what an unjust fate had laid upon them all. As he stretched himself out from his litter and offered his neck without hesitation, his head was cut off. Charging that his hands had written things against Antony, the assassins cut off those as well. And so the head was carried back to Antony and by his order was placed between Cicero's two hands on the Rostra where, as former consul, he had spoken out with remarkable eloquence against Antony that very year.

Livy, *Periochae*, CXX

PART IV
Public Life and Imperial Administration in the Early Empire

The Roman Principate

The beginning of Roman imperial rule took place near Actium, off the western coast of Greece, for it was here that Octavian defeated the combined naval forces of Antony and Cleopatra to become master of the Mediterranean world. After his victory, Octavian gradually assumed autocratic powers under the guise of restoring the Republic and ushered in a period of **Pāx Rōmāna**. Command of the entire Roman Empire thus came into the hands of this one man, Gaius Julius Caesar Octavianus, called **Augustus** ("consecrated" or "holy"). His rule, which ended the Republic (509–27 B.C.), has come to be known as the *Principate,* from the unofficial title **prīnceps** ("first citizen"). The next 500 years of Roman history were dominated by over 95 rulers, or emperors, whose feats and follies established a cult of personality over the more than 50 million people of the Empire. The emperor, whose official title was **Imperātor,** was formally granted his powers by senatorial decree and by ratification of the people, but the real basis of his power was the allegiance of the military. The role of the Senate gradually became ceremonial, and its functions were assumed by a vast bureaucracy, mainly dependent upon the **auctōritās**, or personal prestige, of the emperor himself.

Beginning with Augustus, both the military and civilian populations of the Empire swore an oath of allegiance to the new emperor and renewed it on each anniversary of his accession. The following oath was sworn to Caligula by a community in Spain in A.D. 37:

> I solemnly swear that I will be an enemy to those who I learn are enemies to Gaius Caesar Germanicus. If anyone brings or shall bring danger to him and his welfare, I will not cease to pursue him with arms and deadly war on land and on sea until he has paid the penalty to him; I will hold neither myself nor my children dearer than his welfare; and I will regard as enemies of mine those who have hostile intentions against him. If I knowingly swear or shall swear falsely, then may Jupiter Optimus Maximus and the deified Augustus and all the other immortal gods cause me and my children to be deprived of fatherland, safety, and all good fortune.
>
> *Corpus Inscriptionum Latinarum,* II.172

Augustus

In addition to oaths of allegiance, the relationship between ruler and ruled was fostered by emperor worship, through the imperial cult established by Augustus, and by emperor deification. Julius Caesar was the first Roman ruler to be declared a god posthumously by the Senate, and emperors as early as Caligula began to seek divinity during their reigns.

A Roman Senator of the Empire

C. Plinius Secundus, or Pliny the Younger, perhaps best known for his vivid eyewitness account of the eruption of Vesuvius in A.D. 79, was born to a prosperous landowning family at Comum, in the Cisalpine province of northern Italy. Although a lawyer by vocation, Pliny published hundreds of letters, including his official correspondence with the emperor Trajan, who ruled A.D. 98–117. These letters provide an intimate look at the personal and professional life of a member of the Roman ruling class during the reigns of the emperors Domitian and Nerva, as well as Trajan. Pliny was privileged to witness the reconciliation between Senate and emperor after Domitian and the transition of the Empire into what Gibbon called "the period in the history of the world during which the condition of the human race was most happy and prosperous." As an advocate for the Senate, Pliny prosecuted or defended a number of Roman officials accused of maladministration and embezzlement in their provinces. This, coupled with the fact that he was knowledgeable about financial affairs, having served as head

Trajan

of the state treasury, led to his commission in A.D. 110 as special envoy of the emperor Trajan, with the title **lēgātus Augustī cōnsulārī potestāte**, to deal with problems of inefficiency and corruption in the province of Bithynia-Pontus. The last of Pliny's ten books of epistles contains over 100 letters of correspondence to and from Trajan, in which Pliny asks for advice on such matters as procedure, law, finance, building projects, and security. It is believed that Pliny died in office in Bithynia just before A.D. 114.

Here is a translation of part of an inscription which was placed in the baths at Comum and which records details of Pliny's private life:

> Gaius Plinius Caecilius Secundus, son of Lucius of the tribe Oufentina, consul, augur, praetorian commissioner with full consular power for the province of Pontus and Bithynia, sent to that province in accordance with the Senate's decree by the Emperor Nerva Trajan Augustus, curator of the bed and banks of the Tiber and the sewers of Rome, official of the Treasury of Saturn, official of the military Treasury, praetor, tribune of the people, quaestor of the Emperor, commissioner for the Roman knights, military tribune of the Third Gallic Legion, magistrate of the Board of Ten, left by will public baths at a cost of . . . and an additional 300,000 sesterces for furnishing them, with 1,866,666 sesterces to support a hundred of his freedmen, and subsequently to provide an annual dinner for the people of the city. . . . Likewise in his lifetime he gave 500,000 sesterces for the maintenance of boys and girls of the city and also 100,000 for the upkeep of the library. . . .

Corpus Inscriptionum Latinarum, V.5262

2 **Tua pietās . . . optāverat ut. . . . :** = **Optāverās tibi tuā pietāte ut. . . .** "You had wished, because of your devotion, that. . . ."; **optō,** is followed by an indirect command.

quam tardissimē: "at the latest possible moment."

3 **dī immortālēs:** this phrase probably indicates official, or public, respect for the gods, rather than personal belief on the part of Pliny.

virtūtēs tuās: virtūs here is "virtue," rather than "courage." The thought is that the gods have put Trajan at the helm of state sooner than anticipated, because of Nerva's untimely death.

ad gubernācula reī pūblicae: this metaphor depicts the state as a ship, with the emperor at the helm. The "ship of state" is a common image in literature.

4 **quam suscēperās:** as Nerva's official adopted heir, or Caesar, Trajan had already begun to assume some of the duties of state.

Precor . . . ut . . . omnia . . . contingant: "I pray that all things may turn out. . . ."; **ut . . . contingant** is an indirect command after **precor.**

5 **digna saeculō tuō: dignus** requires an ablative of respect, where we say "worthy of . . ."; **digna** elaborates on the meaning of **prospera.**

6 **optime:** in addressing the Emperor as **optimus,** Pliny foreshadows what will later become the extraordinary title **Optimus,** granted to Trajan alone among all Caesars. Trajan enjoyed the association with Jupiter Optimus Maximus which this title brought, even celebrating it on his coins.

prīvātim et pūblicē: both as a personal individual and as a public official.

7 **Marcus Ulpius Trāiānus:** no contemporary literary account of Trajan's life survives. The surviving accounts of Suetonius, the imperial biographer who wrote chatty and anecdotal lives of the first twelve Caesars, end with Domitian. Subsequent literature omits the lives of Nerva and Trajan and resumes with Hadrian, Trajan's successor.

8 **inūsitātae cīvīlitātis et fortitūdinis:** *genitives of description,* used to denote a quality, when the quality is modified by an adjective. The *ablative of description,* much more commonly found, describes a special or physical characteristic, e.g., **puella eximiā fōrmā,** "a girl of outstanding beauty."

Rōmānī imperiī . . . fīnēs: the territory of the Roman Empire reached its greatest extent under Trajan, who added Dacia, now Rumania, and Mesopotamia, now Iraq.

14 **ad augendum fiscum:** the emperor's private purse, as opposed to the **aerārium,** or State Treasury, of which Pliny had been an official.

15 **immūnitātēs cīvitātibus tribuēns:** the word **immūnitās** means exemption from **mūnera,** or public duties. Public service, an honor for citizens in the early Empire, had become a requirement of public life in provincial communities by Eutropius's day.

20 **Ossa conlāta in urnam auream in Forō:** Trajan's ashes were enshrined in the base of his column in his imperial forum, built just to the northeast of the Roman Forum. The sculpted relief which spirals up the 140-foot (43 meter) column celebrates his victory over the Dacians and tells us much about the imperial army.

63
Emperor and Empire

A. *This letter was written by Pliny to Trajan in* A.D. *98, in celebration of the Emperor's accession upon the sudden death of his adoptive father Nerva.*

C. PLINIUS TRAIANO IMPERATORI

Tua quidem pietās, imperātor sanctissime, optāverat ut quam tardissimē succēderēs patrī; sed dī immortālēs festīnāvērunt virtūtēs tuās ad gubernācula reī pūblicae quam suscēperās admovēre. Precor ergō ut tibi et per tē generī hūmānō prospera omnia, id est digna saeculō tuō, contingant. Fortem tē 5
et hilarem, imperātor optime, et prīvātim et pūblicē optō.

—Pliny, *Letters*, X.1

B. *Although Eutropius, the writer of this passage, lived several hundred years after Trajan, he nonetheless preserves at least the spirit of the popular attitude toward Trajan during the emperor's lifetime.*

Marcus Ulpius Trāiānus rem pūblicam ita administrāvit ut omnibus prīncipibus meritō praeferātur, inūsitātae cīvīlitātis et fortitūdinis. Rōmānī imperiī, quod post Augustum dēfēnsum magis fuerat quam nōbiliter ampliātum, fīnēs longē lātēque diffūdit. Glōriam tamen mīlitārem cīvīlitāte et moder- 10
ātiōne superāvit, Rōmae et per prōvinciās aequālem sē omnibus exhibēns, amīcōs salūtandī causā frequentāns, vel aegrōtantēs vel cum festōs diēs habuissent, convīvia cum īsdem indiscrēta vicissim habēns, saepe in vehiculīs eōrum sedēns, nūllum senātōrem laedēns, nihil iniūstum ad augendum fiscum agēns, per orbem terrārum aedificāns multa, immūnitātēs 15
cīvitātibus tribuēns, nihil nōn tranquillum et placidum agēns. Ob haec per orbem terrārum deō proximus nihil nōn venerātiōnis meruit et vīvus et mortuus. Obiit aetātis annō LXIII, mēnse IX, diē IV; imperiī XIX, mēnse VI, diē XV. Inter dīvōs relātus est solusque omnium intrā urbem sepultus est. Ossa conlāta in urnam auream in Forō, quod aedificāvit, sub columnā 20
posita sunt, cuius altitūdō CXLIV pedēs habet. Huius tantum memoriae dēlātum est ut usque ad nostram aetātem nōn aliter in senātū prīncipibus acclāmētur nisi "Fēlīcior Augustō, melior Trāiānō."

—Eutropius, A *Short History of Rome from its Foundation*, VIII.2–5 (excerpts)

pietās, pietātis (*f*), devotion
sanctus, -a, -um, hallowed, august
gubernāculum, -ī (*n*), rudder, helm
saeculum, -ī (*n*), reign, age
meritō, deservedly
inūsitātus, -a, -um, unusual

cīvīlitās, cīvīlitātis (*f*), politeness, courtesy
ampliō (1), to enlarge, increase
fīnēs, fīnium (*m pl*), territory
longē lātēque, far and wide
aequālis, -is, -e, fair, just
frequentō (1), to visit often
indiscrētus, -a, -um, without prejudice or social distinction
vicissim, in turn, in exchange

iniūstus, -a, -um, improper, unjust
fiscus, -ī (*m*), emperor's private funds
orbis terrārum, world, earth
immūnitās, immūnitātis (*f*), exemption
venerātiō, venerātiōnis (*f*), respect
usque, up to, as far as
nōn aliter = **nihil aliud**
acclāmō (1), to cry out in approval

succēdō, succēdere (3), **successī, successum** (+ *dat.*), to succeed in office
suscipiō, suscipere (3), **suscēpī, susceptum,** to accept, begin, undertake
precor, precārī (1), **precātus sum,** to pray, beg, request
praeferō, praeferre (*irreg.*), **praetulī, praelātum,** to put first, prefer
diffundō, diffundere (3), **diffūdī, diffūsum,** to spread out, extend
obeō, obīre (*irreg.*), **obiī, obitum,** to depart, die

Putō deus fīō. *I think I'm becoming a god!* Said by Vespasian, on his deathbed. (Suetonius, *Vespasian,* 23)

Flattery of the emperor was a reality of imperial political life that Pliny readily understood. In a speech thanking the Emperor for granting him the consulship of A.D. 100, Pliny identifies Trajan as Jove on earth.

> This truly is the concern of an emperor and even of a god—to restore good feeling between rival cities, to restrain angry peoples not by force but by reason, to correct the injustices of government officials, and to undo what should never have been done—finally, like a shooting star, to see and hear all, and to be present and offer assistance whenever called upon. It is in this way that I believe the father of the universe controls all with a nod of his head, whenever he looks down upon the earth and thinks it worthy to reckon the destinies of mortal men among the works of the gods. He is now free of this duty and can turn his full attention to the heavens, since he has given you to us to carry out his responsibility toward the human race.
>
> Pliny, *Panegyric,* 80.3–5

On coin A, Jupiter Optimus Maximus, addressed as **Cōnservātor Pater Patriae,** is shown standing protectively over Trajan dressed in a toga. On coin B, look for the small globe just below the bust of Trajan. This coin is about the size of an American nickel.

Exercise 63a

Coins were used by Roman emperors as instruments of propaganda. Through their coins, which have been found as far away from Rome as India and China, Roman emperors were able to communicate to their subjects the virtues of Roman imperial rule. Study the coin pictured and be ready to discuss its "message" in the light of the preceding English translation of Pliny. What does this coin tell us about Trajan? What message did it send to those who possessed, used, or saw it? What kinds of "messages" do modern coins send?

Exercise 63b

Answer in English the following questions about the reading passages.

1. What is the purpose of Pliny's letter? What is its manner and tone of address?
2. How did those in public life hope to advance themselves during the imperial period? Is there any sign of a self-serving motive on Pliny's part?
3. What characteristics of Trajan as a ruler does Eutropius emphasize?
4. What evidence do we have in this passage that Trajan was a soldier-emperor?
5. What reveals Trajan to be a man of the people? What reputation did he enjoy as a result?
6. What special honor was granted to Trajan at his death? What was his age at death? For how long had he ruled?
7. What revealed Trajan's popularity, even 200 years after his demise?
8. Is there any consistency between what Eutropius and Pliny say about Trajan and what Trajan "says" about himself on his coinage? Were emperors revered by their subjects as gods or men, or both?

VERBS: Impersonal Verbs

You may recall the following sentences from *Pastimes and Ceremonies*:

Mē **taedet** solitūdinis.	*I am tired of being alone.* (literally, *It wearies me. . . .*)
Festīnāre tē **oportet.**	*You must hurry.* (literally, *It is necessary for you to hurry.*)

In each of these examples, the verb is used *impersonally*, that is, with the subject "it" implied in the 3rd person singular form of the verb. Good English often requires a transformation of the impersonal verb into a personal:

Licet nōbīs hīc manēre?	(literally) *Is it allowed for us to stay here?* (better English) *May we stay here?*

Most impersonal verbs belong to the 2nd conjugation, forming their tenses in regular fashion. From **licet, licēre, licuit** come **licet, licēbat, licēbit, licuerat**, and **licuerit**. Remember that *impersonal verbs are found only in the 3rd person singular.*

The Uses of Impersonal Verbs

1. The following impersonal verbs have meanings related to feelings:

Mē **miseret** eius.	*I pity him.*
Mē **paenitet** crūdēlitātis.	*I regret (am sorry for) my cruelty.*
Mē **pudet** errōris.	*I am ashamed of my mistake.*
Mē **taedet** sermōnis.	*I am tired of conversation.*

You will note that these impersonal verbs are accompanied by the accusative of the person who feels and the genitive of the cause of the feeling. Such verbs may also be accompanied by an infinitive phrase describing the cause of the feeling, e.g.:

Nōs **pudet** *male fēcisse.* *We are ashamed of having done poorly.*

2. The following impersonal verbs are found with either the infinitive or the subjunctive.

Infinitive	Subjunctive	
Tē *festīnāre* **oportet.**	**Oportet** *festīnēs.*	*You ought to hurry.*
Tibi *manēre* **licet.**	**Licet** *maneās.*	*You may stay.*
Tibi *exīre* **necesse est.**	**Necesse est** *exeās.*	*You must leave.*

Note: **Licet** and **necesse est** can be used with either the dative, as above, or the accusative, e.g.:

Tē manēre **licet.** *You may stay.*

Other common verbs of this type are **decet,** "it is right" or "it is proper," and **libet**, "it is pleasing" or "it is agreeable."

3. Some ordinary verbs may be used impersonally.

Mihi manēre **placet.**	*I am happy to stay.* (literally, *It pleases me to stay.*)
Nōs īre **iuvat.**	*We are pleased to go.*

Cui peccāre licet, peccat minus. *The one who is allowed to make mistakes makes fewer of them.* (Ovid, *Loves*, III.iv.9)

Miseret tē aliōrum; tuī nec miseret nec pudet. *You take pity on others; but you feel no pity or shame for yourself.* (Plautus, *Trinummus*, 431)

Exercise 63c

Read aloud and translate the following sentences into idiomatic English.

1. Senātuī placuit lēgātōs mittere ad Dāciōs.
2. Nervā mortuō, Trāiānum necesse erat imperātōrem fierī.
3. Decet Trāiānō amīcōs salūtandī causā frequentāre.
4. Oportet epistulam ad imperātōrem scrībās ut eī gratūlēris.
5. Mē nōn sōlum paenitet stultitiae meae sed etiam pudet.
6. Multīs epistulīs scrīptīs, Plīniō festīs diēbus fruī licēbit.
7. Taedet imperātōrem audīre eadem semper.
8. Trāiānus amīcīs aegrōtantibus auxilium dabat quod sē miserēbat eōrum.
9. Nec mē pudet concēdere nescīre quod nesciam.
10. Licuit Trāiānō imperātōrī ossa sua intrā urbem sepelīrī.
11. Optimī imperātōrēs nōn agunt quod libet, sed quod decet.
12. Plīnium laudāvisse Trāiānum nōn paenitet.

Exercise 63d

Translate the following into Latin.

1. I am weary of life.
2. We will be sorry that we did this.
3. Pliny took pity on his slaves.
4. It is proper for a senator to praise the emperor.
5. Trajan must leave Rome at once.

Passive Verbs Used Impersonally

Look at the following sentences:

Pugnātum est ācriter.	*The fight was fierce.* (literally, *It was fought fiercely.*)
Ad summum collem **perventum est.**	*The top of the hill was reached.*
Mihi ab eō **persuadēbātur.**	*He persuaded me.*

The passive of intransitive verbs may be used in the 3rd person singular with an implied subject "it," that is, impersonally, when the writer wishes to emphasize the *action* rather than the person or persons performing the action. English tends to express the same idea either by using a noun or by changing the verb to the active voice.

Exercise 63e

Translate the following into good English.

1. Ad Forum imperātōris salūtandī causā concurritur.
2. Senātōribus ab imperātōre saepe parcitur.

3. Nervā mortuō, vehementer dolēbātur.
4. Cum ventum esset ad domum Plīniī, convīvae intrāvērunt.
5. Dē imperātōre bene narrātur.
6. Cum Dāciīs usque ad noctem pugnābitur.
7. Mox ad Forum Trāiānum perventum est.
8. Plīniō ab amīcō epistulam scrībere persuādēbātur.
9. Quibus senātōribus ab imperātōre favēbitur?
10. Dāciīs persuādērī nōn poterat ut pācem facerent.

> **Tū regere imperiō populōs, Rōmāne, mementō**
> **(hae tibi erunt artēs) pācīque impōnere mōrem,**
> **parcere subiectīs et dēbellāre superbōs.**
> Vergil, *Aeneid*, VI.851–853

Exercise 63f

Make a list of all the modern countries wholly or partly contained within the boundaries of the Roman Empire during the time of Trajan, as illustrated by the map below. Consult a modern atlas for assistance, as necessary.

An Imperial Building Program

Trajan extended the boundaries of the Roman Empire to the limits of the civilized world, with the exception of India and China. The wealth that poured into Rome from these imperial territories enabled Trajan to undertake a massive building program, to the extent that the Emperor Constantine later called him **Parietāria**, "Wallflower," because his name was inscribed on so many walls. He built baths, aqueducts, roads, and bridges at home and abroad, and, in keeping with his imperial vision of Rome as a cosmopolis, he constructed a huge market, which was supplied by his new harbor at Ostia. His crowning achievement was the last and greatest of the imperial **fora**, Trajan's Forum, where the Emperor's remains were laid to rest at the foot of his column celebrating the defeat of the Dacians. It was the Emperor's hope that Rome would become the architectural showpiece of the world, much as the Athens of Pericles had been, and his coins often boast of this intention. In general, Roman rulers used their buildings as architectural propaganda, to symbolize the material rewards of prosperity under imperial rule and to portray such imperial virtues as **concordia, abundantia, fēlīcitās**, and **aeternitās**. Provincial municipalities often competed for imperial favor by constructing baths, **fora**, theaters, and aqueducts in the image of Rome herself. Pliny, in writing to Trajan of the public works in Bithynia, several times refers to those "whose utility and beauty will be most worthy of your age."

Trajan's Column

2 **Lēx Pompēia:** after conquering the Greek East, Pompey established by edict in 65 B.C. the law under which the new Roman province of Bithynia would be governed.

būlēn: Greek *boulê* = Roman **senātus** or, more properly, a **decuriō** or "town council." The language and culture of Bithynia were mainly Greek. For the places mentioned in this reading, refer to the map on p. 90.

ā cēnsōribus leguntur: municipal censors, on the Roman model, selected from ex-magistrates the **decuriōnēs**, or those who would serve for life on the town council. Later in the Empire, councilmen were chosen from the wealthier property owners, who then went on to hold magistracies.

3 **dare pecūniam:** in the more Romanized western provinces, an honorary fee, the **honōrārium decuriōnātūs**, was generally paid by those selected to local senates by the censor of the town.

indulgentia tua: with the special permission of the emperor a local town council could appoint to its own body a person of special distinction as a civic honor. In certain cities of Bithynia, these honorary councilmen had begun to pay the **honōrārium**, perhaps as a source of municipal income.

4 **super lēgitimum numerum:** usually several hundred, but this varied.

5 **Anicius . . . iussit īnferre:** Anicius, a previous governor, had established the **honōrārium decuriōnātūs** for all councilmen in a few cities.

7 **aliud aliīs, . . . īnferre:** "to make a payment . . . which varied from one city to another."

Superest . . . ut . . . dispiciās: "it remains for you to consider. . . ."; the result clause serves as the subject of **superest**, used impersonally.

9 **ā tē cōnstituī decet:** the subject is the previous **quod**-clause, the ruling that will result from Trajan's consideration of the matter (**dispiciās**, 7).

13 **dēbeant necne:** "whether or not they ought. . . ."; **dēbeant** is subjunctive in a double indirect question with **necne**. This indirect question serves as the subject of **nōn potest statuī**, following.

14 **sequendam . . . putō:** supply **esse**, "in my opinion, must be followed. . . ."; the omission of **esse** is very common in Pliny.

17 **Nīcomēdīae et Nīcaeae:** Nicomedia was the provincial capital of Bithynia and Nicaea its chief rival. Both were self-governing cities under the general control of the Roman governor.

quīdam . . . in opus damnātī: these were non-Roman provincial subjects who were sentenced **in opus**, to the mines or quarries, or **in lūdum**, to serve at or in the games. Convicted criminals lost freedom and citizenship and were reduced to the status of slaves. Crimes warranting such punishment were theft, forgery, arson, and sacrilege.

18 **pūblicōrum servōrum:** the **pūblicī servī** were a privileged class of slaves who earned a salary by assisting municipal officials as clerks and by serving the state in other menial capacities. Pliny states elsewhere that public slaves were even used to guard prisoners, evidently an impropriety. Communities were apparently either using convicts to perform public work in order to avoid the costly purchase of slaves or the public slaves themselves were using convicts for their own work.

64
Local Government and Security in the Provinces

Pliny's correspondence with Trajan during his tenure as imperial legate of Bithynia-Pontus reveals much about how the Romans governed their empire. The following selections deal with problems of provincial government and security that are typical of an empire whose size and diversity demanded an ever-increasing centralization of government in the hands of the emperor in Rome.

A. Pliny consults Trajan on a matter of municipal government.

C. PLINIUS TRAIANO IMPERATORI

Lēx Pompēia, domine, quā Bīthȳnī et Ponticī ūtuntur, eōs quī in būlēn ā cēnsōribus leguntur, dare pecūniam nōn iubet; sed eī quōs indulgentia tua quibusdam cīvitātibus super lēgitimum numerum adicere permīsit et singula mīlia dēnāriōrum et bīna intulērunt. Anicius deinde Maximus prōcōnsul 5
eōs etiam quī ā cēnsōribus legerentur, dumtaxat in paucissimīs cīvitātibus, aliud aliīs, iussit īnferre. Superest ergō, ut ipse dispiciās, an in omnibus cīvitātibus certum aliquid omnēs quī deinde būleutae legentur dēbeant prō introitū dare. Nam, quod in perpetuum mānsūrum est, ā tē cōnstituī decet, cuius factīs dictīsque dēbētur aeternitās. 10

—Pliny, *Letters*, X.112

B. Trajan gives his reply.

TRAIANUS PLINIO

Honōrārium decuriōnātūs omnēs, quī in quāque cīvitāte Bīthȳniae decuriōnēs fīunt, īnferre dēbeant necne, in ūniversum ā mē nōn potest statuī. Id ergō, quod semper tūtissimum est, sequendam cuiusque cīvitātis lēgem putō. 15

—Pliny, *Letters*, X.113

C. In this letter, Pliny asks Trajan what to do about condemned criminals who have been found performing the duties of public slaves.

C. PLINIUS TRAIANO IMPERATORI

In plērīsque cīvitātibus, domine, maximē Nīcomēdīae et Nīcaeae, quīdam vel in opus damnātī vel in lūdum similiaque hīs genera poenārum pūblicōrum servōrum officiō ministeriōque funguntur atque etiam ut pūblicī servī annua accipiunt. Quod ego cum audīssem, diū multumque haesitāvī, 20 quid facere dēbērem. Nam et reddere poenae post longum tempus plērōsque iam senēs, et, quantum adfirmātur, frūgāliter modestēque vīventēs nimis sevērum arbitrābar, et in pūblicīs officiīs retinēre damnātōs nōn satis honestum putābam; eōsdem rursus ā rē pūblicā pascī ōtiōsōs inūtile, nōn pascī etiam perīculōsum exīstimābam. Necessāriō ergō rem tōtam, dum tē cōnsulerem in suspēnsō relīquī. 25

—Pliny, *Letters*, X.31

20 **audīssem:** = **audīvissem.**

21 Note the parallel indirect statements: **reddere . . . sevērum arbitrābar** and **retinēre . . . honestum putābam** and **pascī . . . inūtile . . . perīculōsum exīstimābam.** The infinitives each act as the subject of an understood verb, **esse,** which completes its clause. The first clause means, then, "I decided that restoring . . . was heartless."

23 **nōn satis honestum:** "not appropriate to public service (**honōs**)." The use of convicts might compromise the confidential nature of some duties performed by public slaves, such as record-keeping or guarding prisoners.

25 **perīculōsum:** some of these prisoners could be trained gladiators who might cause serious trouble.

dum tē cōnsulerem: "until I could consult you. . . ."; **dum** is found with the present or imperfect subjunctive when denoting expectancy.

Bīthȳnī et Ponticī, the people of Bithynia and Pontus

būlē, būlēs (*f*) (Greek word, usually spelled *boulê*), senate or town council in a Greek city

cēnsor, cēnsōris (*m*), censor, one who enrolls senators

dumtaxat, at most, not more than

būleuta, -ae (*m*) (Greek word, usually spelled **bouleutês**), senator or councilman in a Greek city

introitus, -ūs (*m*), entrance, admission

honōrārium decuriōnātūs, admission fee for the senate

in ūniversum, in general

maximē, especially, notably

damnō (1), to condemn, sentence

ministerium, -ī (*n*), service, employment

annuum, -ī (*n*), yearly salary

quantum adfirmātur, by all accounts

frūgāliter, with thrift, restraint

sevērus, -a, -um, heartless

ōtiōsus, -a, -um, free from public duty, not working

necessāriō (*adverb*), necessarily, unavoidably

legō, legere (3), **lēgī, lēctum,** to choose, select

īnferō, īnferre (*irreg.*), **intulī, illātum,** to pay

supersum, superesse (*irreg.*), **superfuī,** to remain, be left

dispiciō, dispicere (3), **dispexī, dispectum,** to consider, reflect on

statuō, statuere (3), **statuī, statūtum,** to lay down a rule, establish

Exercise 64a

Answer the following questions in English with reference to the specified lines of the reading passage.

1. Does provincial law provide for payment of a fee by newly-enrolled town councilmen? (A.2–3)
2. What particular new councilmen have paid a fee? (A.3–5)
3. What decision did Anicius make that has caused confusion? (A.5–7)
4. What does Pliny want Trajan to decide? (A.7–9)
5. What is the emperor's response to Pliny? (B.14–15)
6. What different problem does Pliny explain in the third passage? (C.16–20)
7. What extenuating circumstances cause Pliny's hesitation? (C.21–23)
8. What dilemma does he face regarding the criminals? (C.24–25)

Exercise 64b

1. To what extent have the cities of Bithynia-Pontus, an area of Greek culture, adopted institutions of Roman government? How did Rome insure its political control over the government of provincial communities?
2. Did communities of Bithynia-Pontus have any local autonomy? What is the evidence for this?
3. In passage C, what do we learn about Pliny as a person? As an administrator?

Exercise 64c

After reading passage C above, imagine that you are the Emperor Trajan. Write in English a letter of reply to Pliny, outlining your proposed solution to the problem and the reasons behind your decision.

A Town Councilman from Pompeii

The following inscription commemorates the civic generosity of Numerius Popidius Celsinus, who rebuilt the Temple of Isis, which had been totally destroyed by earthquake. Celsinus was elected to the city council of Pompeii at the age of six out of gratitude to the real donor, Numerius Popidius Ampliatus, his father, who was ineligible for election to the council of decurions because he had been born a slave.

N(umerius) Popidius N(umeriī) f(īlius) Celsinus
aedem Īsidis terrae mōtū conlāpsam
ā fundāmentō p(ecūniā) s(uā) restituit. Hunc decuriōnēs ob līberālitātem
cum esset annōrum sex ōrdinī suō grātīs adlēgērunt.

Corpus Inscriptionum Latinarum, X.846

VERBS: Relative Clause of Characteristic

For some time now, you have seen examples of the following type of subjunctive clause:

Et sunt **quī** dē viā Appiā **querantur, taceant** dē Cūriā! (59:9)
And there are those **who complain** *about the Appian Way (affair), (yet)* **keep silent** *about the Curia!* (Speaking of unnamed persons)

Neque erat quisquam omnium **quīn** (=**quī nē**) in eius diēī cāsū suārum omnium fortūnārum ēventum cōnsistere **exīstimāret**. (61:11–12)
Nor was there anyone **who did not think** *that the outcome of all his fortunes rested on the events of that day.*

Each of these sentences has a dependent clause introduced by a relative pronoun and containing a verb or verbs in the subjunctive. This type of clause is called a *relative clause of characteristic*, because it characterizes or describes an antecedent as a general or indefinite type, rather than as a specific and definite person or thing. Observe the following examples:

Iste est vir **quem** omnēs **timent**.	*He is (in fact) the man* **whom** *everyone* **fears**.
Iste est vir **quem** omnēs **timeant**.	*He is the (type of) man* **whom** *everyone* **fears (would fear)**.

The relative clause of characteristic is especially common after such expressions as **est quī, sunt quī, nēmō est quī**, and **quis est quī**, and it is usually translated with phrases such as "of the sort that . . . ," "the kind of . . . ," or "of such a kind. . . ." Here are some examples:

Quis est **quī** hoc **faciat**?	*Who is there* **of the sort who would do** *this?*
Sunt **quī dīcant. . . .**	*There are those* **who say**. . . .
Is nōn est **quī** hoc **dīcat**.	*He is not* **the kind of person who says (would say)** *this.*
Nēmō est **quīn sciat. . . .**	*There is no one* **who does not know. . . .** *(=Everyone knows. . . .)*

Exercise 64d

Read aloud and translate the following sentences.

1. Quae cīvitās est quae nōn dēlērī possit?
2. Is erat Augustus quī iniūriae ignōsceret.
3. Nēmō fuit omnium pūblicōrum servōrum quīn damnātus esset.
4. Quid est quod in hāc prōvinciā Plīnium nōn vexet?
5. Nōn is sum quī scelestōs laudem.
6. Nūllus imperātor tam sapiēns est quīn aliquandō erret.

7. Plērīque decuriōnēs fuērunt quī honōrārium nōn intulerant.
8. Plīnius multa scrībit quae sentiat.
9. Quis est cui possessiō lībertātis nōn sit cāra?
10. Numquam cognōvī imperātōrem quī sibi nōn optimus vidērētur.
11. Plīnius multa scrīpsit quae Trāiānus vix intellēxit.
12. Sunt quī putent Bīthȳniam molestissimam omnium prōvinciārum esse.

Difficilius est prōvinciās obtinēre quam facere; vīribus parantur, iūre retinentur. *It is harder to hold onto provinces than to acquire them; they are obtained by might but retained by justice.* (Florus, *Epitome,* II.II.30)

Trajan's Reply

Translate Trajan's reply to Pliny about the convicts who were serving as public slaves. Can you locate the relative clause of characteristic? Compare Trajan's reply with your own.

Meminerimus idcircō tē in istam prōvinciam missum, quoniam multa in eā ēmendanda appāruerint. Erit autem hoc maximē corrigendum. Quī igitur intrā hōs proximōs decem annōs damnātī nec ūllō idōneō auctōre līberātī sunt, hōs oportēbit poenae suae reddī; sī quī vetustiōrēs invenientur et senēs ante annōs decem damnātī, distribuāmus illōs in ea ministeria, quae nōn longē ā poenā sint. Solent enim 5 eiusmodī hominēs ad balineum, ad purgātiōnēs cloācārum, item mūnītiōnēs viārum et vīcōrum darī.

—Pliny, *Letters,* X.32

meminerimus, let us remember
idcircō, for that reason
ēmendanda, to be in need of reform
erit . . . corrigendum, will have to be corrected
hoc = the use of prisoners as public slaves
ūllus, -a, -um, any
auctor, auctōris (*m*), authority
vetustus, -a, -um, of long standing
eiusmodī, of this kind
balineum, -ī (*n*), public bath
purgātiō, purgātiōnis (*f*), a cleaning
cloāca, -ae (*f*), sewer, drain
mūnītiō, mūnītiōnis (*f*), construction, repair
vīcus, -ī (*m*), side street

Building Up the Meaning XVI

Clauses of Doubt, Causal Clauses, and Relative Clauses of Purpose

Here is a summary of several new types of subjunctive clauses which you have seen in recent readings:

1. Clause of Doubt

Nōn dubitāvī **quīn** et **scrīberem** ad tē et grātiās tibi **agerem**. (60:32)

I did not doubt **that I would write** *to you and* **thank** *you.*

Sentences showing doubt or hesitation consist of the following pattern:

Dubitō. . . . *I doubt.* . . .
Nōn dubitō. . . . *I have no doubt.* . . .
Quis dubitat . . . ? *Who would doubt* . . . ?
Nōn dubium est. . . . *There is no doubt.* . . .
] + **quīn** + subjunctive

Thus,

Quis dubitat **quīn** Trāiānus optimus imperātor **fuerit**?

Who doubts **that** *Trajan* **was** *the best of emperors?*

2. Causal Clauses

Quoniam multa in eā ēmendanda **appāruerint**. . . . ("Trajan's Reply," p. 97, lines 1–2)

Since *many things* **seemed** *in need of reform there.* . . .

Quoniam cōnfīdō mē celeriter ad urbem ventūrum esse. . . . (60:34)

Since I am confident *that I will return quickly to Rome.* . . .

A clause introduced by **quod, quoniam**, or **quia**, meaning "since" or "because," is found with the subjunctive when *it gives a reason as viewed by someone other than the writer*, as in the first sentence below. When the reason given *is that of the writer*, the indicative is used, as in the second sentence below.

Meus pater mē pūnīvit **quod** domum sērius **redierim**.

My father punished me **because I came** *home too late.* (his alleged reason, which may or may not be the true reason)

Meus pater mē pūnīvit **quod** domum sērius **rediī**.

My father punished me **because I came** *home too late.* (a fact, as I maintain)

3. Relative Clause of Purpose

Scīpiō et Plancus . . . referrī ad senātum dē patriciīs convocandīs, **quī** interrēgem **prōderent**, nōn sunt passī. (57:11–13)

Scipio and Plancus did not allow the Senate to be consulted concerning assembling the patricians **to elect** *an interrex.*

The relative pronoun **quī, quae, quod** is often used as the equivalent of **ut** in introducing a purpose clause. The relative ties the purpose clause more directly to a specific person or thing: in the sentence above, the antecedent of **quī** is **patriciīs**. Any case may be used, e.g.:

Plīnius epistulās scrīpsit **quibus** nōtissimus **fieret**.

Pliny wrote letters **in order to become** *famous.*

Exercise 64e

In each sentence below, identify the type of indicative or subjunctive clause as causal, doubt, characteristic, purpose, or regular relative, and then read the sentence aloud and translate it.

1. Fīēbant tandem aliī ex aliīs interrēgēs quia comitia cōnsulāria habērī nōn poterant.
2. In castrīs Pompeī vidēre licuit multa quae victōriae fidūciam dēsignārent.
3. Cicerō, quod ēloquentissimus ōrātor esset, lēctus est quī ad plēbem ōrātiōnem habēret.
4. Plīnius damnātōs pūnīvit quod sine auctōre līberātī essent.
5. Caesar equitēs praemittit quī cornū sinistrum hostis circumveniant.
6. Quod ubi Caesar animadvertit, quartae aciēī, quam īnstituerat ex cohortium numerō, dedit signum.
7. Pūblicī servī annuum accipiunt quō cibum sibi emant.
8. Nōn dubium erat quīn aliquī būleutārum honōrārium decuriōnātūs īnferrent.
9. Duae trirēmēs in nāvem D. Brūtī, quae ex īnsignī facile agnōscī poterat, sē incitāvērunt.
10. Neque erat quisquam omnium quīn in eius diēī cāsū suārum omnium fortūnārum ēventum cōnsistere exīstimāret.
11. Bīthȳnī lēgātōs Rōmam mīsērunt quī auxilium ab imperātōre peterent.
12. Plīnius nōn dubitāvit quīn Trāiānus senibus lībertātem datūrus esset.

Word Study XVII

Here are some **sententiae** written in French, Italian, and Spanish, together with their English translations. Using the related Romance words, write the same **sententiae** in Latin, using a separate sheet of paper.

1. O Liberté, O Liberté, que de crimes on commet on ton nom! (French)
   O Liberty, O Liberty, how many crimes are committed in your name!

   crīmen, crīminis (*n*)　　　　**lībertās, libertātis** (*f*)

2. Non ogni fiore fa buon odore. (Italian)
   Not every flower makes a sweet smell.

   odor, odōris (*m*)

3. Rey nuevo, ley nueva. (Spanish)
   New king, new law.

2 **dēferēbantur:** Christians were identified by informers, presumably fellow provincials. **Dēlātōrēs** (the term is derived from the 4th principal part of **dēferō**), "informers," were common and notorious during the Empire.

3 **an essent:** "whether or not they were. . . ."; understand **utrum** in a double indirect question.

4 **dūcī:** "led to execution." Organized persecution of Christians did not begin until the 3rd century A.D., but provincial governors, under imperial mandate to keep the peace, often used summary police powers to suppress Christians charged with disobedience, immorality, or treason.

Neque . . . dubitābam . . . dēbēre: "I had no doubt that. . . ."; **dubitō** is found with an infinitive in writers of the Empire.

6 **inflexibilem obstinātiōnem:** there had been no formal edict of Trajan to suppress Christians; Pliny was acting on his own authority in punishing them for their obstinate rejection of his authority. During the Republic and Empire, certain cults were banned owing to criminal or scandalous behavior of their members, rather than because of religious prejudice. The Romans were generally tolerant of religious diversity and allowed the survival of various gods alongside those of the state religion but were annoyed at Christians who refused to recognize the validity of other gods and forms of worship and who actively solicited converts.

7 **adnotāvī in urbem remittendōs:** "I ruled that they should be sent back to Rome"; **quōs** is the subject of **remittendōs (esse)**. Roman citizens could appeal to Caesar for trial in Rome, as did St. Paul to Nero.

8 **diffundente sē crīmine plūrēs speciēs incidērunt:** "as the accusations spread, more cases came to light."

10 **cum:** introducing **appellārent** (10), **supplicārent** (12), and **maledīcerent** (12).

praeeunte mē: Pliny dictated the formula of the oath or prayer.

11 **imāginī tuae:** dative with **supplicārent** and antecedent of **quam**. Emperor worship was not compulsory, but there was a cult of the emperor established in each province as a focus of political loyalty to Rome. Adoration of the emperor's statue, as a pledge of allegiance, was rejected by Christians as a form of idolatry. Later in the 2nd century, this rejection became the basis for a charge of **maiestās**, or treason.

12 **maledīcerent Chrīstō: maledīcere** means "to curse," with the curse itself serving as the direct object and the recipient the indirect object.

18 **Adfirmābant:** the subject is those Christians who had been accused but were no longer participating and were being held for Trajan's judgment. Pliny here begins a description of the main elements in Christian liturgy.

19 **quod essent solitī:** "because they had been accustomed. . . ."; why is the verb subjunctive here? What preceding word reveals that this is not Pliny's opinion?

20 **statō diē:** Sunday, the day after the Jewish Sabbath.

sēcum invicem: chanting back and forth, in alternate verses.

21 **nē fūrta . . . abnegārent:** indirect commands after **sacrāmentō . . . obstringere** (parallel to **nōn in scelus aliquod**). Some scholars think that this list is a reference to the Ten Commandments.

65
Religion and the State during the Empire

This letter of Pliny contains the earliest and most complete pagan account of the official Roman attitude toward Christians. Pliny asks Trajan for guidance in dealing with the Christians in his province and relates what initiative he has taken thus far.

At the beginning of his letter Pliny confesses, "I am not at all sure whether a pardon ought to be granted to anyone retracting his beliefs, or if he has once professed Christianity he shall gain nothing by renouncing it; and whether it is the mere name of Christian which is punishable, even if innocent of the crime, or rather the crimes associated with the name." He continues:

C. PLINIUS TRAIANO IMPERATORI

Interim, in eīs quī ad mē tamquam Chrīstiānī dēferēbantur, hunc sum secūtus modum. Interrogāvī ipsōs an essent Chrīstiānī. Cōnfitentēs iterum ac tertiō interrogāvī supplicium minātus: persevērantēs dūcī iussī. Neque enim dubitābam quālecumque esset quod fatērentur, pertināciam certē et 5
inflexibilem obstinātiōnem dēbēre pūnīrī. Fuērunt aliī similis āmentiae, quōs, quia cīvēs Rōmānī erant, adnotāvī in urbem remittendōs.

Mox ipsō tractātū, ut fierī solet, diffundente sē crīmine plūrēs speciēs incidērunt. Prōpositus est libellus sine auctōre multōrum nōmina continēns. Quī negābant esse sē Chrīstiānōs aut fuisse, cum praeeunte mē deōs ap- 10
pellārent et imāginī tuae, quam propter hoc iusseram cum simulācrīs nūminum adferrī, tūre ac vīnō supplicārent, praetereā maledīcerent Chrīstō, quōrum nihil cōgī posse dicuntur quī sunt rē vērā Chrīstiānī, dīmittendōs putāvī.

Aliī ab indice nōminātī esse sē Chrīstiānōs dīxērunt et mox negāvērunt; 15
fuisse quidem sed dēsiisse, quīdam ante triennium, quīdam ante plūrēs annōs, nōn nēmō etiam ante vīgintī. Hī quoque omnēs et imāginem tuam deōrumque simulācra venerātī sunt et Chrīstō maledīxērunt. Adfirmābant autem hanc fuisse summam vel culpae suae vel errōris, quod essent solitī statō diē ante lūcem convenīre, carmenque Chrīstō quasi deō dīcere sēcum 20
invicem sēque sacrāmentō nōn in scelus aliquod obstringere, sed nē fūrta,

nē latrōcinia, nē adulteria committerent, nē fidem fallerent, nē dēpositum appellātī abnegārent. Quibus perāctīs mōrem sibi discēdendī fuisse rūrsusque coeundī ad capiendum cibum, prōmiscuum tamen et innoxium; quod ipsum facere dēsiisse post ēdictum meum, quō secundum mandāta tua hetaeriās esse vetueram. Quō magis necessārium crēdidī ex duābus ancillīs, quae ministrae dicēbantur, quid esset vērī, et per tormenta quaerere. Nihil aliud invēnī quam superstitiōnem prāvam et immodicam. 25

—Pliny, *Letters*, X.96 (excerpts)

(Trajan's reply appears on p. 106)

22 **nē dēpositum appellātī abnegārent:** a **dēpositum** is something entrusted. In the absence of banks, property could be left with friends for safekeeping to be returned on demand, a trust apparently commonly abused.

23 **mōrem . . . fuisse** and **quod . . . dēsiisse** (24–25): continuation of the indirect statement after **adfirmābant** (18).

discēdendī . . . coeundī ad capiendum cibum: note the use of gerunds and gerundives here.

24 **cibum, prōmiscuum tamen et innoxium:** Christians were suspected of ritual murder, cannibalism, and the drinking of blood, all associated with the Eucharist.

25 **secundum mandāta tua hetaeriās esse vetueram:** these **hetaeriae** (Greek) or **collēgia** (Latin) were political and social clubs with a long history of political disruption dating back to the Republic. Members of **hetaeriae** enjoyed meals in common, thus the Christian *agapê* or fellowship meal.

26 **quae ministrae dīcēbantur: ministra** is the Latin translation of the feminine form of *diakonos*, the Greek word for servant (cf. **ancilla**), which gives the English word *deacon(ess)*. Slaves could be tortured to give evidence.

supplicium, -ī (*n*), punishment
quāliscumque, quāliscumque, quālecumque, of whatever kind
pertinācia, -ae (*f*), stubbornness
obstinātiō, obstinātiōnis (*f*), determination
āmentia, -ae (*f*), madness
adnotō (1), to make a ruling
trāctātus, -ūs (*m*), investigation
speciēs, speciēī (*f*), example, case
libellus, -ī (*m*), notice, poster
nūmen, nūminis (*n*), divine power, god
tūs, tūris (*n*), incense
supplicō (1) (+ *dat.*), to offer worship to
index, indicis (*m*), spy, informer
triennium, -ī (*n*), three-year period
carmen, carminis (*n*), song, hymn
invicem, back and forth
sacrāmentum, -ī (*n*), oath
fūrtum, -ī (*n*), theft, fraud
latrōcinium, -ī (*n*), robbery
adulterium, -ī (*n*), adultery
appellō (1), to call by name
abnegō (1), to refuse, deny
prōmiscuus, -a, -um, common, ordinary
innoxius, -a, -um, harmless
secundum (+ *acc.*), according to
hetaeria, -ae (*f*), political club or association
ministra, -ae (*f*), attendant
prāvus, -a, -um, depraved, perverse
immodicus, -a, -um, excessive

dēferrō, dēferre (*irreg.*), **dētulī, dēlātum,** to inform against, accuse
cōnfiteor, cōnfitērī (2), **cōnfessus sum,** to confess
minor, minārī (1), **minātus sum,** to threaten
fateor, fatērī (2), **fassus sum,** to admit, confess
prōpōnō, prōpōnere (3), **prōposuī, prōpositum,** to put forth
dēsinō, dēsinere (3), **dēsiī,** to stop, cease
veneror, venerārī (1), **venerātus sum,** to worship
sistō, sistere (3), **stitī, statum,** to establish
obstringō, obstringere (3), **obstrinxī, obstrictum,** to bind up, tie to
fallō, fallere (3), **fefellī, falsum,** to betray, falsify
peragō, peragere (3), **perēgī, perāctum,** to carry through, complete

Exercise 65a

Answer the following questions in English with reference to the specified lines of the reading passage.

1. How were Christians identified in Bithynia? (2)
2. What were Pliny's investigative procedures? (3–4)
3. Why did Pliny think that Christians were deserving of punishment? What Latin words did he use to characterize their attitude? (5–6)
4. What was the penalty for refusal to deny being a Christian? What happened to Christians who were Roman citizens? (4 and 6–7)
5. What was the reason for the sharp increase in accusations? (8–9)
6. What tests were suspects required to pass in order to prove their "innocence"? (10–14)
7. From where did Pliny get his information? What were the **summae culpae** of the Christians? (15–17 and 18–23)
8. What Roman misconception about Christian beliefs do the words **prōmiscuus** and **innoxius** reveal? (24)
9. What concession did the Christians make to Roman law? (25–26)
10. How did Pliny attempt to confirm what he had heard about Christians? (26–27)

Exercise 65b

1. What seems to have been Pliny's attitude toward Christians? Apathy? Fear? Hatred? Amazement? Do you think his treatment of them was just?
2. What were the dangers inherent in the Roman method of identifying Christians? Can you think of similar circumstances in modern history?
3. For what political reasons might the emperor have been suspicious of Christians?
4. Did Roman citizens and provincial subjects receive equal treatment under the law?
5. How did the average imperial Roman view the gods? Recall what Petronius wrote on the subject (54:24–30).

Religion in the Provinces

Roman gods were sometimes adopted wholesale in the provinces and fused with local deities. This can be seen clearly in Britain, where the Roman army was the main vehicle of Romanization. Here is an inscription from a small altar dedicated by a soldier in payment of a vow to **Mars Brāciāca**, "Mars in Pants." The word **brācae** refers to the trousers or breeches worn by Gallic barbarians, but never by Greeks or Romans. Although this altar was found in Britain, the soldier was serving in a unit of provincial auxiliaries from Aquitania, in southwestern Gaul (see the map on p. 90).

Deō Martī Brāciācae
Q. Sittius Caeciliān(us) Praef(ectus) Coh(ortī) I. Aquītānō
V(ōtum) S(olvit)

VERBS: Gerundive of Obligation

Scelestī **pūniendī sunt.**	*Criminals* **must be punished.**
Epistula **erat scrībenda.**	A *letter* **had to be written.**
Sacrāmentum **dīcendum erit.**	*The oath* **will have to be sworn.**

You will recognize the forms **pūniendī, scrībenda,** and **dīcendum** as gerundives, verbal adjectives characterized by **-nd-** and translated in the passive. When used with a form of **esse,** provided or understood, the gerundive is known as a *gerundive of obligation* and is translated "must be . . . ," "should be . . . ," "has to be. . . ." This use of the gerundive is commonly called the *passive periphrastic,* the term *periphrastic* meaning "roundabout" and referring to the use of a helping or auxiliary verb, such as **sunt, erat,** or **erit,** as above.

Compare the following two sentences:

Crūdēlitās vītanda est.	*Cruelty must be avoided.*
Crūdēlitās **tibi** vītanda est.	*Cruelty must be avoided* **by you.**

In English, the second sentence may also be translated

You must avoid cruelty.

The dative has become the subject in English and the verb is now translated as active. Consider the following sentences:

Nōbīs eundum est Rōmam.	*We must go to Rome.* (literally, *It must be gone by us to Rome.*)
Fūrī fugiendum erat.	*The thief had to run away.*
Mihi statim ēgrediendum erit.	*I will have to leave at once.*

Unlike the previous examples, in these sentences the gerundive is used *impersonally*, that is, with the neuter singular ending **-um** together with a 3rd person singular form of the verb **esse** and is translated literally by the word "it." These sentences must be transformed into the active in English translation with the dative supplying the subject. With the impersonal use of the gerundive of obligation, the dative expresses the agent by whom the action is to be carried out rather than a prepositional phrase with **ā** or **ab**, as is usual with passive verbs. This use of the dative is commonly called the *dative of agent*. Observe the following examples:

Omnibus Chrīstiānīs ē Bīthȳniā discēdendum erat. (dative of agent)
All Christians had to leave Bithynia.
Bīthȳnia **ab omnibus Chrīstiānīs** relinquēbātur. (**ā/ab** + abl.)
Bithynia was being abandoned by all Christians.

Carthāgō dēlenda est! *Carthage must be destroyed!* Exclaimed by Cato the Elder at Senate meetings during the Punic Wars.

Exercise 65c

Read aloud and translate each of the following sentences.

1. Lēgēs omnibus cīvibus observandae sunt.
2. Plīnius ā Trāiānō quaerēbat quae cōnsilia capienda essent dē Chrīstiānīs.
3. Quī negābant sē Chrīstiānōs esse dīmittendī erant.
4. Dī immortālēs cīvibus Rōmānīs semper venerandī sunt.
5. Plīnius putāvit eōs quī cīvēs Rōmānī erant Rōmam remittendōs esse.
6. Ā Plīniō Chrīstiānīs persuādendum erat ut simulācrum Trāiānī venerārentur.
7. Ūniversus hic mundus ūna cīvitās commūnis deōrum atque hominum exīstimanda sit.
8. Vigilandum erit semper; multae īnsidiae sunt bonīs.
9. Fallendī cupiditās nōbīs vītanda erit.
10. Plīnius adnotāvit Chrīstiānōs propter pertināciam pūniendōs esse.

Exercise 65d

Complete the following sentences by supplying the appropriate form from the pool on page 106, and then translate the completed sentences.

1. Sī nōbīscum venīre nōn vīs, ________ domī manendum est.
2. Cum Plīnius revocātus esset, ________ Rōmam erat regrediendum.
3. Hic puer ________ est laudandus quod mē maximē adiūvit.

4. Fātum est suum ________ ferendum.
5. Ubi Rōmam perveniētis, ad Circum Maximum ________ eundum erit.

nōbīs	vōs	mihi	ego	tibi	cuique	nōs	tū	vōbīs	eī	quisque

Trajan on the Christians

Read Trajan's reply to Pliny's letter concerning the Christians, and then answer in English the following questions. Note the use of gerunds and gerundives.

Āctum quem dēbuistī, mī Secunde, in excutiendīs causīs eōrum, quī Chrīstiānī ad tē dēlātī fuerant, secūtus es. Neque enim in ūniversum aliquid, quod quasi certam fōrmam habeat, cōnstituī potest. Conquīrendī nōn sunt; sī dēferantur et arguantur, pūniendī sunt, ita tamen ut, quī negāverit sē Chrīstiānum esse idque rē ipsā manifestum fēcerit, id est supplicandō dīs nostrīs, quamvīs suspectus in praeteritum, 5 veniam ex paenitentiā impetret. Sine auctōre vērō prōpositī libellī in nūllō crīmine locum habēre dēbent. Nam et pessimī exemplī nec nostrī saeculī est.

—Pliny, *Letters*, X.97

āctum, -ī (*n*), procedure
causa, -ae (*f*), case
certam fōrmam, a fixed rule
manifestus, -a, -um, clear, evident
quamvīs, although
in praeteritum, formerly
venia, -ae (*f*), pardon
paenitentia, -ae (*f*), repentance
impetrō (1), to obtain, secure
pessimī exemplī, the worst sort of precedent (genitive of description)

excutiō, excutere (3), **excussī, excussum,** to examine, inspect
conquīrō, conquīrere (3), **conquīsīvī, conquīsītum,** to hunt down, seek out
arguō, arguere (3), **arguī, argūtum,** to accuse, denounce

Exercise 65e

1. How does Trajan feel about the way in which Pliny has been handling the situation thus far?
2. Is Pliny to seek out Christians? How does the construction **conquīrendī nōn sunt** (3) reinforce Trajan's wishes?
3. What is to happen to the Christians who are accused? Is there any contradiction between the fact that Christians are not to be hunted down but are to be punished, if found?
4. How does Trajan address Pliny's uncertainty about Christians who deny their beliefs?
5. What previous practice described by Pliny will Trajan not tolerate?

The abbreviation **Q.E.D.**, for **quod erat dēmōnstrandum**, *which was to be shown*, is often found following mathematical proofs and solutions to problems.

PART V
Daily Life in the Early Empire

The last three chapters of this book deal with aspects of Roman private life: the settings in which Romans lived in city and country, the everyday activities of rich and poor, and their relationships with members of their **familia**, which included slaves and freedmen as well as blood relatives.

Most of the texts you are about to read were written by Pliny the Younger, whom you have already met in some of his more public roles, and his older contemporary, the poet Martial (A.D. c. 40–104). Martial was a native of the village of Bilbilis in northeastern Spain but came to Rome as a young man and lived there for thirty-five years; he achieved considerable fame (though not much fortune) as a writer of epigrams, short poems that made witty comments on the passing scene. When he finally retired to Bilbilis shortly before A.D. 100, a generous and cultured woman named Marcella seems to have acted as his patron, providing him with a small estate and also with the stimulating conversation he sorely missed after he left Rome. The exact date of his death is unknown, but he seems to have lived only a few years after returning to Spain.

In addition to these literary texts you will also read some documents written by or for ordinary Romans without much pretension to advanced education or culture: epitaphs expressing the grief and affection family members felt for one another, inscriptions on the iron collars of runaway slaves (which incidentally show us what Romans used for "street addresses"), and some of the signs and notices that met their eyes as they walked down the street.

SOME ROMAN STREET SIGNS

NO LOITERING: **Ōtiōsīs locus hīc nōn est. Discēde, morātor.** *This is no place for idlers. Go away, loiterer.*

POST NO BILLS: **Quis hīc ūlla scrīpserit, tābēscat neque nōminētur.** *Whoever writes anything here, may he waste away and never be spoken of.*

LOST PROPERTY: **Urna aēnea periit dē tabernā. Sīquis rettulerit, dabuntur H-S LXV. Sī fūrem dabit unde rem servāre possīmus, H-S XX.** *A copper pot has disappeared from this shop. If someone returns it, 65 sesterces will be paid him. If he hands over the thief, from whom we can recover the article, 20 sesterces.*

2 **inque . . . erat:** i.e., the shopkeepers' activities, the effective **līmen** of their establishments, extended beyond the architectural **līmen** and into the streets. This encroachment was halted by the emperor Domitian in an edict of A.D. 92; in this sense he "ordered the streets to grow wider" (3).

5 **catēnātīs . . . lagōnīs:** a form of advertising for a wineshop.

6 **mediō . . . lutō:** ablative of place where without a preposition (common in poetry).

7 **caeca novācula:** the street-corner barber's razor (or the cutpurse's knife?) is "unseen" because of the milling crowd, and hence more dangerous.

8 **nigra:** from the smoke of the cooking-fire.

9 **servant:** "are keeping to," "are staying inside."

10 **magna:** "just one big."

> **Quid Rōmae faciam? Mentīrī nesciō.** *What am I to do in Rome? I don't know how to lie.* (Juvenal III.41)

1 **cōgitandī . . . quiēscendī:** genitives dependent on **locus** in the next line.
Sparse: a friend of Martial, protected by his wealth from urban discomfort.

2 **Negant vītam:** i.e., they make city life unbearable; the rest of the poem illustrates what Martial means by this.

3 **pistōrēs:** with the noise of their heavy millstones, grinding the flour for the next morning's baking.

5 **ōtiōsus:** while waiting for customers.
quatit mēnsam: to attract the attention of potential customers by rattling the heap of coins on it.

6 **Nerōniānā . . . massā:** "with his heap (of coins minted in the reign) of Nero" (A.D. 54–68), who debased the currency.

7 **palūcis malleātor Hispānae:** "the hammerer of Spanish gold dust," perhaps a maker of gold leaf for gilding.

8 **nitentī:** with specks of gold embedded in it after long use.

9 **turba . . . entheāta Bellōnae:** "Bellona's raving mob," a reference to the Eastern cult of Ma-Bellona, introduced to Rome in the early first century B.C. and characterized by frenzied dancing and loud music.

10 **fasciātō . . . truncō:** "his body swathed (in bandages)," descriptive ablative. A beggar, mutilated in a shipwreck, has worked up a convincing line of patter (**loquāx**) describing the catastrophe and his desperate need of alms.

11 **sulpurātae . . . mercis:** "of sulfured merchandise," either sulfur-tipped sticks used as matches or glassware repaired with sulfur, used like glue. Perhaps the peddler's eye condition was caused by his contact with the chemical.

14 **ad cubīle est Rōma:** to the tired poet who can't get to sleep, it is as if the city's entire population were standing beside his bed, making a racket and keeping him awake.
Taediō fessīs: taediō is ablative of cause with **fessīs; fessīs** is dative with **libuit** (15); with **fessīs** supply **nōbīs** (= **mihi**).

66
Environments

A. Martial rejoices at the solving of an urban traffic problem.

The Streets of Rome

Abstulerat tōtam temerārius īnstitor urbem
  inque suō nūllum līmine līmen erat.
Iussistī tenuīs, Germānice, crēscere vīcōs,
  et modo quae fuerat sēmita, facta via est.
Nūlla catēnātīs pīla est praecincta lagōnīs 5
  nec praetor mediō cōgitur īre lutō,
stringitur in dēnsā nec caeca novācula turbā,
  occupat aut tōtās nigra popīna viās.
Tōnsor, caupo, coquus, lanius sua līmina servant.
  Nunc Rōma est, nūper magna taberna fuit. 10

—Martial, *Epigrams* VII.61

īnstitor, īnstitōris (*m*), shopkeeper
tenuis, -is, -e, slender, narrow
modo (*adverb*), recently
sēmita, -ae (*f*), path
catēnō (1), to chain
pīla, -ae (*f*), pillar
lagōna, -ae (*f*), bottle
caecus, -a, -um, blind, unseen
tōnsor, tōnsōris (*m*), barber

praecingō, praecingere (3), **praecinxī, praecinctum**, to gird, wrap around

B. Amidst the noises of a great city, Martial "can't hear himself think."

The Sounds of Rome

Nec cōgitandī, Sparse, nec quiēscendī
in urbe locus est pauperī. Negant vītam
lūdī magistrī māne, nocte pistōrēs,
aerāriōrum marculī diē tōtō;
hinc ōtiōsus sordidam quatit mēnsam 5
Nerōniānā nummulārius massā,
illinc palūcis malleātor Hispānae
trītum nitentī fūste verberat saxum;
nec turba cessat entheāta Bellōnae,
nec fasciātō naufragus loquāx truncō, 10
nec sulpurātae lippus īnstitor mercis.
Tū, Sparse, nescīs ista nec potēs scīre.
Nōs trānseuntis rīsus excitat turbae,
et ad cubīle est Rōma. Taediō fessīs
dormīre quotiēns libuit, īmus ad vīllam. 15

—Martial, *Epigrams* XII.57 (abridged)

aerārius, -ī (*m*), coppersmith
marculus, -ī (*m*), hammer
hinc, from this place, here
nummulārius, -ī (*m*), moneychanger
massa, -ae (*f*), mass, heap
illinc, from that place, there
nitēns, -ntis, shining, glittering
naufragus, -ī (*m*), shipwrecked man
loquāx, loquācis, talkative
truncus, -ī (*m*), trunk, body
lippus, -a, -um, bleary-eyed
cubīle, cubīlis (*n*), bed
taedium, -ī (*n*), annoyance
fessus, -a, -um, weary
quotiēns, as often as, whenever

quatiō, quatere (3), ——, **quassum,** to shake
terō, terere (3), **trīvī, trītum,** to rub, wear away

SOME ROMAN "STREET ADDRESSES"
(inscribed on runaway slaves' collars)

Tenē mē quia fūgī. Redūc mē ad Flōram ad tōnsōrēs. *Detain me, because I have run away. Return me to Barbers' Street near (the temple of) Flora.*

Tenē mē, nē fugiam, et revocā mē in Forō Trāiānī in purpurēticā ad Pacasium dominum meum. *Detain me so that I do not escape, and return me to my master Pacasius in Dyers' Street in the Forum of Trajan.*

1 **nemus:** the first of a long series of subjects of the verb **sunt** (7).
textilis: "woven"; because the shoots of the grapevine that casts the shade are intertwined.
supīnī: "low-lying," probably because these vines are supported by poles or low arbors and hence are closer to the ground than those trained on trees, as the Romans sometimes did.
2 **ductile:** "channeled"; Martial's vineyard is artificially irrigated.
3 **biferō . . . Paestō:** "rose gardens not about to yield (i.e., not inferior) to twice-bearing Paestum." This town on the coast south of Naples was famous for its commercial rose plantations, which produced two crops a year.
4 **quod . . . holus:** having lived thirty-five years (7) in the mild Italian climate, Martial regards as a special blessing a kitchen-garden that produces winter vegetables even in northeastern Spain; **holus** is the antecedent of **quod**, as **turris** of **quae** (6).
5 **anguilla:** "eel(s)," singular used collectively; they were kept live in a tank or fish-pond, for food.
6 **similēs . . . avēs:** i.e., doves white like the dovecote they inhabit.
7 **dominae:** this word is the ancestor of It. *donna*, Sp. *doña*, and Fr. *dame*, and has much the same meaning here, "(my) lady."
reversō: supply **mihi**.
8 **Marcella:** though she is otherwise unknown, Martial refers to this woman in several poems with gratitude and admiration; she was evidently a native of Bilbilis and a generous benefactor to the poet.
rēgna: poetic plural for singular.
9 **Nausicaā** (*nom.*): a princess, daughter of King Alcinoös, encountered by Odysseus as he was returning home from the Trojan War (*Odyssey*, Books VI–VIII).

Exercise 66a

Using reading passages A–C *as guides, give the Latin for:*

1. It pleased the emperor to order all shopkeepers to remain in their shops. (A.1–4)
2. Consuls were forced to walk in the middle of the street. (A.6)
3. Barbers, cooks, (and) butchers had to stay inside their own thresholds. (A.9; use gerundive of obligation.)
4. What had recently been (one) big shop was becoming a city again. (A.10)
5. There was opportunity at Rome for neither writing nor sleeping. (B.1–2)
6. Rome was full of noise which (was such that it) woke the poet up. (B.13) (Use a relative clause of characteristic.)
7. Whenever it pleases him to go to Rome, the passing crowds deny (him) sleep. (B.15)
8. A villa was given to the poet (after he) returned home. (C.7–8)
9. If a king had granted him his kingdom, the poet would have refused. (C.9–10)
10. He preferred his own wooded pastures, fountains, (and) meadows to ("than") the most magnificent gardens. (C.10)

C. Martial describes the Spanish farm where he spent his last years.

A Poet's Country "Estate"

Hoc nemus, hī fontēs, haec textilis umbra supīnī
 palmitis, hoc riguae ductile flūmen aquae,
prātaque, nec biferō cessūra rosāria Paestō,
 quodque viret Iānī mēnse nec alget holus,
quaeque natat clausīs anguilla domestica lymphīs, 5
 quaeque gerit similēs candida turris avēs,
mūnera sunt dominae: post septima lūstra reversō
 hās Marcella domōs parvaque rēgna dedit.
Sī mihi Nausicaā patriōs concēderet hortōs,
 Alcinoō possem dīcere, "Mālō meōs." 10

—Martial, *Epigrams* XII.31

nemus, nemoris (*n*), wooded pasture
fōns, fontis (*m*), fountain, spring
palmes, palmitis (*m*), vine-branch
riguus, -a, -um, watering, irrigating
flūmen, flūminis (*n*), river, stream
prātum, -ī (*n*), meadow, grass
vireō (2), to be green, flourish
domesticus, -a, -um, tame
lympha, -ae (*f*), water
candidus, -a, -um, white
turris, turris (*f*), tower, dovecote
lūstrum, -ī (*n*), five-year period
patrius, -a, -um, of a father, ancestral

1 **Lāriī lacūs**: now Lake Como, in the far north of Italy above Milan.
plūrēs vīllae: supply **sunt**.
ut . . . ita: "as they . . . so (also) they . . . ," or "they both . . . and. . . ."

2 **exercent**: "keep (me) busy."
saxīs: dative with a compound verb (**impōnō**), "set on the rocks," i.e., on cliffs along the lakeshore.
mōre Bāiānō: "in the style of Baiae."

3 **illam . . . hanc**: "the former . . . the latter"; the two pronouns (and their derivatives **illīc** and **hīc**, 7–8) are used in this sense throughout this letter.

4 **cothurnīs . . . socculīs**: the **cothurnus** was a high-heeled, thick-soled boot worn by tragic actors to give extra height and dignity; the **socculus** was a low shoe worn by comic actors; Pliny whimsically compares them to the elevated and water-level situations of his two villas.

5 **utrīque**: dative of possession; supply **est**.
dīversitāte: ablative of cause (not comparison) with **iūcundior**; translate with "by" or "because of."

6 **lacū**: ablative with **ūtitur**, which here means "commands a view of."

7 **duōs**: supply **sinūs** from the preceding line.
illīc: i.e., at "Tragedy"; **hīc** in the next line refers to "Comedy."
gestātiō: "promenade," for riding (in a litter or on horseback).

8 **longō līmite**: "in a long line."
xystō . . . īnflectitur: "it (the **gestātiō** at "Comedy") curves gently in a walkway." The **xystus** was lined with shade trees and was intended for recreational walking, as the **gestātiō** for riding.

9 **haec frangit**: supply **fluctūs** from the preceding clause. At "Comedy" the waves of the lake break against the foundations of the villa.
possīs: potential subjunctive, "you would be able to," "you could."

10 **piscārī**: with this infinitive, and **iacere** in the next line, supply **possīs** from the preceding line.

Two villas with colonnades and gardens (from a Pompeian mural).

D. Pliny describes the attractions of two of his many villas.

A Rich Man's Country Estates

Lāriī lacūs in lītore plūrēs vīllae meae, sed duae ut maximē dēlectant ita exercent. Altera imposita saxīs mōre Bāiānō lacum prōspicit, altera aequē mōre Bāiānō lacum tangit. Itaque illam "Tragoediam," hanc appellāre "Cōmoediam" soleō; illam, quod quasi cothurnīs, hanc quod quasi socculīs, sustinētur. Sua utrīque amoenitās, et utraque possidentī ipsā dīversitāte iūcundior. Haec lacū propius, illa lātius ūtitur; haec ūnum sinum mollī curvāmine amplectitur, illa ēditissimō dorsō duōs dirimit; illīc rēcta gestātiō longō līmite super lītus extenditur, hīc spatiōsissimō xystō leviter īnflectitur; illa fluctūs nōn sentit, haec frangit; ex illā possīs dēspicere piscantēs, ex hāc ipse piscārī hāmumque dē cubiculō ac paene etiam dē lectulō ut ē nāviculā iacere.

—Pliny, *Letters* IX.7 (abridged)

lacus, -ūs (*m*), lake
amoenitās, amoenitātis (*f*), charm, pleasantness
sinus, -ūs (*m*), curve, bay
mollis, -is, -e, soft, gentle
ēditus, -a, -um, raised, high
dorsum, -ī (*n*), back, ridge
illīc, in that place, there
rēctus, -a, -um, straight
līmes, līmitis (*m*), path, line
spatiōsus, -a, -um, spacious
leviter, lightly, slightly
fluctus, -ūs (*m*), wave
hāmus, -ī (*m*), hook
lectulus, -ī (*m*), bed

prōspiciō, prōspicere (3), **prōspēxī, prōspectum**, to look out (over)
sustineō, sustinēre (2), **sustinuī, sustentum**, to hold up, support
possideō, possidēre (2), **possēdī, possessum**, to possess, own
dirimō, dirimere (3), **dirēmī, dirēmptum**, to separate, divide
īnflectō, īnflectere (3), **īnflēxī, īnflexum**, to bend, curve
dēspiciō, dēspicere (3), **dēspēxī, dēspectum**, to look down on
piscor, piscārī (1), **piscātus sum**, to fish

Summary of Case Usages

Genitive

1. Possessive: **Servī baculum vīlicī timent.** (11:10)
2. Objective: **Augēbat factī invidiam uxor Clōdiī.** (58:23)
3. Subjective: **Mūnera sunt dominae.** (66C:7)
4. Partitive: **Quid ille nōbīs bonī fēcit?** (55:21)
5. With **causā/grātiā**: **Ardeat amōris et dēsīderī meī causā.** (56c:5)
6. Descriptive: **Ūnus (gladiātor) alicuius flātūrae fuit.** (55:25)
7. With impersonal verbs: **Mē taedet sōlitūdinis.** (49:3)
8. With special verbs: **Diī eius colōniae miserentur.** (54:23–24)
9. With special adjectives: **Immemor terrōris nocturnī, fābulam nārrābat.** (21:4)

Dative

1. Indirect object: **Eucleidēs mandāta servīs dabat.** (21:4–5)
2. Possessive: **Sua utrīque amoenitās (est).** (66D:5)
3. Of agent: **Crūdēlitās tibi vītanda est.** (Chapter 65, page 104)
4. Of reference: **Spectātōribus admīrātiōnī fuērunt leōnēs.** (47:1–2)
5. Of purpose: **Spectātōribus admīrātiōnī fuērunt leōnēs.** (When these two usages occur together, they are called the double dative.)
6. Of separation: **Arma nōbīs adēmērunt.** (40:20)
7. With compound verbs: **Sī pīrātīs resistēmus, necābimur.** (40:19)
8. With special verbs: **Servō illī parvō numquam parcet.** (48:11)
9. With special adjectives: **puer . . . parentibus cārissimus.** (Chapter 52, page 101)

Ablative (a conflation of three separate cases in primitive Latin)

I. Separative Uses (the true ablative)
   1. Place from which (with **ab, dē, ex**): **(Possīs) hāmum dē lectulō ut ē nāviculā iacere.** (66D:10–11)
      Without preposition (names of towns, small islands): **Brundisiō profectus est.**
   2. Of separation: **Fīet vir vīnō abstinentissimus.** (32e:28)
   3. Of respect: **Erant uterque audāciā pārēs.** (57:8)
   4. Of comparison: **Quis est mē miserior?** (35:3)

II. Local Uses (of a "place," **locus**, in space or time)
   1. Place where (with **in, sub**): **Lacūs in lītore plūrēs vīllae (sunt).** (66D:1)
      Without preposition: **Sōl caelō serēnō lūcēbat.** (49:1)
   2. Time when: **Illō tempore annōna prō lutō erat.** (54:15)

III. Instrumental Uses
   1. Means: **Thisbē amōre capta est.** (43:3–4)
   2. Agent: **Rīma ab amantibus inventa est.** (43:7–8)
   3. Accompaniment: **Cum patre fīliōque suō nāvigāvit.** (36:6)
   4. Manner: **Līberōs maximō cum gaudiō salūtāvit.** (22:9)
   5. Description: **Puer eximiā pulchritūdine (fuit).** (Chapter 52, page 101)
   6. With certain deponents: **In spēluncā habitābāmus, eōdem cibō vescentēs.** (47:20–21)
   7. Degree of difference: **Multō libentius tē vidēbō.** (34:10)
   8. Ablative absolute: **Pӯramō vīsō, amōre capta est.** (43:3–4)

PLINY ON THE DEATH OF MARTIAL: **Audiō Valerium Martiālem dēcessisse et molestē ferō. Erat homō ingeniōsus, acūtus, ācer, et quī plūrimum in scrībendō et salis habēret et fellis nec candōris minus.** *I hear that Valerius Martial has died and I am grieved by the news. He was a man of great talent, clever and lively, one who had in his writing both wit and venom, and frankness as well.* (Pliny, *Letters* III.21)

Exercise 66b

Complete the Latin sentences, identify the usage of each word that you supply, and translate the sentences.

1. Uxōrī __________ (Clodius') nūllus __________ (of death) metus erat.
2. Illum paenitet __________ __________ (his crimes).
3. Oblīvīscēbātur __________ __________ (her friends).
4. Ars __________ __________ (for art's sake). (Motto of MGM Films)
5. Hic liber nōn est __________ (for students) idōneus.
6. Milō bonōrum __________ (in the support) cōnfīdēbat.
7. Rēs pūblica __________ (to Cicero) __________ __________ (a cause of the greatest concern) fuit.
8. Aurum __________ (by you) tangendum nōn est.
9. Clōdius et Milō __________ (in crime) pārēs erant.
10. Poēta dōnum __________ __________ (his lady's) __________ __________ (with great joy) accēpit.
11. Mārtiālis poēta __________ (much) melior __________ (than Cicero) fuit.
12. Cicerō __________ __________ (Greek literature) ūtēbātur.

Exercise 66c

1. Roman poets liked to "bracket" a line with two closely related words such as verb and object or noun and modifier, set at beginning and end. Find four examples in passages A and B.
2. What is the effect of repeating the demonstrative **hic** four times at the beginning of passage C? (Hint: "demonstrative" is a derivative of **dēmōnstrāre**, "to show," "to point out.") Why would **ille** have been less effective here? How does Pliny's repetition of **hic** in passage D differ from Martial's?
3. Judging from passages A, B, and C, did Martial prefer city life or country life? Where did he actually live for most of his life? Do you find his attitude inconsistent or insincere? Does anyone in our own society have a similar ambivalence about urban living?
4. Pliny's description of "Tragedy" and "Comedy" (passage D) is a kind of stylistic balancing act, each feature of one villa carefully contrasted with a corresponding feature of the other, expressed in syntactically parallel clauses. Identify eight examples of such parallels. How does Pliny introduce variety into these parallels? Does the artificiality of Pliny's style make you doubt the sincerity of his affection for the villas, or does the care he takes with his writing express his sincere affection?

67
The Daily Round

1 **Erret:** jussive, here and throughout. The object of Martial's curse is a rival poet who writes libelous verse against respectable people.
pontis . . . et clīvī: translate with *from* rather than *of*; these were favorite haunts of beggars, probably because they slowed down traffic.
2 **ultimus:** i.e., the most wretched of all.
3 **canīnās:** i.e., fit only for dogs.
4 **Illī:** dative of reference.
5 **fornix:** often the only shelter the urban poor could find; they could not be "closed." Martial in his anger is wishing for the impossible.
7 **Orcīniānā . . . spondā:** "the couch of Orcus" (the underworld), i.e., a bier.
8 **fīla:** of the man's life, spun and eventually cut by the three Fates.
9 **sentiat . . . lītem:** i.e., remain conscious to the very end, so that as he dies he will see dogs already beginning to squabble over his body.
10 **mōtō . . . pannō:** "by shaking his ragged garment."

2 **ille . . . ille . . . ille:** "one man . . . another . . . another."
3 **diē:** antecedent of the relative pronoun **quō.**
4 **necessāria:** supply **videntur** from the following clause.
5 **sēcesseris:** i.e., from the city to the country.
6 **in Laurentīnō meō:** for Pliny's Laurentine villa, see Chapter 7, pp. 37–38.
7 **corporī:** i.e., for physical exercise, meals, baths, etc.
8 **audīsse:** supply **paeniteat** from the following phrase, "it is a matter of regret (to me) to. . . ."
9 **strepitum . . . discursum . . . labōrēs:** i.e., of the city (Rome); objects of **relinque** (10); **multum** is adverbial with **ineptōs.**
ut prīmum: "as soon as."

Exercise 67a

Using readings A and B as guides, give the Latin for:

1. The beggar has become hoarse from ("by") begging for bread. (A.1–3)
2. If his final hour comes soon, he will be very fortunate. (A.6–8)
3. Dogs and rapacious birds will feed on his body. (A.9–10)
4. Pliny had to attend a wedding. (Use gerundive of obligation.) (B.2)
5. He said he had used up so many days in trivial matters. (B.5–6)
6. Pliny is urging his friend to abandon city life. (B.8–10)

A. **A Beggar's Life in the City**

Erret per urbem pontis exul et clīvī,
interque raucōs ultimus rogātōrēs
ōret canīnās pānis improbī buccās.
Illī December longus et madēns brūma
claususque fornix trīste frīgus extendat: 5
vocet beātōs clāmitetque fēlīcēs
Orcīniānā quī feruntur in spondā.
At cum suprēmae fīla vēnerint hōrae
diēsque tardus, sentiat canum lītem
abigatque mōtō noxiās avēs pannō. 10

—Martial, *Epigrams* X.5 (abridged)

exul, exulis (*m*), exile, outcast
raucus, -a, -um, hoarse
rogātor, rogātōris (*m*), beggar
improbus, -a, -um, bad, vile
madēns, madentis, wet, moist
brūma, -ae (*f*), winter
fornix, fornicis (*m*), arch
frīgus, frīgoris (*n*), cold
suprēmus, -a, -um, last, final
fīlum, -ī (*n*), thread
līs, lītis (*f*), quarrel, dispute
noxius, -a, -um, harmful, rapacious

abigō, abigere (3), **abēgī, abāctum,** to drive away

B. **A Gentleman's Life in the City**

Sī quem interrogēs, "Hodiē quid ēgistī?" respondeat: "Officiō togae virīlis interfuī; spōnsālia aut nūptiās frequentāvī; ille mē ad signandum testāmentum, ille in advocātiōnem, ille in cōnsilium rogāvit." Haec quō diē fēceris, necessāria; eadem, si cotīdiē fēcisse tē reputēs, inānia videntur, multō magis, cum sēcesseris. Tunc enim subit recordātiō: "Quot diēs quam frīgidīs rēbus 5
absūmpsī!" Quod ēvenit mihi, postquam in Laurentīnō meō aut legō aliquid aut scrībō aut etiam corporī vacō, cuius fultūrīs animus sustinētur. Nihil audiō quod audīsse, nihil dīcō, quod dīxisse paeniteat. Proinde tū quoque strepitum istum inānemque discursum et multum ineptōs labōrēs, ut prīmum fuerit occāsiō, relinque tēque studiīs vel ōtiō trāde. Valē. 10

—Pliny, *Letters* I.9 (abridged)

nūptiae, -ārum (*f pl*), wedding
advocātiō, advocātiōnis (*f*), (legal) counsel
inānis, -is, -e, empty, pointless
recordātiō, recordātiōnis (*f*), recollection
frīgidus, -a, -um, cold, trivial
fultūra, -ae (*f*), support
proinde, therefore
discursus, -ūs (*m*), a running back and forth or around
ineptus, -a, -um, silly, foolish
ōtium, -ī (*n*), leisure

intersum, interesse (*irreg.*), **interfuī** (+ *dat.*), to be present, attend
sēcēdō, sēcēdere (3), **sēcessī, sēcessum,** to withdraw, retire
subeō, subīre (*irreg.*), **subiī, subitum,** to come up, occur
absūmō, absūmere (3), **absūmpsī, absūmptum,** to consume, use up

1 **Mē**: in the opening lines, here omitted, Martial describes the hectic life being led in Rome by his friend Juvenal, the satirist; the rest of the poem contrasts Martial's simple existence in rural Spain, hence the emphatic position of the pronoun at the beginning of this line.
repetīta: this word and **mea** (2) modify **Bilbilis** (3).
2 **rūsticum:** supply **mē** from line 1.
3 **aurō . . . et superba ferrō:** there were gold and iron mines nearby.
5 **Boterdum Plateamque:** nearby villages whose names sounded "rather uncouth" (**crassiōra**, 6) to the ears of citified Romans.
Celtibērīs . . . terrīs: i.e., in that part of Spain where the native (Iberian) population had received an admixture of Celtic blood from the north.
7 **improbōque somnō:** ironic; "sleeping in," as Martial does now, is "shameless" from the point of view of a hard-driving city dweller like Juvenal.
9 **tōtum . . . quidquid . . . vigilāveram:** "all the staying-up I did."
10 **ter dēnōs:** "thrice ten."
11 **petentī:** supply **mihi**.
12 **proxima:** i.e., the first that comes to hand.
13 **Surgentem:** supply **mē**.
superbā . . . strue cultus: "graced with a magnificent pile."
15 **quem:** the antecedent is **focus** (13).

Roman Timekeeping

The Roman **hōra** was not a fixed period of time like the modern hour, but a fraction (one twelfth) of the daylight of a given day. Since days and nights are not of equal length throughout the year, the length of a **hōra** varied: on the longest day (June 21), when there are about fifteen hours of daylight, the **hōra** was about 1¼ hours long; on the shortest day (December 21), only about 45 minutes. After-dark hours (**hōrae noctis**) were reckoned in the same way but were less important due to the expense and inefficiency of artificial lighting. The fixed points in this system were noon and midnight, which in all seasons occurred at the end of the sixth **hōra**.

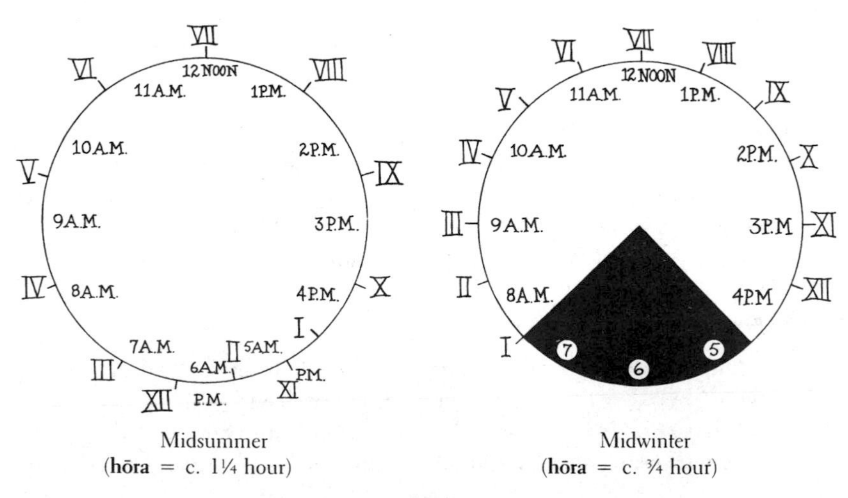

Midsummer
(**hōra** = c. 1¼ hour)

Midwinter
(**hōra** = c. ¾ hour)

C. **A Poet's Life in the Country**

Mē multōs repetīta post Decembrēs
accēpit mea rūsticumque fēcit
aurō Bilbilis et superba ferrō.
Hīc pigrī colimus labōre dulcī
Boterdum Plateamque (Celtibērīs 5
haec sunt nōmina crassiōra terrīs):
ingentī fruor improbōque somnō
quem nec tertia saepe rumpit hōra,
et tōtum mihi nunc repōnō quidquid
ter dēnōs vigilāveram per annōs. 10
Ignōta est toga, sed datur petentī
ruptā proxima vestis ā cathēdrā.
Surgentem focus excipit superbā
vīcīnī strue cultus īlicētī,
multā vīlica quem corōnat ōllā. 15
Sīc mē vīvere, sīc iuvat perīre.
—Martial, *Epigrams* XII.18 (abridged)

piger, -gra, -grum, lazy, indolent
dulcis, -is, -e, sweet, pleasant
ignōtus, -a, -um, unknown
cathēdra, -ae (*f*), chair
focus, -ī (*m*), fireplace
struēs, struis (*f*), heap, pile
īlicētum, -ī (*n*), oak-grove
ōlla, -ae (*f*), pot

repetō, repetere (3), **repetīvī, repetītum,** to seek again, return to
repōnō, repōnere (3), **reposuī, repositum,** to put back, repay

Pars magna Ītaliae est, sī vērum admittimus, in quā nēmō togam sūmit nisi mortuus. *There's a large part of Italy (if we admit the truth) in which no one wears a toga unless he's dead.* (Juvenal III.171–172)

Martial's retirement from the stress of urban living was permanent and occurred near the end of his life. Pliny, like other wealthy Romans, could "retire" whenever he wished to one of his seven villas (cf. Chapter 7, pages 37–38, and reading passage 66D). His favorite of them all was in the foothills of the Apennines, north of Rome in Tuscany. In a letter he describes his daily routine when he was in residence there during the summer.

You ask how I organize my day in summertime at my Tuscan villa. I wake up when I please, usually about the first hour, often earlier, rarely later. The window-shutters remain closed, for in silence and darkness I am wonderfully free and removed from all distractions, and left to myself; I do not follow my eyes with my mind, but rather my mind with my eyes, which see only what the mind sees so long as they see nothing else. If I have work in progress, I think; I think like one actually writing and revising, sometimes only short passages, sometimes longer ones, so that they can be composed and remembered whether the subject is difficult or easy. I call in my stenographer and, letting in the daylight, I dictate what I have composed. He goes away, is called back again, and again dismissed.

At the fourth or fifth hour (for I have no fixed and precise schedule), as the weather suggests, I go to the terrace or the covered portico, work out the rest, and dictate it. I get into my carriage, and there I do the same thing I did while lying in bed or walking; my concentration lasts longer when refreshed by this change of scene. I take another short nap, then go for a walk; after that I read, aloud and with concentration, a Greek or Latin speech, not so much for the sake of my voice as for my digestion; though the voice too is strengthened. I take another walk, oil myself and take some exercise, and bathe. While I dine a book is read to me if I am with my wife or only a few friends; after dinner we have a comic actor or a lyre-player. Then I take a walk with members of my household, some of whom are quite well educated. Thus the evening is passed in various kinds of conversation, and even the longest day is quickly laid to rest.

Sometimes certain details of this routine are modified. For instance, if I have stayed in bed or walked longer than usual, after the nap and the reading I go for a ride, not in my carriage but on horseback, which is briefer because faster. Friends from nearby towns sometimes interrupt me and appropriate part of my day; sometimes, too, by this timely interruption they come to my rescue when I am tired. Occasionally I go hunting, but never without my notebooks, so that even if I catch nothing I don't come back empty-handed. Some time is also devoted to my tenants—not enough, as it seems to them; their farmers' complaints enhance my literary studies and citified pursuits. Farewell.

—Pliny, *Letters* IX.36

1 **litterās meās**: the letter you have just read in translation.
2 **exigerem . . . permūtem**: what tenses of the subjunctive, and why?
hōc: Pliny's daily schedule in summertime.
3 **Nihil**: supply **permūtō** from the preceding sentence.
multumque . . . sūmitur: i.e., he either goes to bed later or gets up earlier.
4 **agendī**: "of pleading (a case in court)."
5 **frequēns**: supply **est.**
cōmoedō vel lyristae: "for a comic actor (to give readings) or a lyre-player."
locus: supply **est.**
6 **memoriae . . . prōficitur**: "(my) memory benefits" (literally, "benefit is done to my memory").
7 **addās . . . licet**: = **licet (tibi) addere,** "you may add to this."
8 **media**: supply **sunt.**
ut . . . acquīrunt: i.e., his working-days are no shorter, and a little of the night is put to use as well. Supply **sīc** before **dē,** to balance **ut**: "as (on the one hand), so (on the other). . . ."

Exercise 67b

Using the "clocks" on *page 118**, answer the following questions with full Latin sentences:*

1. Quotā hōrā surgere solēs aestāte? Hieme?
2. Quotā hōrā cubitum īvistī proximā nocte?
3. Quota hōra nunc est?
4. Quotā hōrā cēnāre solet familia tua?
5. Quotā hōrā ad lūdum hodiē vēnistī?
6. Quotā hōrā surgis Sāturnī diē? Sōlis diē?

Exercise 67c

Answer in English the following questions:

1. How late does Martial sleep in the country? Why? (C.8–10)
2. What is the implication of **Ignōta est toga**? (C.11)
3. What details suggest that Bilbilis is an unsophisticated, backwoods kind of place? (C.2, 6, 12, 15)
4. How does Pliny's routine change in winter? (D.3–4, 5–6)
5. Why do you think Pliny makes these adjustments? (D.4)

D. A Gentleman's Life in the Country

Scrībis pergrātās tibi fuisse litterās meās, quibus cognōvistī quemadmodum in Tuscīs ōtium aestātis exigerem; requīris quid ex hōc in Laurentīnō hieme permūtem. Nihil, nisi quod merīdiānus somnus eximitur, multumque dē nocte vel ante vel post diem sūmitur, et sī agendī necessitās īnstat, quae frequēns hieme, nōn iam cōmoedō vel lyristae post cēnam locus, sed 5
illa quae dictāvī identidem retractantur, ac simul memoriae frequentī ēmendātiōne prōficitur. Habēs aestāte hieme cōnsuētūdinem; addās hūc licet vēr et autumnum, quae inter hiemem aestātemque media, ut nihil dē diē perdunt, dē nocte parvulum acquīrunt. Valē.

—Pliny, *Letters* IX.40

pergrātus, -a, -um, very welcome
permūtō (1), to change, modify
merīdiānus, -a, -um, of noon, midday
retractō (1), to rework, revise
ēmendātiō, ēmendātiōnis (*f*), emendation, correction
cōnsuētūdō, cōnsuētūdinis (*f*), custom, habit
vēr, vēris (*n*), spring

exigō, exigere (3), **exēgī, exāctum,** to spend (time)
requīrō, requīrere (3), **requīsīvī, requīsītum,** to ask, inquire

Word Study XVIII

Latin Suffixes in the Romance Languages

You have learned some of the ways in which words are formed from other words in Latin by the addition of prefixes and suffixes. Knowing the principles of word-formation, as you have discovered, makes it possible to increase your Latin vocabulary with a minimum of memorizing. These same principles will also enable you to recognize hundreds of words in the Romance languages. Some of the Latin suffixes you have already learned, and their Romance equivalents, are shown below.

LATIN	ITALIAN	SPANISH	FRENCH
-tās, -tātis (*f*)	-tà (*f*)	-dad (*f*)	-té (*f*)
ūnitās	unità	unidad	unité
-tiō, -tiōnis (*f*)	-zione (*f*)	-ción (*f*)	-tion (*f*)
nātiō	nazione	nación	nation
-tor, -tōris (*m*)	-tore (*m*)	-dor (*m*)	-teur (*m*)
ōrātor	oratore	orador	orateur
-entia, -ae (*f*)	-enza (*f*)	-encia (*f*)	-ence (*f*)
scientia	scienza	ciencia	science
-ōsus, -a, -um	-oso, -a	-oso, -a	-eux, euse
verbōsus	verboso	verboso	verbeux

The adverb in the Romance languages is an interesting special case: it derives from Latin phrases of the type _(adjective)_ **mente,** e.g., **firmā mente,** "with a firm mind," "firmly." This type of ablative of manner was used so extensively that **mente** eventually lost most of its original meaning and became a suffix changing the preceding adjective into an adverb.

LATIN	ITALIAN	SPANISH	FRENCH
_______ mente	-mente	-mente	-ment
firmā mente	fermamente	firmemente	fermement

68
Familia

The Romans were a strongly family-oriented people, as is abundantly attested not only in their literature but also in the visual arts and in subliterary texts such as epitaphs and letters. Even so undomestic a soul as the philosopher-poet Lucretius, a contemporary of Cicero, could paint a touching picture of the **praemia vītae,** "life's prizes": a happy home, a good wife, and "sweet children who run to meet you and snatch a kiss, touching your heart with unspoken delight." There is an element of idealization in this, of course, as there is in the conventional phrase often found in the epitaphs of Roman spouses, "they lived together so many years **sine ūllā querēlā,**" "without a single complaint." So conventional was this sentiment, in fact, that it was frequently reduced to the mere abbreviation **s.u.q.** Yet genuine feeling sometimes seems to break through formula and rhetoric, in the epitaphs as in literature, in unpretentious phrases like "I put these words on her tomb so that people reading them would know how much we loved each other." Another Roman husband put it even more simply and briefly: "we worked well together." The small jet engagement medallions illustrated here symbolize the hope for this kind of enduring loyalty and affection in marriage. As the readings in this chapter show, the strong sense of responsibility and affection summed up in the word **pietās** often extended to the family slaves and freedmen as well as spouse and children.

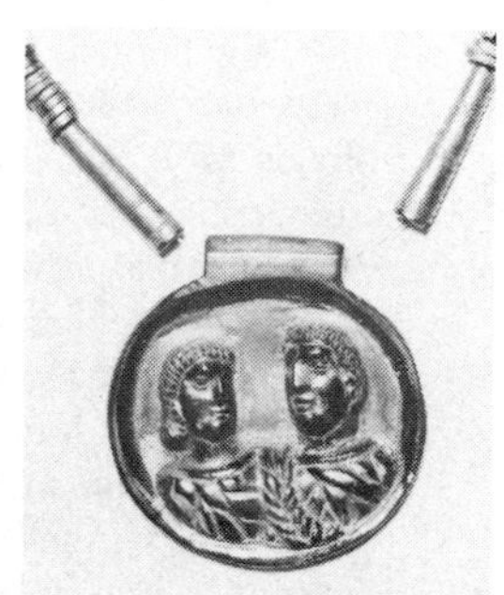

2 **tuī**: genitive of **tū**; objective genitive with **dēsīderiō.**
In causā (est): "is responsible."
3 **quod**: "the fact that . . ." (as also in 3 and 4).
abesse: i.e., from each other.
Inde est: "Hence. . . ." or "This is the reason for. . . ."
4 **in imāgine tuā**: "in imagining you," "dreaming of you."
quibus: the antecedent is **hōrīs**.
5 **diaetam**: a Greek word meaning "apartment" or "living quarters," i.e., a suite of rooms for Calpurnia's personal use.
ipsī: with **pedēs**, "of their own accord."
6 **aeger**: "sick (at heart)," "dejected."
līmine: what kind of ablative?
7 **quō**: the antecedent is **tempus**.
lītibus: "lawsuits"; Pliny was a prominent lawyer.
8 **requiēs**: supply **est.**

Uxor, vīvāmusque ut vīximus et teneāmus
nōmina, quae prīmō sūmpsimus in thalamō,
nec ferat ūlla diēs, ut commūtēmur in aevō,
quīn tibi sim iuvenis tūque puella mihi.

Wife, let us live as we have lived and let us keep the names we gave each other on our wedding night; may the day never come when we change in old age, but let me be forever your young lover and you my girl.

Ausonius, c. A.D. 350

1 **mihi**: dative of separation, with the three verbs compounded with **ex.**
3 **oculīs**: dative with the compound **obversantur.**
labōrēs . . . precēs . . . honor: all in reference to Avitus' abortive political career: "exertions . . . campaigning . . . office."
meruit tantum: "only earned (but never held)"; Avitus was elected to an aedileship (9) but died before taking office.
4 **animō**: supply **meō**; dative with the compound **redit.**
lātus clāvus: the "broad (purple) stripe" of the senatorial tunic. Under the Empire, the privilege of wearing it was granted to senators' sons who, though not yet senators themselves, were about to begin their political careers.
5 **suffrāgia mea**: i.e., occasions on which I "got out the vote" for you.
6 **adulēscentiā**: like us, the Romans were especially grieved at the death of a child or young person with most of his life ahead of him.
grandis nātū: "elderly." The gender of **parēns** is ambiguous, but it is clear from line 10 that Avitus' mother is meant.
7 **ante**: adverbial, "(only) a year ago."
8 **sustulerat**: a Roman husband "picked up" his wife's newborn child from the ground to symbolize his acceptance of it as his own and his willingness to raise it, which he was not otherwise obligated to do.

A. A Husband in Love

C. PLINIUS CALPURNIAE SUAE S.

Incrēdibile est, quantō dēsīderiō tuī tenear. In causā amor prīmum, deinde quod nōn cōnsuēvimus abesse. Inde est, quod magnam partem noctium in imāgine tuā vigil exigō, inde, quod interdiū, quibus hōrīs tē vīsere solēbam, ad diaetam tuam ipsī mē, ut vērissimē dīcitur, pedēs dūcunt; quod dēnique 5 aeger et maestus ac similis exclūsō, vacuō līmine recēdō. Ūnum tempus hīs tormentīs caret, quō in forō et amīcōrum lītibus conteror. Aestimā tū, quae vīta mea sit, cui requiēs in labōre, in miseriā cūrīsque sōlācium. Valē.

—Pliny, *Letters* VII.5

vigil, vigilis, awake, sleepless
maestus, -a, -um, sad
vacuus, -a, -um, empty
aestimō (1), to estimate, judge
requiēs, requiētis (*f*), rest

cōnsuēscō, cōnsuēscere (3), **cōnsuēvī, cōnsuētum,** to be accustomed
vīsō, vīsere (3), **vīsī, vīsum,** to go to see, visit
exclūdō, exclūdere (3), **exclūsī, exclūsum,** to shut out, exclude
recēdō, recēdere (3), **recessī, recessum,** to withdraw, retire
careō, carēre (2), **caruī, caritum** (+ *abl.*), to be without, lack
conterō, conterere (3), **contrīvī, contrītum,** to wear out, exhaust

B. Death of a Young Husband and Father

Omnia mihi studia, omnēs cūrās, omnia āvocāmenta exēmit, excussit, ēripuit dolor, quem ex morte Iūnī Avītī gravissimum cēpī. Obversantur oculīs cassī labōrēs et īnfructuōsae precēs et honor, quem meruit tantum. Redit animō ille lātus clāvus in penātibus meīs sūmptus; redeunt illa prīma, illa postrēma suffrāgia mea, illī sermōnēs, illae cōnsultātiōnēs. Adficior 5 adulēscentiā ipsīus, adficior necessitūdinum cāsū. Erat illī grandis nātū parēns, erat uxor, quam ante annum virginem accēperat; erat fīlia, quam paulō ante sustulerat. Tot spēs, tot gaudia diēs ūnus in adversa convertit. Modo dēsignātus aedīlis, recēns marītus, recēns pater intāctum honōrem, orbam mātrem, viduam uxōrem, fīliam pupillam īgnāramque patris relīquit. 10

—Pliny, *Letters* VIII.23 (abridged)

āvocāmentum, -ī (*n*), diversion, recreation
cassus, -a, -um, empty, useless
īnfructuōsus, -a, -um, fruitless
prex, precis (*f*), prayer, request
penātēs, penātium (*m pl*), household gods, home
suffrāgium, -ī (*n*), vote
necessitūdō, necessitūdinis (*f*), necessity, (personal) connection, relative
adversum, -ī (*n*), calamity
orbus, -a, -um, bereaved
viduus, -a, -um, deprived, widowed
pūpilla, -ae (*f*), orphan
īgnārus, -a, -um, ignorant of, not knowing (+ *gen.*)

excutiō, excutere (3), **excussī, excussum,** to shake out, drive out
obversor, obversārī (1), **obversātus sum** (+ *dat.*), to hover before, appear to
adficiō, adficere (3), **adfēcī, adfectum,** to affect, afflict
sufferō, sufferre (*irreg.*), **sustulī, sublātum,** to take up

Pliny on Disciplining Children

A man was scolding his son because the boy was spending rather lavishly on horses and dogs. I said to him, after the young man had left, "See here, did you never do anything your father could object to? Have you never done—indeed, do you not even now do, things that your son would blame you for just as severely, if suddenly he were the father and you the son? Don't we all make mistakes of one kind or another? One man is self-indulgent in one thing, others in another, isn't that so?"

Because of our affection for each other, I am sending you this example of exaggerated severity by way of a warning not to treat your own son too strictly and harshly. Remember that he is a child and that you used to be one too, and therefore exercise your parental authority in such a way as never to forget that you are a man and the father of a man. Farewell.

—Pliny, *Letters* IX.12

1 **fuerās:** translate as simple past.
Charidēme: vocative of **Charidēmus,** Latinized form of a Greek name; slaves in responsible positions such as that of **paedagōgus,** in which a good education was necessary or desirable, were often of Greek origin.
2 **puerī:** supply **meī** (genitive of **ego**), "of (me as a) boy."
3 **mihi:** dative of reference; may be translated as a possessive with **barbā.**
sūdāria: "towels," placed around Martial's neck when his beard is trimmed.
4 **labrīs:** i.e., with his beard or mustache when he kisses her.
5 **tibi:** dative of reference, here (as often) indicating the person in whose eyes the statement is true.
Tē . . . pavet: Charidemus is a household tyrant!
8 **mihi:** with **licēre,** parallel to **tibi.**
9 **Corripis, observās:** supply **mē** as direct object; **corripis** = "scold."
dūcis: we say "heave" rather than "draw."
10 **ferulīs:** which he no doubt used on Martial as a child.
11 **Tyriōs . . . capillōs:** to wear "Tyrian-purple clothes" and use scented hair oil were marks of the fashionable Roman dandy and regarded as decadent by the conservative older generation.
12 **fēcerat:** here = **fēcisset.**
13 **nostrōs . . . trientēs:** "the cups (of wine) I drink." The **triēns** was equivalent to about five ounces.
15 **lībertum Catōnem:** both Cato the Elder (234–149 B.C.) and his great-grandson Cato the Younger (95–46 B.C.) had long been bywords for uncompromising integrity and puritanical conservatism; Martial may have either or both in mind.

Exercise 68a

Answer in English the following questions on readings A and B.

1. In his wife's absence, how does Pliny spend his nights? His days? (A.2–5)
2. What does the phrase **ut vērissimē dīcitur** imply? (A.4)
3. What gives Pliny some relief from his longing for his wife? (A.6)
4. What was the nature of Pliny's friendship with Avitus? What did Pliny do with and for the young man that he remembers now with sorrow? (B.4–5)
5. What three unusual circumstances make Avitus' death particularly sad? (B.3, 6, 10)
6. Judging from reading B, what were the most important things in life to a young Roman aristocrat? (B.9–10)

C. For this **paedagōgus**, the boy he raised will never grow up.

Martial's Old Tutor

Cūnārum fuerās mōtor, Charidēme, meārum
   et puerī custōs adsiduusque comes.
Iam mihi nigrēscunt tōnsā sūdāria barbā
   et queritur labrīs puncta puella meīs,
sed tibi nōn crēvī. Tē noster vīlicus horret,   5
   tē dispēnsātor, tē domus ipsa pavet:
lūdere nec nōbīs nec tū permittis amāre,
   nīl mihi vīs et vīs cuncta licēre tibi.
Corripis, observās, quereris, suspīria dūcis,
   et vix ā ferulīs temperat īra tua.   10
Sī Tyriōs sūmpsī cultūs unxīve capillōs,
   exclāmās, "Numquam fēcerat ista pater!"
et numerās nostrōs adstrictā fronte trientēs,
   tamquam dē cellā sit cadus ille tuā.
Dēsine: nōn possum lībertum ferre Catōnem.   15
   Esse virum iam mē dīcet amīca tibi.

—Martial, *Epigrams* XI.39

cūnae, -ārum (*f pl*), cradle
adsiduus, -a, -um, constant
barba, -ae (*f*), beard
labrum, -ī (*n*), lip
horreō (2), to tremble at, dread
suspīrium, -ī (*n*), sigh
adstrictus, -a, -um, drawn together
cella, -ae (*f*), storeroom, cellar
cadus, -ī (*m*), (wine-)jar

tondeō, tondēre (2), **totondī, tōnsum,** to shave, trim
pungō, pungere (3), **pupugī, punctum,** to prick
paveō, pavēre (2), **pāvī,** to be terrified of

1 **D.M.S.: Dīs Mānibus Sacrum,** "sacred to the deified spirits," a common formula in Roman epitaphs. Sometimes, as here, it is syntactically independent of the rest of the inscription; sometimes, as in the next epitaph, it is followed by a dependent genitive, "sacred to the . . . spirits *of* so-and-so."
cuius: a Greek genitive of comparison, "than whom"; such Grecisms are common in subliterary texts, which were often written by people from the Greek-speaking East, who had learned Latin rather imperfectly.
2 **certus:** supply **sum,** governing an indirect statement.
ita: the writer apparently anticipates a result clause but never gets around to it; omit in translating.
3 **in diem:** "every day."
4 **quam . . . tam:** "both . . . and."
mōrum: "character," a common meaning of **mōs** in the plural.
ideō: anticipating **ut,** "for this reason, . . . that. . . ."; omit in translating.
5 **b(ene) m(erentī) f(ēcit):** supply **hoc monumentum** as direct object.

7 **iam:** an important adverb here: the parents are proud of her precocity.
8 **f(ēcērunt) d(ē) s(uō):** "made (this monument) at their own expense."

11 **maledīxit:** this verb commonly means "to curse," but here it may have its root sense, "spoke ill of" or "spoke a harsh word to."
12 **multum ponderis aurī:** two partitive genitives strung together rather awkwardly; **magnum pondus** would be better, and you may so translate it.
13 **caelātūrae Clōdiānae:** "of Clodian engraving," a technique for engraving on precious metals; this explains why Zosimus was entrusted with quantities of gold and silver.

Dē mortuīs nīl nisi bonum. *Of the dead, (speak) nothing but good.*

Exercise 68b

Answer in English the following questions on readings C and D:

1. What, specifically, does Charidemus do that proves Martial is still a child to him? (C.7, 11–12, 13–14)
2. In what ways was Zosimus an ideal slave? (D.11–14)
3. Charidemus (C) and Zosimus (D) are examples of skilled slaves (later freed) employed in positions of considerable responsibility. Compare the two men in the following respects: 1) kind of responsibility, 2) personality, 3) relationship to the author, 4) nature of the document, and the effect this has on the portrayal of the man.
4. What were Urbana's virtues as a wife? (D.1, 3, 4)
5. To whom does **legentēs** (D.5) refer?
6. How many months old was Cornelia Anniana when she died? (D.8)

D. Epitaphs for Family Members

A Well-Loved Wife

D.M.S. Urbānae coniugī dulcissimae et castissimae ac rārissimae, cuius praeclārius nihil fuisse certus. Hōc etiam titulō honōrārī meruit, quae ita mēcum cum summā iūcunditāte atque simplicitāte in diem vītae suae ēgit quam affectiōnī coniugālī tam industriā mōrum suōrum. Haec ideō adiēcī, ut legentēs intellegant, quantum nōs dīlēxerimus. Paternus b(ene) m(erentī) f(ēcit). 5

castus, -a, -um, chaste
titulus, -ī (*m*), inscription
iūcunditās, iūcunditātis (*f*), pleasantness
simplicitās, simplicitātis (f), frankness

A Baby Just Learning to Talk

D(īs) m(ānibus) Cornēliae Anniānae fīliae iam garrulae, bīmulae nōndum, quae vīxit annum ūnum m(ēnsēs) III d(iēs) X; dulcissim(ae) parentēs f(ēcērunt) d(ē) s(uō).

garrulus, -a, -um, prattling
bīmulus, -a, -um, two years old

A Trustworthy Freedman

D(īs) m(ānibus) M(arcī) Canuleī Zōsimī, vīx(it) ann(ōs) XXVIII, fēcit patrōnus līb(ertō) bene merentī. Hic in vītā suā nūllī maledīxit, sine voluntāte patrōnī nihil fēcit, multum ponderis aurī arg(entīque) penes eum semper fuit, concupīvit ex eō nihil umquam. Hic arte caelātūrae Clōdiānae ēvīcit omnēs. 10

pondus, ponderis (*n*), weight, quantity
argentum, -ī (*n*), silver
penes (+ *acc.*), in the possession of
ēvincō, ēvincere (3), **ēvīcī, ēvictum,** to conquer, surpass

ON TOMBS

Aedēs aedificat dīves, sapiēns monumentum. Hospitium est illud corporis, hic domus est. *The rich man builds himself a mansion, the wise man a tomb. The former is a mere inn for the body, the latter a true home.*

Homō es: resiste et tumulum contemplā meum. *You are mortal: stop, and consider my tomb.*

Carpis sī quī viās, paulum hīc dēpōne labōrem. Cūr tantum properās? Nōn est mora dum legis, audī. *You who are traveling this road, lay down your burden here for a moment. Why are you hurrying so? It doesn't take long to read (this). Listen!*

FORMS

I. Nouns

Number Case	1st Declension	2nd Declension			3rd Declension			4th Declension		5th Declension
	Fem.	*Masc.*	*Masc.*	*Neut.*	*Masc.*	*Fem.*	*Neut.*	*Fem.*	*Neut.*	*Masc.*
Singular										
Nom.	puélla	sérvus	púer	báculum	páter	vōx	nṓmen	mánus	génū	díēs
Gen.	puéllae	sérvī	púerī	báculī	pátris	vṓcis	nṓminis	mánūs	génūs	diḗī
Dat.	puéllae	sérvō	púerō	báculō	pátrī	vṓcī	nṓminī	mánuī	génū	diḗī
Acc.	puéllam	sérvum	púerum	báculum	pátrem	vṓcem	nṓmen	mánum	génū	díem
Abl.	puéllā	sérvō	púerō	báculō	pátre	vṓce	nṓmine	mánū	génū	díē
Plural										
Nom.	puéllae	sérvī	púerī	bácula	pátrēs	vṓcēs	nṓmina	mánūs	génua	díēs
Gen.	puellā́rum	servṓrum	puerṓrum	baculṓrum	pátrum	vṓcum	nṓminum	mánuum	génuum	diḗrum
Dat.	puéllīs	sérvīs	púerīs	báculīs	pátribus	vṓcibus	nōmínibus	mánibus	génibus	diḗbus
Acc.	puéllās	sérvōs	púerōs	bácula	pátrēs	vṓcēs	nṓmina	mánūs	génua	díēs
Abl.	puéllīs	sérvīs	púerīs	báculīs	pátribus	vṓcibus	nōmínibus	mánibus	génibus	diḗbus

II. Adjectives

Number Case	*1st and 2nd Declension*			*3rd Declension*		
	Masc.	*Fem.*	*Neut.*	*Masc.*	*Fem.*	*Neut.*
Singular						
Nominative	mágnus	mágna	mágnum	ómnis	ómnis	ómne
Genitive	mágnī	mágnae	mágnī	ómnis	ómnis	ómnis
Dative	mágnō	mágnae	mágnō	ómnī	ómnī	ómnī
Accusative	mágnum	mágnam	mágnum	ómnem	ómnem	ómne
Ablative	mágnō	mágnā	mágnō	ómnī	ómnī	ómnī
Plural						
Nominative	mágnī	mágnae	mágna	ómnēs	ómnēs	ómnia
Genitive	magnṓrum	magnā́rum	magnṓrum	ómnium	ómnium	ómnium
Dative	mágnīs	mágnīs	mágnīs	ómnibus	ómnibus	ómnibus
Accusative	mágnōs	mágnās	mágna	ómnēs	ómnēs	ómnia
Ablative	mágnīs	mágnīs	mágnīs	ómnibus	ómnibus	ómnibus

II. Adjectives (continued)

Adjectives have *positive*, *comparative*, and *superlative* forms. You can usually recognize the comparative by the letters **-ior**(-) and the superlative by ***-issimus, -errimus,*** or ***-illimus,*** e.g.:

ignāvus, *lazy*	ignāvior	ignāvissimus, -a, -um
pulcher, *beautiful*	pulchrior	pulcherrimus, -a, -um
facilis, *easy*	facilior	facillimus, -a, -um

The comparative form uses the endings of 3rd declension adjectives, except for the ablative singular, which ends in **-e**, the genitive plural, which ends in **-um**, and the nominative and accusative plural, neuter, which end in **-a**.

Some adjectives are irregular in the comparative and superlative, e.g.:

bonus, *good*	melior, *better*	optimus, *best*
malus, *bad*	peior, *worse*	pessimus, *worst*
magnus, *big*	maior, *bigger*	maximus, *biggest*
parvus, *small*	minor, *smaller*	minimus, *smallest*
multus, *much*	plūs, *more*	plūrimus, *most, very much*
multī, *many*	plūrēs, *more*	plūrimī, *most, very many*

III. Demonstrative Adjectives and Pronouns

Number Case	*Masc.*	*Fem.*	*Neut.*	*Masc.*	*Fem.*	*Neut.*
Singular						
Nom.	hic	haec	hoc	ílle	ílla	íllud
Gen.	húius	húius	húius	illī́us	illī́us	illī́us
Dat.	húic	húic	húic	íllī	íllī	íllī
Acc.	hunc	hanc	hoc	íllum	íllam	íllud
Abl.	hōc	hāc	hōc	íllō	íllā	íllō
Plural						
Nom.	hī	hae	haec	íllī	íllae	ílla
Gen.	hṓrum	hā́rum	hṓrum	illṓrum	illā́rum	illṓrum
Dat.	hīs	hīs	hīs	íllīs	íllīs	íllīs
Acc.	hōs	hās	haec	íllōs	íllās	ílla
Abl.	hīs	hīs	hīs	íllīs	íllīs	íllīs

The intensive adjective **ipse, ipsa, ipsum** has the same endings as **ille, illa, illud** except **ipsum** in neuter nominative and accusative singular. The demonstrative **iste, ista, istud** has the same endings as **ille, illa, illud.**

Number Case	*Masc.*	*Fem.*	*Neut.*	*Masc.*	*Fem.*	*Neut.*
Singular						
Nom.	is	éa	id	ī́dem	éadem	ídem
Gen.	éius	éius	éius	eiúsdem	eiúsdem	eiúsdem
Dat.	éī	éī	éī	eī́dem	eī́dem	eī́dem
Acc.	éum	éam	id	eúndem	eándem	ídem
Abl.	éō	éā	éō	eṓdem	eā́dem	eṓdem
Plural						
Nom.	éī	éae	éa	eī́dem	eaédem	éadem
Gen.	eṓrum	eā́rum	eṓrum	eōrúndem	eārúndem	eōrúndem
Dat.	éīs	éīs	éīs	eī́sdem	eī́sdem	eī́sdem
Acc.	éōs	éās	éa	eṓsdem	eā́sdem	éadem
Abl.	éīs	éīs	éīs	eī́sdem	eī́sdem	eī́sdem

IV. Indefinite Adjectives and Pronouns

Number Case	*Masc.*	*Fem.*	*Neut.*	*Masc.*	*Fem.*	*Neut.*
Singular						
Nom.	quī́dam	quaédam	quóddam	áliquī	áliqua	áliquod
Gen.	cuiúsdam	cuiúsdam	cuiúsdam	álicuius	álicuius	álicuius
Dat.	cuídam	cuídam	cuídam	álicui	álicui	álicui
Acc.	quéndam	quándam	quóddam	áliquem	áliquam	áliquod
Abl.	quṓdam	quā́dam	quṓdam	áliquō	áliquā	áliquō
Plural						
Nom.	quī́dam	quaédam	quaédam	áliquī	áliquae	áliqua
Gen.	quōrúndam	quārúndam	quōrúndam	aliquṓrum	aliquā́rum	aliquṓrum
Dat.	quibúsdam	quibúsdam	quibúsdam	alíquibus	alíquibus	alíquibus
Acc.	quṓsdam	quā́sdam	quaédam	áliquōs	áliquās	áliqua
Abl.	quibúsdam	quibúsdam	quibúsdam	alíquibus	alíquibus	alíquibus

The indefinite pronoun **quīdam, quaedam, quiddam** has the same forms as the indefinite adjective, except for **quiddam** in the neuter nominative and accusative singular. The indefinite pronoun **aliquis, aliquis, aliquid** has the regular forms of the interrogative adjective **quis, quis, quid,** as do the indefinite pronouns **quisque, quisque, quidque** and **quisquam, quisquam, quidquam (quicquam)**. The indefinite adjective **quisque, quaeque, quodque** has the same forms as the relative pronoun **quī, quae, quod** except for **quis-** in the masculine nominative singular.

V. Adverbs

Latin adverbs may be formed from adjectives of the 1st and 2nd declensions by adding ***-ē*** to the base of the adjective, e.g., **strēnuē,** "strenuously," from **strēnuus, -a, -um.** To form an adverb from a 3rd declension adjective, add ***-iter*** to the base of the adjective or ***-ter*** to bases ending in **-nt-**, e.g., **breviter,** "briefly," from **brevis, -is, -e,** and **prūdenter,** "wisely," from **prūdēns, prūdentis.**

The comparative ends in ***-ius.***
The superlative ends in ***-issimē, -errimē,*** or ***-illimē,*** e.g.:

lentē, *slowly*	lentius	lentissimē
fēlīciter, *luckily*	fēlīcius	fēlīcissimē
dīligenter, *carefully*	dīligentius	dīligentissimē
celeriter, *quickly*	celerius	celerrimē
facile, *easily*	facilius	facillimē

Some adverbs are irregular:

bene, *well*	melius, *better*	optimē, *best*
male, *badly*	peius, *worse*	pessimē, *worst*
magnopere, *greatly*	magis, *more*	maximē, *most*
paulum, *little*	minus, *less*	minimē, *least*
multum, *much*	plūs, *more*	plūrimum, *most*

Some adverbs are not formed from adjectives:

diū, *for a long time*	diūtius	diūtissimē
saepe, *often*	saepius	saepissimē
sērō, *late*	sērius	sērissimē

VI. Personal and Demonstrative Pronouns

	Singular					*Plural*				
Case	*1st*	*2nd*	*3rd*			*1st*	*2nd*	*3rd*		
			Masc.	*Fem.*	*Neut.*			*Masc.*	*Fem.*	*Neut.*
Nom.	égo	tū	is	éa	id	nōs	vōs	éī	éae	éa
Gen.	méī	túī	éius	éius	éius	nóstrī	véstrī	eṓrum	eā́rum	eṓrum
Dat.	míhi	tíbi	éī	éī	éī	nṓbīs	vṓbīs	éīs	éīs	éīs
Acc.	mē	tē	éum	éam	id	nōs	vōs	éōs	éās	éa
Abl.	mē	tē	éō	éā	éō	nṓbīs	vṓbīs	éīs	éīs	éīs

VII. Reflexive Pronoun

Case	*Singular*	*Plural*
Nom.	—	—
Gen.	súī	súī
Dat.	síbi	síbi
Acc.	sē	sē
Abl.	sē	sē

VIII. Relative and Interrogative Pronouns and Adjectives

	Singular			*Plural*		
Case	*Masc.*	*Fem.*	*Neut.*	*Masc.*	*Fem.*	*Neut.*
Nom.	quī	quae	quod	quī	quae	quae
Gen.	cúius	cúius	cúius	quṓrum	quā́rum	quṓrum
Dat.	cúi	cúi	cúi	quíbus	quíbus	quíbus
Acc.	quem	quam	quod	quōs	quās	quae
Abl.	quō	quā	quō	quíbus	quíbus	quíbus

The interrogative pronoun **Quis . . . ?** has the same forms as the relative pronoun except for the nominative masculine singular **Quis . . . ?** and the nominative and accusative neuter singular **Quid . . . ?** In the singular, the feminine has the same forms as the masculine. In the plural, all forms are the same as those of the relative pronoun.

IX. Regular Verbs Active: Infinitive, Imperative, Indicative

			1st Conjugation	*2nd Conjugation*	*3rd Conjugation*		*4th Conjugation*
Present Infinitive			parā́re	habḗre	míttere	iácere (-iō)	audī́re
Imperative			párā	hábē	mítte	iáce	aúdī
			parā́te	habḗte	míttite	iácite	audī́te
Present	*Singular*	1	párō	hábeō	míttō	iáciō	aúdiō
		2	párās	hábēs	míttis	iácis	aúdīs
		3	párat	hábet	míttit	iácit	aúdit
	Plural	1	parā́mus	habḗmus	míttimus	iácimus	audī́mus
		2	parā́tis	habḗtis	míttitis	iácitis	audī́tis
		3	párant	hábent	míttunt	iáciunt	aúdiunt
Imperfect	*Singular*	1	parā́bam	habḗbam	mittḗbam	iaciḗbam	audiḗbam
		2	parā́bās	habḗbās	mittḗbās	iaciḗbās	audiḗbās
		3	parā́bat	habḗbat	mittḗbat	iaciḗbat	audiḗbat
	Plural	1	parābā́mus	habēbā́mus	mittēbā́mus	iaciēbā́mus	audiēbā́mus
		2	parābā́tis	habēbā́tis	mittēbā́tis	iaciēbā́tis	audiēbā́tis
		3	parā́bant	habḗbant	mittḗbant	iaciḗbant	audiḗbant

IX. Regular Verbs Active: Indicative, Infinitive (continued)

Future	*Singular*	1	parā́bō	habḗbō	míttam	iáciam	aúdiam
		2	parā́bis	habḗbis	míttēs	iáciēs	aúdiēs
		3	parā́bit	habḗbit	míttet	iáciet	aúdiet
	Plural	1	parā́bimus	habḗbimus	mittḗmus	iaciḗmus	audiḗmus
		2	parā́bitis	habḗbitis	mittḗtis	iaciḗtis	audiḗtis
		3	parā́bunt	habḗbunt	míttent	iácient	aúdient
Perfect Infinitive			parāvísse	habuísse	mīsísse	iēcísse	audīvísse
Perfect	*Singular*	1	parā́vī	hábuī	mī́sī	iḗcī	audī́vī
		2	parāvístī	habuístī	mīsístī	iēcístī	audīvístī
		3	parā́vit	hábuit	mī́sit	iḗcit	audī́vit
	Plural	1	parā́vimus	habúimus	mī́simus	iḗcimus	audī́vimus
		2	parāvístis	habuístis	mīsístis	iēcístis	audīvístis
		3	parāvḗrunt	habuḗrunt	mīsḗrunt	iēcḗrunt	audīvḗrunt

IX. Regular Verbs Active: Indicative (continued)

Tense	Number	Person					
Pluperfect	Singular	1	parā́veram	habúeram	mī́seram	iḗceram	audī́veram
		2	parā́verās	habúerās	mī́serās	iḗcerās	audī́verās
		3	parā́verat	habúerat	mī́serat	iḗcerat	audī́verat
	Plural	1	parāverā́mus	habuerā́mus	mīserā́mus	iēcerā́mus	audīverā́mus
		2	parāverā́tis	habuerā́tis	mīserā́tis	iēcerā́tis	audīverā́tis
		3	parā́verant	habúerant	mī́serant	iḗcerant	audī́verant
Future Perfect	Singular	1	parā́verō	habúerō	mī́serō	iḗcerō	audī́verō
		2	parā́veris	habúeris	mī́seris	iḗceris	audī́veris
		3	parā́verit	habúerit	mī́serit	iḗcerit	audī́verit
	Plural	1	parāvérimus	habuérimus	mīsérimus	iēcérimus	audīvérimus
		2	parāvéritis	habuéritis	mīséritis	iēcéritis	audīvéritis
		3	parā́verint	habúerint	mī́serint	iḗcerint	audī́verint

X. Regular Verbs Passive: Indicative

			1st Conjugation	*2nd Conjugation*	*3rd Conjugation*		*4th Conjugation*
Present	*Singular*	1	pórtor	móveor	míttor	iácior	aúdior
		2	portā́ris	movḗris	mítteris	iáceris	audī́ris
		3	portā́tur	movḗtur	míttitur	iácitur	audī́tur
	Plural	1	portā́mur	movḗmur	míttimur	iácimur	audī́mur
		2	portā́minī	movḗminī	mittíminī	iacíminī	audī́minī
		3	portántur	movéntur	mittúntur	iaciúntur	audiúntur
Imperfect	*Singular*	1	portā́bar	movḗbar	mittḗbar	iaciḗbar	audiḗbar
		2	portābā́ris	movēbā́ris	mittēbā́ris	iaciēbā́ris	audiēbā́ris
		3	portābā́tur	movēbā́tur	mittēbā́tur	iaciēbā́tur	audiēbā́tur
	Plural	1	portābā́mur	movēbā́mur	mittēbā́mur	iaciēbā́mur	audiēbā́mur
		2	portābā́minī	movēbā́minī	mittēbā́minī	iaciēbā́minī	audiēbā́minī
		3	portābántur	movēbántur	mittēbántur	iaciēbántur	audiēbántur

X. Regular Verbs Passive: Indicative (continued)

Future	*Singular*	1	portā́bor	movḗbor	míttar	iáciar	aúdiar
		2	portā́beris	movḗberis	mittḗris	iaciḗris	audiḗris
		3	portā́bitur	movḗbitur	mittḗtur	iaciḗtur	audiḗtur
	Plural	1	portā́bimur	movḗbimur	mittḗmur	iaciḗmur	audiḗmur
		2	portābíminī	movēbíminī	mittḗminī	iaciḗminī	audiḗminī
		3	portābúntur	movēbúntur	mitténtur	iaciéntur	audiéntur

		PERFECT PASSIVE		PLUPERFECT PASSIVE		FUTURE PERFECT PASSIVE	
Singular	1	portā́tus, -a	sum	portā́tus, -a	éram	portā́tus, -a	érō
	2	portā́tus, -a	es	portā́tus, -a	érās	portā́tus, -a	éris
	3	portā́tus, -a, -um	est	portā́tus, -a, -um	érat	portā́tus, -a, -um	érit
Plural	1	portā́tī, -ae	súmus	portā́tī, -ae	erā́mus	portā́tī, -ae	érimus
	2	portā́tī, -ae	éstis	portā́tī, -ae	erā́tis	portā́tī, -ae	éritis
	3	portā́tī, -ae, -a	sunt	portā́tī, -ae, -a	érant	portā́tī, -ae, -a	érunt

XI. Regular Verbs Active: Subjunctive

			1st Conjugation	*2nd Conjugation*	*3rd Conjugation*		*4th Conjugation*
Present	*Singular*	1	párem	hábeam	míttam	iáciam	aúdiam
		2	párēs	hábeās	míttās	iáciās	aúdiās
		3	páret	hábeat	míttat	iáciat	aúdiat
	Plural	1	parḗmus	habeā́mus	mittā́mus	iaciā́mus	audiā́mus
		2	parḗtis	habeā́tis	mittā́tis	iaciā́tis	audiā́tis
		3	párent	hábeant	míttant	iáciant	aúdiant
Imperfect	*Singular*	1	parā́rem	habḗrem	mítterem	iácerem	audī́rem
		2	parā́rēs	habḗrēs	mítterēs	iácerēs	audī́rēs
		3	parā́ret	habḗret	mítteret	iáceret	audī́ret
	Plural	1	parārḗmus	habērḗmus	mitterḗmus	iacerḗmus	audīrḗmus
		2	parārḗtis	habērḗtis	mitterḗtis	iacerḗtis	audīrḗtis
		3	parā́rent	habḗrent	mítterent	iácerent	audī́rent

XI. Regular Verbs Active: Subjunctive (continued)

			1st Conjugation	*2nd Conjugation*	*3rd Conjugation*		*4th Conjugation*
Perfect	*Singular*	1	parā́verim	habúerim	mī́serim	iḗcerim	audī́verim
		2	parā́veris	habúeris	mī́seris	iḗceris	audī́veris
		3	parā́verit	habúerit	mī́serit	iḗcerit	audī́verit
	Plural	1	parāvérimus	habuérimus	mīsérimus	iēcérimus	audīvérimus
		2	parāvéritis	habuéritis	mīséritis	iēcéritis	audīvéritis
		3	parā́verint	habúerint	mī́serint	iḗcerint	audī́verint
Pluperfect	*Singular*	1	parāvíssem	habuíssem	mīsíssem	iēcíssem	audīvíssem
		2	parāvíssēs	habuíssēs	mīsíssēs	iēcíssēs	audīvíssēs
		3	parāvísset	habuísset	mīsísset	iēcísset	audīvísset
	Plural	1	parāvissḗmus	habuissḗmus	mīsissḗmus	iēcissḗmus	audīvissḗmus
		2	parāvissḗtis	habuissḗtis	mīsissḗtis	iēcissḗtis	audīvissḗtis
		3	parāvíssent	habuíssent	mīsíssent	iēcíssent	audīvíssent

XII. Regular Verbs Passive: Subjunctive

			1st Conjugation	2nd Conjugation	3rd Conjugation		4th Conjugation
Present	Singular	1	párer	hábear	míttar	iáciar	aúdiar
		2	parḗris	habeā́ris	mittā́ris	iaciā́ris	audiā́ris
		3	parḗtur	habeā́tur	mittā́tur	iaciā́tur	audiā́tur
	Plural	1	parḗmur	habeā́mur	mittā́mur	iaciā́mur	audiā́mur
		2	parḗminī	habeā́minī	mittā́minī	iaciā́minī	audiā́minī
		3	paréntur	habeántur	mittántur	iaciántur	audiántur
Imperfect	Singular	1	parā́rer	habḗrer	mítterer	iácerer	audī́rer
		2	parārḗris	habērḗris	mitterḗris	iacerḗris	audīrḗris
		3	parārḗtur	habērḗtur	mitterḗtur	iacerḗtur	audīrḗtur
	Plural	1	parārḗmur	habērḗmur	mitterḗmur	iacerḗmur	audīrḗmur
		2	parārḗminī	habērḗminī	mitterḗminī	iacerḗminī	audīrḗminī
		3	parāréntur	habēréntur	mitteréntur	iaceréntur	audīréntur

The perfect passive subjunctive consists of the perfect passive participle plus the present subjunctive of the verb **esse** (see p. 147), e.g., **parātus sim**. The pluperfect passive subjunctive consists of the perfect passive participle plus the imperfect subjunctive of the verb **esse** (see p. 147), e.g., **parātus essem**.

XIII. Irregular Verbs: Infinitive, Imperative, Indicative

			ésse	pósse	vélle	nṓlle
Infinitive			ésse	pósse	vélle	nṓlle
Imperative			es	—	—	nṓlī
			éste	—	—	nōlī́te
Present	*Singular*	1	sum	póssum	vólō	nṓlō
		2	es	pótes	vīs	nōn vīs
		3	est	pótest	vult	nōn vult
	Plural	1	súmus	póssumus	vólumus	nṓlumus
		2	éstis	potéstis	vúltis	nōn vúltis
		3	sunt	póssunt	vólunt	nṓlunt
Imperfect	*Singular*	1	éram	póteram	volḗbam	nōlḗbam
		2	érās	póterās	volḗbās	nōlḗbās
		3	érat	póterat	volḗbat	nōlḗbat
	Plural	1	erā́mus	poterā́mus	volēbā́mus	nōlēbā́mus
		2	erā́tis	poterā́tis	volēbā́tis	nōlēbā́tis
		3	érant	póterant	volḗbant	nōlḗbant
Future	*Singular*	1	érō	póterō	vólam	nṓlam
		2	éris	póteris	vólēs	nṓlēs
		3	érit	póterit	vólet	nṓlet
	Plural	1	érimus	potérimus	volḗmus	nōlḗmus
		2	éritis	potéritis	volḗtis	nōlḗtis
		3	érunt	póterunt	vólent	nṓlent

XIII. Irregular Verbs: Infinitive, Imperative, Indicative (cont.)

Infinitive			mā́lle	ī́re	férre	férrī	fíerī
Imperative			—	ī	fer	férre	—
			—	ī́te	férte	ferímini	—
Present	*Singular*	1	mā́lō	éō	férō	féror	fī́ō
		2	mā́vīs	īs	fers	férris	fīs
		3	mā́vult	it	fert	fértur	fit
	Plural	1	mā́lumus	ī́mus	férimus	férimur	fī́mus
		2	māvúltis	ī́tis	fértis	feríminī	fī́tis
		3	mā́lunt	éunt	férunt	ferúntur	fī́unt
Imperfect	*Singular*	1	mālḗbam	ī́bam	ferḗbam	ferḗbar	fīḗbam
		2	mālḗbās	ī́bās	ferḗbās	ferēbā́ris	fīḗbās
		3	mālḗbat	ī́bat	ferḗbat	ferēbā́tur	fīḗbat
	Plural	1	mālēbā́mus	ībā́mus	ferēbā́mus	ferēbā́mur	fīēbā́mus
		2	mālēbā́tis	ībā́tis	ferēbā́tis	ferēbā́minī	fīēbā́tis
		3	mālḗbant	ī́bant	ferḗbant	ferēbántur	fīḗbant
Future	*Singular*	1	mā́lam	ī́bō	féram	férar	fī́am
		2	mā́lēs	ī́bis	férēs	ferḗris	fī́ēs
		3	mā́let	ī́bit	féret	ferḗtur	fī́et
	Plural	1	mālḗmus	ī́bimus	ferḗmus	ferḗmur	fīḗmus
		2	mālḗtis	ī́bitis	ferḗtis	ferḗminī	fīḗtis
		3	mā́lent	ī́bunt	férent	feréntur	fī́ent

Note: perfect, pluperfect, and future perfect tenses are formed regularly from the perfect stem plus the regular endings for each tense. These tenses of **fīō** are made up of the participle **factus, -a, -um** plus **sum, eram**, and **erō** respectively.

XIV. Irregular Verbs: Subjunctive

Present	*Singular*	1	sim	póssim	vélim	nṓlim
		2	sīs	póssīs	vélīs	nṓlīs
		3	sit	póssit	vélit	nṓlit
	Plural	1	sī́mus	possī́mus	velī́mus	nōlī́mus
		2	sī́tis	possī́tis	velī́tis	nōlī́tis
		3	sint	póssint	vélint	nṓlint
Imperfect	*Singular*	1	éssem	póssem	véllem	nṓllem
		2	éssēs	póssēs	véllēs	nṓllēs
		3	ésset	pósset	véllet	nṓllet
	Plural	1	essḗmus	possḗmus	vellḗmus	nōllḗmus
		2	essḗtis	possḗtis	vellḗtis	nōllḗtis
		3	éssent	póssent	véllent	nṓllent
Perfect	*Singular*	1	fúerim	potúerim	volúerim	nōlúerim
		2	fúeris	potúeris	volúeris	nōlúeris
		3	fúerit	potúerit	volúerit	nōlúerit
	Plural	1	fuérimus	potuérimus	voluérimus	nōluérimus
		2	fuéritis	potuéritis	voluéritis	nōluéritis
		3	fúerint	potúerint	volúerint	nōlúerint
Pluperfect	*Singular*	1	fuíssem	potuíssem	voluíssem	nōluíssem
		2	fuíssēs	potuíssēs	voluíssēs	nōluíssēs
		3	fuísset	potuísset	voluísset	nōluísset
	Plural	1	fuissḗmus	potuissḗmus	voluissḗmus	nōluissḗmus
		2	fuissḗtis	potuissḗtis	voluissḗtis	nōluissḗtis
		3	fuíssent	potuíssent	voluíssent	nōluíssent

XIV. Irregular Verbs: Subjunctive (continued)

Tense	Number	Person					
Present	*Singular*	1	mā́lim	éam	féram	férar	fī́am
		2	mā́līs	éās	férās	feráris	fī́ās
		3	mā́lit	éat	férat	ferā́tur	fī́at
	Plural	1	mālī́mus	eā́mus	ferā́mus	ferā́mur	fīā́mus
		2	mālī́tis	eā́tis	ferā́tis	ferā́minī	fīā́tis
		3	mā́lint	éant	férant	ferántur	fī́ant
Imperfect	*Singular*	1	mā́llem	ī́rem	férrem	férrer	fíerem
		2	mā́llēs	ī́rēs	férrēs	ferrḗris	fíerēs
		3	mā́llet	ī́ret	férret	ferrḗtur	fíeret
	Plural	1	māllḗmus	īrḗmus	ferrḗmus	ferrḗmur	fierḗmus
		2	māllḗtis	īrḗtis	ferrḗtis	ferrḗminī	fierḗtis
		3	mā́llent	ī́rent	férrent	ferréntur	fíerent
Perfect	*Singular*	1	mālúerim	ī́verim	túlerim	lā́tus sim	fáctus sim
		2	mālúeris	ī́veris	túleris	lā́tus sīs	fáctus sīs
		3	mālúerit	ī́verit	túlerit	lā́tus sit	fáctus sit
	Plural	1	māluérimus	īvérimus	tulérimus	lā́tī sī́mus	fáctī sī́mus
		2	māluéritis	īvéritis	tuléritis	lā́tī sī́tis	fáctī sī́tis
		3	mālúerint	ī́verint	túlerint	lā́tī sint	fáctī sint
Pluperfect	*Singular*	1	māluíssem	īvíssem	tulíssem	lā́tus éssem	fáctus éssem
		2	māluíssēs	īvíssēs	tulíssēs	lā́tus éssēs	fáctus éssēs
		3	māluísset	īvísset	tulísset	lā́tus ésset	fáctus ésset
	Plural	1	māluissḗmus	īvissḗmus	tulissḗmus	lā́tī essḗmus	fáctī essḗmus
		2	māluissḗtis	īvissḗtis	tulissḗtis	lā́tī essḗtis	fáctī essḗtis
		3	māluíssent	īvíssent	tulíssent	lā́tī éssent	fáctī éssent

XV. Infinitives

Present		*Perfect*	
Active	*Passive*	*Active*	*Passive*
1 paráre	parárī	parāvísse	parátus, -a, -um ésse
2 habḗre	habḗrī	habuísse	hábitus, -a, -um ésse
3 míttere	míttī	mīsísse	míssus, -a, -um ésse
4 audíre	audírī	audīvísse	audítus, -a, -um ésse

Future
Active
1 parātúrus, -a, -um ésse
2 habitúrus, -a, -um ésse
3 missúrus, -a, -um ésse
4 audītúrus, -a, -um ésse

XVI. Participles

Present		*Perfect*	
Active	*Passive*	*Active*	*Passive*
1 párāns, parántis			parátus, -a, -um
2 hábēns, habéntis			hábitus, -a, -um
3 míttēns, mitténtis			míssus, -a, -um
4 aúdiēns, audiéntis			audítus, -a, -um

Future
Active
1 parātúrus, -a, -um
2 habitúrus, -a, -um
3 missúrus, -a, -um
4 audītúrus, -a, -um

VOCABULARY

A

ā, ab (+ *abl.*), by, from, away from

67 **ábigō, -ígere** (3), **-ḗgī, -ā́ctum**, to drive away

65 **ábnegō** (1), to refuse, deny

56 **ábsēns, -ntis**, absent

ábstinēns, -ntis, refraining from

ábsum, abésse (*irreg.*), **ā́fuī**, to be away, be distant from

67 **absū́mō, -ere** (3), **-psī, -ptum**, to consume, use up

ac, and

áccidō, -ere (3), **-ī**, to happen

accípiō, -ípere (3), **-ḗpī, -éptum**, to receive, get

58 **acclāmā́tiō, -ṓnis** (*f*), loud outcry

63 **acclā́mō** (1), to cry out in approval

accúrrō, -rrere (3), **-rrī, -rsum**, to run towards, up to

58 **ā́cer, ā́cris, ā́cre**, fierce

62 **ācérrimē**, very fiercely

62 **ā́crius**, more fiercely

59 **acérbus, -a, -um**, bitter, hideous, appalling

62 **aciēs, -ḗī** (*f*), battle line

58 **acquī́rō, -rere** (3), **-sī́vī, -sī́tum**, to acquire, gain

65 **ā́ctum, -ī** (*n*), procedure

58 **ā́cta, -ṓrum** (*n pl*), public records

ad (+ *acc.*), to, towards, at, near

áddō, -ere (3), **-idī, -itum**, to add

ádeō, so much, to such an extent

68 **adfíciō, -ícere** (3), **-ḗcī, -éctum**, to affect, move

64 **adfírmō** (1), to affirm, assert, swear

60 **adflī́gō, -gere** (3), **-xī, -ctum**, to strike down

55 **adhíbeō, -ḗre** (2), **-uī, -itum**, to offer, give to

adhū́c, still, as yet

56 **adíciō, -ícere** (3), **-iḗcī, -iéctum**, to add

ádimō, -ímere (3), **-ḗmī, -ḗmptum** (+ *dat.*), to take away (from)

ádiuvō, -iuvā́re (1), **-iū́vī, -iū́tum**, to help

63 **adminístrō** (1), to administer

admīrā́tiō, -ṓnis (*f*), amazement, wonder

admóveō, -movḗre (2), **-mṓvī, -mṓtum**, to move towards, bring to

65 **ádnotō** (1), to make a ruling

adórior, -ī́rī (4), **-tus sum**, to attack

68 **adsíduus, -a, -um**, constant

63 **adsístō, -ere** (3), **ádstitī**, to stand by, help

68 **adstríctus, -a, -um**, drawn together, contracted

ádsum, -ésse (*irreg.*), **-fuī**, to be present, near

68 **adulēscéntia, -ae** (*f*), youth

65 **adultérium, -ī** (*n*), adultery

54 **adū́rō, -ū́rere** (3), **-ū́ssī, -ū́stum**, to set on fire, burn, scorch

68 **advérsum, -ī** (*n*), calamity, misfortune

67 **advocā́tiō, -ṓnis** (*f*), (legal) counsel

58 **advocā́tus, -ī** (*m*), supporter

aedifícium, -ī (*n*), building

aedíficō (1), to build

54 **aedī́lis, -is** (*m*), aedile

68 **aéger, -gra, -grum**, ill, disturbed

aegrṓtō (1), to be ill

63 **aémulus, -a, -um**, rivalling, vying

63 **aequā́lis, -is, -e**, fair, just

56 **aéquē**, equally

66 **aerā́rius, -ī** (*m*), coppersmith

59 **aes, aéris** (*n*), copper; money

aes aliḗnum, debt ("another's money")

aéstās, -ā́tis (*f*), summer

68 **aéstimō** (1), to estimate, judge

61 **aétās, -ā́tis** (*f*), age, time of life, old age

64 **aetérnitās, -ā́tis** (*f*), eternity

68 **afféctiō, -ṓnis** (*f*), affection

áfferō, -rre (*irreg.*), **áttulī, allā́tum**, to bring, bring to, bring in

áger, ágrī (*m*), field, land

in ágrum, in depth (as opposed to frontage)

61 **ágger, -eris** (*m*), earthen wall, earthwork

58 **ágmen, -inis** (*n*), column, band

agnṓscō, -ṓscere (3), **-ṓvī, -itum**, to recognize

ágō, ágere (3), **ḗgī, ā́ctum**, to do; speak (publicly), plead (a case); celebrate (a holiday)

grā́tiās ágere (+ *dat.*), to thank

60 **ā́la, -ae** (*f*), wing

66 **álgeō, -gḗre** (2), **-sī**, to be cold, feel the cold

63 **aliquándō**, sometimes

áliquī, áliqua, áliquod, some (or other), any

áliquis, áliquid, someone, something

sī quis (quis = áliquis), if anyone

55 **áliquot** (*indeclinable*), some, a few

57 **áliter**, otherwise
55 **alíubī**, elsewhere, somewhere else
álius, ália, áliud, other, another
56 **álligō** (1), to tie
58 **álloquor, -quī** (3), **-cū́tus sum**, to speak to, address
álter, áltera, álterum, the one, the other (of two), the second
61 **altitū́dō, -inis** (*f*), height
áltus, -a, -um, tall, high
ámbō, ámbae, ámbō, both
63 **ambítiō, -ṓnis** (*f*), ambition, political campaigning (57)
ámbulō (1), to walk, walk around
58 **ambū́rō, -ū́rere** (3), **-ússī, -ústum**, to scorch, burn near
60 **ā́mēns, -ntis**, mad, insane
65 **āméntia, -ae** (*f*), madness
68 **amī́ca, -ae** (*f*), girlfriend
amī́cus, -ī (*m*), friend
57 **amī́cus, -a, -um**, friendly
59 **āmíttō, -íttere** (3), **-ī́sī, -íssum**, to lose
ámō (1), to like, love
66 **amoénitās, -ā́tis** (*f*), pleasantness, charm
ámor, -ṓris (*m*), love
amphitheā́trum (also **amphitheā́ter**), **-ī** (*n*), amphitheater
56 **ámphora, -ae** (*f*), amphora, large two-handled earthenware jar
ampléctor, -ctī (3), **-xus sum**, to embrace
55 **ampléxō** (1), to embrace
63 **ámpliō** (l), to enlarge, increase
59 **amplitū́dō, -inis** (*f*), grandeur, majesty
61 **ámplus, -a, -um**, eminent, important
an, or, whether
ancílla, -ae (*f*), slave woman
66 **anguílla, -ae** (*f*), eel
60 **ánima, -ae** (*f*), soul, darling
animadvértō, -tere (3), **-tī, -sum**, to notice
ánimus, -ī (*m*), mind, spirit, heart
54 **annṓna, -ae** (*f*), (price of) grain
ánnus, -ī (*m*), year
64 **ánnuum, -ī** (*n*), yearly salary
ánte (+ *acc.*), before, in front of
ánte (*adverb*), before, previously
ánteā, before, previously
61 **antecḗdō, -dere** (3), **-ssī, -ssum**, to anticipate, precede
ā́nulus, -ī (*m*), ring
apériō, -ī́re (4), **-uī, -tum**, to open
appā́reō, -ḗre (2), **-uī, -itum**, to appear
65 **appéllō** (1), to call, call on, invoke
appropínquō (1), (+ *dat.*), to approach, draw near to
áqua, -ae (*f*), water
62 **áquila, -ae** (*f*), eagle, insignia of a legion

ā́ra, -ae (*f*), altar
64 **árbitror, -ā́rī** (1), **-ā́tus sum**, to think
árcus, -ūs (*m*), arch
árdeō, -dḗre (2), **-sī**, to burn, blaze
ā́rea, -ae (*f*), open space, site, (city) square
68 **argéntum, -ī** (*n*), silver
65 **árguō, -úere** (3), **-uī, -ū́tum**, to accuse, denounce
árma, -ṓrum (*n pl*), arms, weapons
armā́tus, -a, -um, armed
ars, -tis (*f*), skill, art
61 **artifícium, -ī** (*n*), skill
54 **as, ássis** (*m*), as, a small coin comparable to a penny
55 **ásinus, -ī** (*m*), ass, donkey
átque, and, also
58 **ā́trium, -ī** (*n*), atrium, main room of a Roman house
54 **attíneō, -ḗre** (2), **-uī**, to concern
64 **aúctor, -ṓris** (*m*), author, authority
57 **auctṓritās, -ā́tis** (*f*), authority, influence
57 **audā́cia, -ae** (*f*), daring, recklessness
54 **audā́cter**, boldly, with confidence
54 **audā́culus, -a, -um**, bold, courageous
aúdeō, -dḗre (2), **-sus sum**, to dare
aúdiō (4), to hear, listen to
aúferō, -rre (*irreg.*), **ábstulī, ablā́tum**, to carry away, take away
aúgeō, -gḗre (2), **-xī, -ctum**, to increase
aúreus, -a, -um, golden
aúrum, -ī (*n*), gold
aut, or
aútem, however, but, moreover
67 **autúmnus, -ī** (*m*), autumn
auxílium, -ī (*n*), help
ávis, -is (*m/f*), bird
68 **āvocāméntum, -ī** (*n*), diversion, recreation

B

báculum, -ī (*n*), stick
64 **balíneum, -ī** (*n*), public bath
68 **bárba, -ae** (*f*), beard
62 **bárbarus, -a, -um**, barbarian, foreign
55 **bā́rō, -ṓnis** (*m*), lout
58 **basílica, -ae** (*f*), public courthall
59 **beā́tus, -a, -um**, happy
60 **bellíssimē**, most comfortably, elegantly
béllum, -ī (*n*), war
béne, well
61 **benefáciō, -fácere** (3), **-fḗcī, -fáctum**, to do a service (to), benefit
56 **benefícium, -ī** (*n*), kindness, favor
54 **benígnus, -a, -um**, kind, friendly
55 **bēstiā́rius, -ī** (*m*), animal fighter (in the arena)
bíbō, -ere (3), **-ī**, to drink

66 **bífer, -era, -erum,** that bears (fruit or flowers) twice (a year)
68 **bímulus, -a, -um,** two years old
55 **bínī, -ae, -a,** two each
bónus, -a, -um, good
54 **bóna, -ṓrum** (*n pl*), goods, material possessions
bōs, bóvis (*m/f*), ox, cow
brévis, -is, -e, short, brief
60 **brévitās, -ā́tis** (*f*), brevity, shortness
67 **brū́ma, -ae** (*f*), winter
54 **bū́b(u)lus, -a, -um,** of or belonging to an ox
54 **búcca, -ae** (*f*), cheek, mouthful
64 **bū́lē, -ēs** (*f*), senate or town council in a Greek city
64 **būleúta, -ae** (*m*), senator or councilor in a Greek city
55 **burdubásta, -ae** (*m*), stick (?) (as an insult to a feeble gladiator)

C

58 **cadā́ver, -eris** (*n*), corpse
cádō, -ere (3), **cécidī, cā́sum,** to fall
68 **cádus, -ī** (*m*), (wine)jar
66 **caécus, -a, -um,** blind, hidden, unseen
55 **caédō, -dere** (3), **cecī́dī, -sum,** to cut, beat, cut down, kill
68 **caelātū́ra, -ae** (*f*), engraving
caélum, -ī (*n*), the sky, heaven
55 **caldicerébrius, -a, -um,** hotheaded, impulsive
56 **candēlā́brum, -ī** (*n*), candelabrum, candle- or lampstand
57 **candidā́tus, -ī** (*m*), candidate
66 **cándidus, -a, -um,** white
67 **canī́nus, -a, -um,** of or belonging to a dog
cánis, -is (*m/f*), dog
capillā́tus, -a, -um, with long hair
capíllī, -ṓrum (*m pl*), hair
cápiō, -ere (3), **cḗpī, -tum,** to take, capture
cáput, -itis (*n*), head
68 **cáreō, -ḗre** (2), **-uī, -itum** (+ *abl.*), to be without, lack
65 **cármen, -inis** (*n*), song, hymn
55 **carnā́rium, -ī** (*n*), butcher-shop, slaughterhouse
cā́rus, -a, -um, dear, beloved
68 **cássus, -a, -um,** empty, useless
61 **cástra, -ṓrum** (*n pl*), camp
68 **cástus, -a, -um,** chaste
54 **cásula, -ae** (*f*), little house, hut
61 **cā́sus, -ūs** (*m*), fall, outcome, happening, misfortune
56 **catélla, -ae** (*f*), puppy
66 **catḗnō** (1), to chain
67 **cathédra, -ae** (*f*), chair
caúda, -ae (*f*), tail
54 **caúniae, -ā́rum** (*f pl*), figs from Caunus (in Asia Minor)
caúpō, -ṓnis (*m*), innkeeper
caúsa, -ae (*f*), cause, reason, case
genitive + **caúsā,** for the sake of
60 **cēdō, -dere** (3), **-ssī, -ssum,** to retreat, yield, be inferior to
celéritās, -ā́tis (*f*), speed
celériter, quickly
68 **célla, -ae** (*f*), storeroom, cellar
cḗna, -ae (*f*), dinner
cḗnō (1), to dine, eat dinner
60 **cḗnseō, -ḗre** (2), **-uī, -um,** to be of the opinion, think
64 **cḗnsor, -ṓris** (*m*), censor, one who enrolls senators
54 **centḗnī, -ae, -a,** a hundred each
56 **céntiēs,** a hundred times
55 **centōnā́rius, -ī** (*m*), maker of patchwork, rag dealer
céntum, a hundred
62 **centū́riō, -ṓnis** (*m*), centurion, leader of 100 men
56 **cerebéllum, -ī** (*n*), brain, heart
cértus, -a, -um, certain
cértē, certainly, at least
55 **cḗterum,** for the rest, moreover
cíbus, -ī (*m*), food
56 **cícarō, -ṓnis** (*m*), small boy, pet
58 **cíngō, -gere** (3), **-xī, -ctum,** to equip, strap on
56 **cíngulum, -ī** (*n*), belt, leash
56 **cínis, -eris** (*m*), ashes
56 **círcā** (+ *acc.*), around, near
circúmeō, -ī́re (*irreg.*), **-iī, -itum,** to go around, surround
59 **circumscrī́bō, -bere** (3), **-psī, -ptum,** to confine, keep in bounds
58 **circúmstō, -ā́re, -etī,** to stand around
64 **circumvéniō, -enī́re, -ḗnī, -éntum,** to surround
56 **cítō,** quickly, soon
62 **cítō** (1), to spur on, rouse up
60 **cīvī́lis, -is, -e,** civil
63 **cīvī́litās, -ā́tis** (*f*), politeness, courtesy
cī́vis, -is (*m*), citizen
57 **cī́vitās, -ā́tis** (*f*), state
67 **clā́mitō** (1), to call
67 **clā́mō,** (1), to shout
clā́mor, -ṓris (*m*), shout, shouting
61 **clássis, -is** (*f*), fleet
claúdō (clūdō), -dere (3), **-sī, -sum,** to shut, close
68 **clā́vus, -ī** (*m*), stripe
lātus clāvus, a broad purple stripe on a senator's tunic, one of the insignia of his rank
54 **clī́vus, -ī** (*m*), slope, hill

64 **cloā́ca, -ae** (*f*), sewer, drain

58 **cṓdex, -icis** (*m*), ledger, tablet

65 **cóeō, -ī́re** (*irreg.*), **-iī, -itum,** to come together, meet

coépī, -ísse, -tum, to begin (perfect system only used)

59 **coérceō** (2), to check, restrain

cṓgitō (1), to think, consider

58 **cognā́tus, -ī** (*m*), relative, kinsman

cognṓscō, -ṓscere (3), **-ṓvī, -itum,** to find out, learn, hear of

cṓgō, -ere (3), **coḗgī, coā́ctum,** to compel, force

56 **cohḗrēs, -ḗdis** (*m*), joint heir

62 **cóhors, -rtis** (*f*), cohort, one-tenth of a legion

62 **cohórtor, -ā́rī** (1), **-ā́tus sum,** to encourage

57 **collḗga, -ae** (*m*), colleague, partner

65 **collḗgium, -ī** (*n*), club, association

54 **collū́dō, -dere** (3), **-sī, -sum,** to act in collusion (with)

cólō, -ere (3), **-uī, cúltum,** to cultivate, inhabit

54 **colṓnia, -ae** (*f*), colony, town

55 **cólor, -ṓris** (*m*), color, complexion

55 **cólubra, -ae** (*f*), snake

56 **colúmba, -ae** (*f*), dove

63 **colúmna, -ae** (*f*), column, pillar

54 **comédō, -ésse** (*irreg.*), **-ḗdī, -ḗsum,** to eat up, eat

cómes, -itis (*m/f*), companion

57 **comítia, -ṓrum** (*n pl*), electoral assembly of the people

61 **cómminus** (*adverb*), at close quarters, hand to hand

commíttō, -íttere (3), **-ī́sī, -íssum,** to bring together; entrust

púgnam (ríxam) commíttere, to join battle, start a fight

commū́nis, -is, -e, common, joint

66 **comoédia, -ae** (*f*), comedy

67 **comoédus, -ī** (*m*), comic actor, comedian

cómparō (1), to buy, obtain, get ready

62 **compéllō, -éllere** (3), **-ulī, -úlsum,** to force, drive

59 **compériō, -ī́re, -ī, -tum,** to find out for certain

63 **compéscō, -ere** (3), **-uī,** to check, curb, restrain

57 **competī́tor, -ṓris** (*m*), fellow candidate, opponent

complū́rēs, -ēs, -a, several

61 **compórtō** (1), to bring together, collect

54 **cómputō** (1), to add up, count, figure out

59 **concḗdō, -dere** (3), **-ssī, -sum,** to grant

cóncidō, -ere (3), **-ī,** to fall down

56 **concupī́scō, -ī́scere** (3), **ī́vī, -ī́tum,** to long for

61 **concúrsus, -ūs** (*m*), a running together, collision

64 **condíciō, -ṓnis** (*f*), situation, position, status

60 **(sē) cṓnferō, -rre** (*irreg.*), **cóntulī, collā́tum,** to take oneself, flee

confíciō, -ícere (3), **-ḗcī, -éctum,** to accomplish, finish, overwhelm

65 **cōnfíteor, -fitḗrī** (2), **-féssus sum,** to confess, admit

61 **cōnflī́gō, -gere** (3), **-xī, -ctum,** to collide

58 **cṓnfluō, -ere** (3), **-xī,** to flow together

cōnfúgiō, -úgere (3), **-ū́gī,** to flee for refuge

58 **cóngruō, -ere** (3), **-uī,** to agree with

68 **coniugā́lis, -is, -e,** belonging to marriage, conjugal

61 **coniúngō, -gere** (3), **-xī, -ctum** (+ *dat.*), to join

68 **cóniūnx, -ugis** (*m/f*), spouse, husband, wife

61 **conlabefī́ō, -fíerī** (*irreg.*), **-fáctus sum,** to fall in, collapse, break up

cṓnor, -ā́rī (1), **-ā́tus sum,** to try

62 **conquī́rō, -rere** (3), **-sī́vī, -sī́tum,** to procure, obtain, seek out

61 **cōnscéndō, -dere** (3), **-dī, -sum,** to board ship

61 **cṓnsequor, -quī** (3), **-cū́tus sum,** to follow, catch up to, overtake

59 **cōnsérvō** (1), to preserve

60 **cōnsī́derō** (1), to consider, think about, make plans

cōnsílium, -ī (*n*), plan, deliberation, advice

61 **cṓnspicor, -ā́rī** (1), **-ā́tus sum,** to catch sight of

58 **cōnspū́tō** (1), to spit on (in contempt)

cōnstítuō, -úere (3), **-uī, -ū́tum,** to decide, determine

58 **cṓnstō, -ā́re** (1), **-itī** (+ *abl.*), to depend on, be based on

68 **cōnsuḗscō, -escere** (3), **-ḗvī, -ḗtum,** to be accustomed

67 **cōnsuētū́dō, -inis** (*f*), custom, habit

cōnsul, -lis (*m*), consul

57 **cōnsulā́ris, -is, -e,** belonging to a consul, consular

57 **cōnsulā́tus, -ūs** (*m*), consulship

cṓnsulō, -ere (3), **-uī, -tum,** to consult, decide

68 **cōnsultátiō, -ṓnis** (*f*), consultation, discussion

62 **conténdō, -dere** (3), **-dī, -tum,** to hurry, try to reach

68 **cónterō, -térere** (3), **-trī́vī, -trī́tum,** to wear out, exhaust

contíneō, -inḗre (2), -ínuī, -éntum, to hold together, hold in position, contain
56 contíngō, -íngere (3), -igī, -áctum, to befall, happen to
58 cṓntiō, -ṓnis (*f*), public meeting
cóntrā (+ *acc.*), opposite, in front of, facing; equivalent to, worth its weight in
65 contrā́rius, -a, -um, contrary, opposite
61 convéllō, -éllere (3), -éllī, -úlsum, to tear away, weaken
convéniō, -enī́re (4), -ḗnī, -éntum, to come together, meet, assemble
convértō, -tere (3), -tī, -sum, to turn (around)
58 convī́cium, -ī (*n*), insult
convī́va, -ae (*m*), guest (at a banquet)
convī́vium, -ī (*n*), feast, banquet
cónvocō (1), to call together, assemble
56 cōpiṓsus, -a, -um, capacious, large
cóquō, -quere (3), -xī, -ctum, to cook
cóquus, -ī (*m*), cook
cor, córdis (*n*), heart
62 córnū, -ūs (*n*), horn; end of a battle line, wing
corṓna, -ae (*f*), garland, crown
corṓnō (1), to crown, form a ring around, encircle
córpus, -oris (*n*) body
64 córrigō, -ígere (3), -ḗxī, -ḗctum, to correct
corrípiō, -ípere (3), -ípuī, éptum, to seize, scold
56 corrotúndō (1), to round off, "clear" (a profit)
66 cothúrnus, -ī (*m*), raised boot worn by tragic actors
cotī́diē, daily, every day
crās, tomorrow
67 crássus, -a, -um, thick, coarse, uncouth
57 crēbrḗscō, -ḗscere (3), -uī, to increase, gather strength
crḗdō, -ere (3), -idī, -itum, to trust, believe
58 crémō (1), to burn
créō (1), to elect, create
54 crḗscō, -ere (3), crḗvī, crḗtum, to rise, grow, swell
64 crī́men, -inis (*n*), accusation, indictment, crime
crūdḗlis, -is, -e, cruel
crūdḗlitās, -ā́tis (*f*), cruelty
cubículum, -ī (*n*), bedroom
66 cubī́le, -is (*n*), bed
cúbitum ī́re, to go to bed
cúlpa, -ae (*f*), fault, blame
56 cúltus, -a, -um, cultivated, elegant, adorned
68 cúltus, -ūs (*m*), adornment, finery, (fancy) clothing
cum (+ *abl.*), with
cum, when, since, whenever, although
68 cū́nae, -ā́rum (*f pl*), cradle
cū́nctī, -ae, -a, all
65 cupíditās, -ā́tis (*f*), desire, greed
57 cúpidus, -a, -um (+ *gen.*), desirous, eager
cū́ra, -ae (*f*), care, anxiety
cū́ria, -ae (*f*), senate house
54 cūriṓsē, carefully
cū́rō (1), take care of, care about
56 cúrsus, -ūs (*m*), run, course, voyage
66 curvā́men, -inis (*n*), curve
cústōs, -ṓdis (*m*), guard, guardian

D

64 dámnō (1), to condemn, sentence
dē (+ *abl.*), down from, concerning, about
dḗbeō (2), to owe, (one) ought
57 dḗbilis, -is, -e, feeble, powerless
dēcḗdō, -dere (3), -ssī, -ssum, to die
décem, ten
56 dēcérnō, -érnere (3), -rḗvī, -rḗtum, to decide, decree
61 dēcértō (1), to fight to the finish, fight it out
63 décet, -ḗre (2), -uit (+ *acc.*), it is right or fitting for (one to . . .), one ought
55 dēcrépitus, -a, -um, decrepit, feeble
62 decumā́nus, -a, -um, related to the tenth (legion, e.g.)
56 decúria, -ae (*f*), group, panel, board, guild
58 decúriō, -ṓnis (*m*), town councilman
64 decuriōnā́tus, -ūs (*m*), decurionate, office of decurion
dēféndō, -dere (3), -dī, -sum, to defend
62 dēfḗnsiō, -ṓnis (*f*), defense
58 dḗfero, -rre (*irreg.*), dḗtulī, delā́tum, to bring down
dēféssus, -a, -um, weary, tired
61 dēfíciō, -ícere (3), -ḗcī, -éctum, to lack, fail
deínde, then
65 dēlā́tor, -ṓris (*m*), informer, accuser
dēléctō (1), to delight
55 dēléctor, -ā́rī (1), -ā́tus sum, to please, amuse
dḗleō, -ḗre (2), -ḗvī, -ḗtum, to destroy
55 dēlicā́tus, -a, -um, spoiled, fussy, fastidious
54 dēlicā́tus, -ī (*m*), favorite, pet

63 **dēmíttō, -íttere** (3), **-ī́sī, -íssum,** to send down, cast down
dēnā́rius, -ī (*m*), denarius, silver coin
67 **dḗnī, -ae, -a,** ten each, ten
56 **dḗnique,** at last, finally
66 **dḗnsus, -a, -um,** dense
55 **deórsum** (*adverb*), down
65 **dēpósitum, -ī** (*n*), deposit (of money or valuables, for safekeeping)
55 **dēprehéndō, -dere** (3), **-dī, -sum,** to seize, catch
61 **dḗprimō, -ímere** (3), **-éssī, -éssum,** to sink, press down
57 **dēpúgnō** (1), to fight it out
56 **dēsīdérium, -ī** (*n*), desire, longing
dēsī́derō (1), to desire, wish
62 **dēsígnō** (1), to mark, indicate
65 **dḗsinō, -ínere** (3), **-iī, -itum,** to stop, cease
66 **dēspíciō, -ícere** (3), **-éxī, -éctum,** to look down on
62 **dēstítuō, -úere** (3), **-uī, -ū́tum,** to desert, abandon
61 **dḗsum, -ésse** (*irreg.*), **-fuī,** to be lacking
62 **dḗtrahō, -here** (3), **-xī, -ctum,** to drag from, strip off
57 **dētrīméntum, -ī** (*n*), damage, harm
déus, déī (*m*), (*dat.* and *abl. pl.* **dīs**), god
dḗvorō (1), to devour, eat
déxt(e)ra, -ae (*f*), right hand
68 **diaéta, -ae** (*f*) (Greek), room, private apartment
dī́cō, -cere (3), **-xī, -ctum,** to say, tell
65 **måle dī́cere** (+ *dat.*), to speak ill of, insult, curse
57 **dictā́tor, -ṓris** (*m*), dictator, magistrate with absolute power in emergencies
67 **dictō** (1), to dictate
55 **dictā́ta, -ṓrum** (*n pl*), dictated lessons, rules
64 **díctum, -ī** (*n*), thing spoken, word
61 **dīdū́cō, -cere** (3), **-xī, -ctum,** to separate, draw apart
díēs, -ḗī (*m*), day
63 **diffúndō, -úndere** (3), **-ū́dī, -ū́sum,** to spread out, extend
60 **dígnitās, -ā́tis** (*f*), reputation
63 **dígnor, -ā́rī** (1), **-ā́tus sum,** to consider worthy
55 **dígnus, -a, -um,** worthy, deserving
57 **dīlḗctus, -ūs** (*m*), draft of troops, levy
dīligénter, carefully
dī́ligō, -ígere (3), **-ḗxī, -ḗctum,** to love, care for
dīmíttō, -íttere (3), **-ī́sī, -íssum,** to send away, let go
54 **dīrḗctum** (*adverb*), directly, simply, straightforwardly
61 **dīréptiō, -ṓnis** (*f*), breach
66 **dī́rimō, -ímere** (3), **-ḗmī, -ḗmptum,** to separate, divide
60 **dīrípiō, -ípere** (3), **-ípuī, -éptum,** to lay waste, plunder
discḗdō, -dere (3), **-ssī, -ssum,** to depart, leave, go away
64 **discéssus, -ūs** (*m*), separation, departure
díscō, -ere (3), **dídicī,** to learn
67 **discúrsus, -ūs** (*m*), a running back and forth or around
55 **dispēnsā́tor, -ṓris** (*m*), steward, household manager
64 **dīspíciō, -ícere** (3), **-éxī, -éctum,** to consider, reflect on
65 **dísputō** (1), to dispute, argue
64 **distríbuō, -úere, -uī, -ū́tum,** to distribute
díū, for a long time
56 **diū́tius** (*adverb*), longer
66 **dīvérsitās, -ā́tis** (*f*), diversity, difference
63 **dīvī́nus, -a, -um,** divine
63 **dī́vus, -ī** (*m*), god
dō, dáre (1), **dédī, dátum,** to give
dólor, -ṓris (*m*), grief, pain, resentment
55 **doméstícus, -a, -um,** of the house or family, close, intimate, tame
dómina, -ae (*f*), mistress, lady of the house
dóminus, -ī (*m*), master, owner
dómus, -ūs (*f*), house
dómī, at home
65 **dṓnō** (1), to present, give, donate
dórmiō (4), to sleep
66 **dórsum, -ī** (*n*), back, ridge
60 **dúbitō** (1), to hesitate, be in doubt
64 **dúbius, -a, -um,** doubtful
56 **ducéntī, -ae, -a,** two hundred
dū́cō, -cere (3), **-xī, -ctum,** to lead
66 **dúctilis, -is, -e,** led, channeled
67 **dúlcis, -is, -e,** sweet, pleasant
dum, while, as long as
64 **dumtáxat,** at most, not more than
dúo, dúae, dúo, two
58 **dux, -cis** (*m*), leader, general

E

Écce! Look at . . . ! Look!
65 **ēdíctum, -ī** (*n*), edict, proclamation
66 **ḗditus, -a, -um,** raised, high
56 **éffluō, -úere** (3), **-ū́xī,** to flow out, spill
56 **effúndō, -úndere** (3), **-ū́dī, -ū́sum,** to pour out
égo, I
58 **ēíciō, ēícere** (3), **ēiḗcī, ēiéctum,** to throw out
64 **eiúsmodī:** see **modus**
64 **ḗloquēns, -ntis,** eloquent

60 **éloquor, -quī** (3), **-cū́tus sum,** to speak, speak out
67 **ēmendā́tiō, -ṓnis** (*f*), emendation, correction
64 **ēméndō** (1), to correct, reform
61 **ḗminus** (*adverb*), at long range, from a distance
émō, émere (3), **ḗmī, ḗmptum,** to buy
énim (*postpositive*), for
61 **ēnī́tor, -tī** (3), **-sus sum,** to strive, make an effort
57 **ēníxē,** eagerly
66 **entheā́tus, -a, -um,** frenzied, raving
éō, ī́re (*irreg.*), **ī́vī, ítum,** to go
epístula, -ae (*f*), letter
55 **épulum, -ī** (*n*), (public) feast, banquet
55 **éques, -itis** (*m*), horseman, knight; a member of the equestrian class at Rome
60 **équidem,** certainly, surely
62 **equitā́tus, -ūs** (*m*), cavalry
équus, -ī (*m*), horse
érgā (+ *acc.*), towards
54 **érgō,** therefore, so
ērípiō, -ípere (3), **-ípuī, -éptum,** to snatch from, take away
érrō (1), to wander
55 **ésseda, -ae** (*f*), Celtic war-chariot
55 **essedā́rius, -a, -um,** fighting from a chariot
54 **ēsurī́tiō, -ṓnis** (*f*), famine
et, and, also, too
étiam, also, even
58 **etiámsī,** even if, although
60 **étsī,** even if, although
54 **ēvéniō, -enī́re** (4), **-ḗnī, -éntum,** to happen, turn out
61 **ēvéntus, -ūs** (*m*), outcome, consequence, result
68 **ēvíncō, -íncere** (3), **-ī́cī, -íctum,** to conquer, surpass
61 **ḗvocō** (1), to call out, summon
ex, ē (+ *abl.*), from, out of
58 **exardḗscō, -dḗscere** (3), **-sī,** to catch fire, blaze up
excḗdō, -dere (3), **-ssī, -ssum,** to go out, leave
55 **excéllēns, -ntis,** excellent, outstanding
60 **excípiō, -ípere** (3), **-ḗpī, -éptum,** to take in, receive, catch
éxcitō (1), to stir up, excite, rouse, wake up
exclā́mō (1), to cry out, exclaim
68 **exclū́dō, -dere** (3), **-sī, -sum,** to shut out, exclude
65 **excútiō, -tere** (3), **-ssī, -ssum,** to examine, inspect, shake out
56 **exémplar, -ā́ris** (*n*), copy, transcript
61 **exémplum, -ī** (*n*), example, copy, precedent
éxeō, -ī́re (*irreg.*), **-iī, -itum,** to go out, get out, escape
exérceō (2), to exercise, occupy, keep busy
60 **exércitus, -ūs** (*m*), army
63 **exhíbeō** (2), to present, show
67 **éxigō, -ígere** (3), **-ḗgī, -ā́ctum,** to spend (time)
exímius, -a, -um, outstanding
éximō, -ímere (3), **-ḗmī, -ḗmptum,** to remove, omit
61 **exī́stimō** (1), to think, suppose
55 **éxitus, -ūs** (*m*), outcome, end
54 **exṓrō** (1), to pray for (with the implication that your prayer will be answered)
58 **expedī́tus, -a, -um,** lightly equipped
expéllō, -éllere (3), **-ulī, -úlsum,** to drive out, expel
expérior, -ī́rī (4), **-tus sum,** to test, try, experience, undergo
éxplicō (1), to unfold, disentangle, explain
61 **expóscō, -ere** (3), **expopóscī,** to ask for, beg
54 **éxpuō, -úere** (3), **-uī, -ū́tum,** to spit out, spit
59 **exscíndō, -ndere** (3), **-dī, -ssum,** to destroy utterly
59 **exsílium, -ī** (*n*), exile
61 **éxstruō, -ere** (3), **-xī, -ctum,** to pile up, build
exténdō, -dere (3), **-dī, -tum,** to stretch out, extend
59 **extérminō** (1), to drive out, banish
éxtrā (+ *acc.*), outside, out
éxtrahō, -here (3), **-xī, -ctum,** to pull out, drag out
58 **extúrbō** (1), to take by storm
67 **éxul, -lis** (*m*), exile, outcast

F

65 **fáber, -brī** (*m*), craftsman, workman
fā́bula, -ae (*f*), story, fable, fiction
fácilis, -is, -e, easy
fácile, easily
fáciō, -ere (3), **fḗcī, fáctum,** to make, do
56 **fáctum, -ī** (*n*), thing done, deed, fact
57 **fáctiō, -ṓnis** (*f*), gang, political partisans
61 **facúltās, -ā́tis** (*f*), opportunity
65 **fállō, -lere** (3), **fefélli, -sum,** to betray, falsify
56 **fálsus, -a, -um,** false, wrong
58 **fā́ma, -ae** (*f*), rumor, reputation
60 **fámes, -is** (*f*), hunger

família, -ae (*f*), family, household, troupe

familiáris, -is (*m/f*), close friend

66 **fásciō** (1), to bandage, swathe

65 **fáteor, -ērī** (3), **fassus sum,** to admit, confess

56 **fātum, -ī** (*n*), fate, destiny

fáveō, -ēre (2), **fāvī, faútum** (+ *dat.*), to favor, support

55 **fávor, -ōris** (*m*), support, popularity

56 **fávus, -ī** (*m*), honeycomb

fēlīx, -īcis, happy, lucky, fortunate

fēmina, -ae (*f*), woman

férē, almost, approximately

61 **feriō, ferīre** (4), to strike

férō, -rre (*irreg.*), **túlī, lātum,** to carry, bring, bear

61 **férreus, -a, -um,** made of iron

55 **férrum, -ī** (*n*), iron, steel

férula, -ae (*f*), cane

66 **féssus, -a, -um,** weary, tired

60 **festīnātiō, -ōnis** (*f*), haste

festīnō (1), to hurry

55 **féstus, -a, -um,** pertaining to a holiday, festive

fidēlis, -is, -e, faithful

fídēs, -ēī (*f*), good faith, reliability, trust

62 **fīdūcia, -ae** (*f*), confidence

fīlia, -ae (*f*), daughter

fīlius, -ī (*m*), son

55 **fílix, -icis** (*f*), a fern, weed, worthless person

67 **fīlum, -ī** (*n*), thread

fīnis, -is (*m*), end

63 **fīnēs, fīnium** (*m pl*), territory

fīō, fíerī (*irreg.*), **fáctus sum,** to become, be made, be done, happen

63 **físcus, -ī** (*m*), emperor's private funds

55 **flagéllum, -ī** (*n*), whip

58 **flágrō** (1), to blaze, flame

58 **flāmen, -inis** (*m*), priest (of a particular god or deified emperor)

55 **flātūra, -ae** (*f*), breath, fighting spirit

56 **fléō, -ēre** (2), **-ēvī, -ētum,** to weep

66 **flúctus, -ūs** (*m*), wave

66 **flūmen, -inis** (*n*), river, stream

67 **fócus, -ī** (*m*), fireplace

66 **fōns, -ntis** (*m*), fountain, spring

fórās (*adverb*), out of doors, in public

65 **fōrma, -ae** (*f*), rule, formula

67 **fórnix, -icis** (*m*), arch

fórte (*adverb*), by chance

fórtis, -is, -e, brave, strong

63 **fortitūdō, -inis** (*f*), courage

56 **fortūna, -ae** (*f*), fortune, good fortune, prosperity

fórum, -ī (*n*), forum, marketplace

frángō, -ngere (3), **frēgī, -ctum,** to break

frāter, -tris (*m*), brother

55 **frenēticus, -a, -um,** raving mad

67 **fréquēns, -ntis,** frequent

63 **frequénter,** frequently

63 **frequéntō** (1), to frequent, attend, visit frequently

56 **frīgeō, -ēre** (2), to freeze, be cold

67 **frīgidus, -a, -um,** cold, trivial

67 **frīgus, -oris** (*n*), cold

frōns, -ntis (*f*), forehead, front

in frónte, frontage, length of the side of a property fronting on a road

56 **frūgālitās, -ātis** (*f*), frugality, sober habits

64 **frūgāliter,** with thrift, with restraint

54 **frūníscor, -íscī** (3), **-ītus sum,** to enjoy

62 **frúor, -ī** (3), **-ctus sum** (+ *abl.*), to enjoy, have benefit of

55 **fúga, -ae** (*f*), a fleeing, rout, escape

fúgiō, -ere (3), **fūgī,** to flee

67 **fultūra, -ae** (*f*), support

61 **fundāméntum, -ī** (*n*), foundation

62 **fúnditor, -ōris** (*m*), slinger

59 **fūnéstō** (1), to pollute with murder

62 **fúngor, -gī** (3), **-ctus sum** (+ *abl.*), to perform, discharge

fūnus, -eris (*n*), funeral

fūr, -ris (*m*), thief

59 **fúria, -ae** (*f*), frenzy, madness

65 **fūrtum, -ī** (*n*), theft, fraud

fūstis, -is (*m*), club, stick

G

55 **gallīnāceus, -a, -um,** belonging to domestic poultry

55 **gallus gallīnāceus,** poultry-cock, barnyard rooster

68 **gárrulus, -a, -um,** talkative, prattling

gaúdeō, -ēre (2), **gavīsus sum,** to rejoice, enjoy oneself

gaúdium, -ī (*n*), joy

54 **gémitus, -ūs** (*m*), groan

57 **géner, -rī** (*m*), son-in-law

gēns, -tis (*f*), family, clan, nation

génus, -eris (*n*), kind, race

gérō, -rere (3), **-ssī, -stum,** to wear, carry on, lead (a life)

66 **gestātiō, -ōnis** (*f*), a place for riding, promenade

gladiātor, -ōris (*m*), gladiator

gládius, -ī (*m*), sword

61 **glāns, -ndis** (*f*), acorn, acorn-shaped missile shot from a sling

glōria, -ae (*f*), fame, glory

grándis, -is, -e, grown, mature, large

68 **grándis nātū,** advanced in years, elderly

57 **grātiā** (+ *gen.*), for the sake of

grā́tia, -iae (*f*), favor, kindness, gratitude
grā́tiās ágere (+ *dat.*), to thank
gráviter, seriously
63 **gubernā́culum, -ī** (*n*), rudder, helm
61 **gubernā́tor, -ṓris** (*m*), helmsman
57 **gubérnō** (1), to govern, rule
56 **gústō** (1), to taste
56 **gypsā́tus, -a, -um,** sealed with gypsum (plaster of Paris)

H

hábeō (2), to have, hold
60 **hábet sē rēs,** the situation is, things are
hábitō (1), to live, dwell
64 **haésitō** (1), to hesitate, be undecided
66 **hā́mus, -ī** (*m*), hook
56 **hḗrēs, -ḗdis** (*m*), heir
héri, yesterday
65 **hetaéria, -ae** (*f*), political club or association
54 **Heu!** Alas! Ah me!
hic, haec, hoc, this
hīc (*adverb*), here
59 **hícine = hic + -ne**
67 **híems, -mis** (*f*), winter
hílaris, -is, -e, cheerful
66 **hinc,** from here, over here
hódiē, today
66 **hólus, -eris** (*n*), vegetables
hómō, -inis (*m*), man, fellow
61 **honéstus, -a, -um,** respected, best
60 **honéstē,** respectably, honorably
68 **hónor, -ṓris** (*m*), honor, (political) office
64 **honōrā́rium, -ī** (*n*), admission fee
68 **honṓrō** (1), to honor
hṓra, -ae (*f*), hour
56 **hōrológium, -ī** (*n*), clock, sundial
68 **hórreō** (2), to tremble at, dread
54 **horríbilis, -is, -e,** horrible
hórtor, -ā́rī (1), **-ā́tus sum,** to encourage, urge
hórtus, -ī (*m*), garden
hóstis, -is (*m*), enemy
hūc, here, to here
65 **hūmā́nitās, -ā́tis** (*f*), humanity, human kindness
hūmā́nus, -a, -um, human

I

iáceō (2), to lie, be lying down, be at rest, be idle
iáciō, -ere (3), **iḗcī, -tum,** to throw
iáctō (1), to toss
iam, now, already
íbi, there
64 **idcírcō,** for that reason
ī́dem, éadem, ídem, the same
idéntidem, again and again, repeatedly
56 **ídeō,** for this reason, therefore
56 **idṓneus, -a, -um,** suitable, appropriate
54 **iēiū́nium, -ī** (*n*), a fast, fast-day
ígitur, therefore
68 **ignā́rus, -a, -um,** ignorant of, not knowing
58 **ígnis, -is** (*m*), fire
60 **ignṓscō, -ṓscere** (3), **-ṓvī, -ṓtum** (+ *dat.*), to forgive, excuse
67 **ignṓtus, -a, -um,** unknown
67 **īlicḗtum, -ī** (*n*), oak-grove
ílle, ílla, íllud, that, he, she, it
66 **íllīc,** in that place, there
66 **íllinc,** from there, over there
imā́gō, -inis (*f*), likeness, image, mental picture
ímmemor, -ris (+ *gen.*), forgetful
ímmō, rather, on the contrary
ímmō vḗrō, on the contrary, in fact
65 **immódicus, -a, -um,** excessive
immortā́lis, -is, -e, immortal
63 **immū́nitās, -ā́tis** (*f*), immunity, exemption
62 **impedīméntum, -ī** (*n*), baggage
impédiō (4), to hinder, prevent, obstruct
55 **impéndō, -dere** (3), **-dī, -sum,** to spend, pay out
60 **imperā́tor, -ṓris** (*m*), commander, general, emperor
58 **imperī́tus, -a, -um,** ignorant, unskilled
63 **impérium, -ī** (*n*), power, supreme authority, empire
ímperō (1) (+ *dat.*), to order, command
65 **ímpetrō** (1), to obtain, secure by entreaty
ímpetus, -ūs (*m*), attack
56 **ímpleō, -ḗre** (2), **-ḗvī, -ḗtum,** to fill
impṓnō, -ṓnere (3), **-ósuī, -situm,** to place on, set on
67 **ímprobus, -a, -um,** bad, vile, shameless
61 **(dē) imprōvī́sō,** unexpectedly
61 **imprū́dens, -ntis,** ignorant, not expecting, not foreseeing
in (+ *abl.*), in, on, among
in (+ *acc.*), into, towards, until, against
67 **inā́nis, -is, -e,** empty, worthless, pointless
incéndō, -dere (3), **-dī, -sum,** to burn, set on fire
íncidō, -ere (3), **-ī, incā́sum,** to fall into, occur, turn up
62 **incitā́tus, -a, -um,** fast-moving, rapid
68 **incrēdíbilis, -is, -e,** incredible
índe, from there, then, in consequence of that

65 **índex, -icis** (*m*), spy, informer

63 **indiscrétus, -a, -um,** without prejudice or social distinction

56 **indulgéntia, -ae** (*f*), indulgence, kindness

68 **indústria, -ae** (*f*), industry, diligence

62 **indústriē,** with energy

íneō, -íre (*irreg.*), **-iī, -itum,** to go in, enter

67 **inéptus, -a, -um,** silly, foolish

61 **inérmis, -is, -e,** unarmed

59 **īnfélīx, -ícis,** unhappy, unfortunate

58 **ínferō, -re** (*irreg.*), **íntulī, illátum,** to bring in, carry in, inflict on

57 **īnféstus, -a, -um,** hostile

63 **īnféctus, -a, -um,** not done, undone

58 **ínfimus, -a, -um,** lowest, most vile

59 **īnflámmō** (1), to kindle, set aflame

66 **īnfléctō, -ctere** (3), **-xī, -xum,** to bend, curve

65 **īnflexíbilis, -is, -e,** inflexible, stubborn

68 **īnfructuṓsus, -a, um,** fruitless

61 **ínfula, -ae** (*f*), wool headband worn by suppliants

56 **ingemḗscō, -ḗscere** (3), **-uī,** to (begin to) groan

íngēns, -ntis, huge, big, long

59 **ingrátus, -a, -um,** ungrateful

iníciō, -ícere (3), **-iḗcī, -iéctum,** to throw in or on

57 **inimīcítia, -ae** (*f*), hostility

63 **iníquitās, -átis** (*f*), injustice, unfairness

59 **inítium, -ī** (*n*), beginning

64 **iniū́ria, -ae** (*f*), injury, injustice, wrong

63 **iniū́stus, -a, -um,** unjust, improper

65 **innóxius, -a, -um,** innocuous, harmless

ínquit, he (she) says, said

63 **īnsániō** (4), to act crazy

56 **īnscríptiō, -ṓnis** (*f*), inscription

59 **īnsepúltus, -a, -um,** unburied

58 **īnsídiae, -árum** (*f pl*), ambush

61 **īnsígne, -is** (*n*), badge, token, insignia

īnspíciō, -ícere (3), **-éxī, -éctum,** to examine, look at

66 **ínstitor, -ṓris** (*m*), shopkeeper

īnstítuō, -úere (3), **-uī, -ū́tum,** to establish, set up, organize

62 **ínstō, -áre** (1), **-itī,** to pursue eagerly, be at hand, be impending

68 **intáctus, -a, -um,** untouched, unused

62 **ínteger, -gra, -grum,** whole, fresh

intéllegō, -gere (3), **-xī, -ctum,** to understand, realize

ínter (+ *acc.*), between, among

63 **intercḗdō, -dere** (3), **-ssī, -ssum,** to intervene, oppose

60 **interclū́dō, -dere** (3), **-sī, -sum,** to shut off

intérdiū, during the day, by day

62 **interfíciō, -fícere** (3), **-fḗcī, -féctum,** to kill

54 **ínterim,** meanwhile

57 **intérrēx, -ḗgis** (*m*), temporary chief magistrate

intérrogō (1), to ask, question, interrogate

67 **intérsum, -ésse** (*irreg.*), **-fuī** (+ *dat.*), to be present, attend

55 **intestína, -ṓrum** (*n pl*), intestines

íntrā (+ *acc.*), inside, within

intróeō, -íre (*irreg.*), **-iī, -itum,** to enter, go into

64 **intróitus, -ūs** (*m*), entrance, admission

55 **intrōvérsus** (*adverb*), indoors

63 **inūsitátus, -a, -um,** unusual

64 **inū́tilis, -is, -e,** useless, undesirable

58 **ínvehō, -here** (3), **-xī, -ctum,** to speak out against, attack with words

invéniō, -eníre (4), **-ḗnī, -éntum,** to come upon, find

65 **ínvicem,** back and forth, in turn, responsively

58 **invídia, -ae** (*f*), anger, hatred

63 **invísō, -ere** (3), **-ī, -um,** to go to see, inspect

55 **ínvolō** (1), to fly at, attack, carry off

54 **invólvō, -vere** (3), **-vī, -ū́tum,** to wrap in, wrap up

ípse, ípsa, ípsum, himself, herself, itself

54 **ípsimus, -ī** (*m*), master of a household

íra, -ae (*f*), anger

īrátus, -a, -um, angry

is, éa, id, he, she, it, this, that

54 **íste, -a, -ud,** this, that (of yours) (often disparaging)

60 **ístīc,** there (where you are)

íta, thus, in this way

ítaque, and so, therefore

58 **ítem,** likewise, also

íter, -íneris (*n*), journey, road

íterum, again, a second time

iúbeō, -bḗre (2), **-ssī, -ssum,** to order

68 **iucúnditās, -átis** (*f*), pleasantness, charm

iucúndus, -a, -um, pleasant, enjoyable

59 **iū́dex, -icis** (*m*), judge, juror

61 **iūméntum, -ī** (*n*), work animal

iúngō, -gere (3), **-xī, -ctum,** to join, attach

58 **iūs, -iū́ris** (*n*), law, right

62 **iússum, -ī** (*n*), command, bidding

61 **iūstítia, -ae** (*f*), justice

61 **iū́stus, -a, -um,** just, legitimate

61 **iuvéntūs, -ū́tis** (*f*), youth, young men (of military age)

63 **iúvō, -áre** (1), **iū́vī, iū́tum,** to delight, please, help

L

lábor, -ṓris (*m*), work, toil
labṓrō (1), to work, toil, suffer, be in distress
68 **lábrum, -ī** (*n*), lip
56 **lāc, láctis** (*n*), milk
66 **lácus, -ūs** (*m*), lake
laédō, -dere (3), **-sī, -sum,** to harm, injure
66 **lagṓna, -ae** (*f*), bottle
56 **lāmentā́tiō, -ṓnis** (*f*), lamentation, weeping
54 **lānā́tus, -a, -um,** covered with wool
lanísta, -ae (*m*) trainer (of gladiators)
55 **lanistícius, -a, -um,** owned and managed by a **lanista**
lánius, -ī (*m*), butcher
lápis, -idis (*m*), stone
56 **lárgiter,** abundantly, in abundance, (+ *gen.*) plenty (of)
57 **largī́tiō, -ṓnis** (*f*), bribery, bribe
62 **lassitū́dō, -inis** (*f*), exhaustion, weariness
láteō (2), to lie in hiding, hide
61 **laterícius, -a, -um,** made of brick
56 **lāticlā́vius, -a, -um,** fit for a senator, princely
65 **latrōcínium, -ī** (*n*), robbery
63 **lā́tus, -a, -um,** wide, broad
62 **látus, -eris** (*n*), side, flank
laúdō (1), to praise
lávō, -ā́re (1), **lā́vī, -ā́tum** or **lṓtum,** to wash
lectī́ca, -ae (*f*), litter
66 **léctulus, -ī** (*m*), bed
léctus, -ī (*m*), bed, couch
61 **lēgā́tus, -ī** (*m*), second in command
60 **légiō, -ṓnis** (*f*), legion, military unit
64 **lēgítimus, -a, -um,** legal, lawful, prescribed
56 **légō, -ere** (3), **lḗgī, lḗctum,** to read, choose
léō, -ṓnis (*m*), lion
lépus, -oris (*m*), rabbit
66 **léviter,** lightly, slightly
57 **lēx, lḗgis** (*f*), law
65 **libéllus, -ī** (*m*), notice, poster
libénter, gladly
56 **lī́ber, -era, -erum,** free, belonging to freedom
lī́berī, -ṓrum (*m pl*), children
lī́berō (1), to set free
64 **lībértās, -ā́tis** (*f*), liberty, freedom
lībértus, -ī (*m*), freedman
63 **líbet, -ḗre** (2), **-uit** (+ *dat.*), it is pleasing, agreeable
58 **librā́rius, -ī** (*m*), copier, secretary
lícet, -ḗre (2), **-uit** (+ *dat.*), it is allowed
lī́men, -inis (*n*), threshold, doorway
66 **lī́mes, -itis** (*m*), path, line
língua, -ae (*f*), tongue, speech
66 **líppus, -a, -um,** bleary-eyed
67 **līs, lī́tis** (*f*), quarrel, dispute
líttera, -ae (*f*), letter (of the alphabet)
lítterae, -ā́rum (*f pl*), letter, epistle, literature
lī́tus, -oris (*n*), shore
55 **lī́vidus, -a, -um,** black and blue (as by bruising)
lócus, -ī (*m*; *n* in *pl*), place
lóngus, -a, -um, long, tall
lóngē, far
66 **lóquāx, -ā́cis,** talkative
lóquor, -ī (3), **locū́tus sum,** to speak, talk
55 **lṓripēs, -edis,** clubfooted
lū́cet, -ḗre (2), **lū́xit,** to be light, to be day, to shine
lucérna, -ae (*f*), lamp
59 **lūctuṓsus, -a, -um,** distressing, heartbreaking
58 **lū́ctus, -ūs** (*m*), mourning, grief
lū́dō, -dere (3), **-sī, -sum,** to play, have fun
lū́dus, ī (*m*), game, school
58 **lū́geō, -ḗre** (2), **lū́xī, lū́ctum,** to grieve, mourn, lament
59 **lúō, -ere** (3), to pay, suffer, atone for
poénās lúere, to pay the price, suffer punishment
66 **lū́strum, -ī** (*n*), a five-year period
58 **lútō** (1), to cover with mud, make dirty
lútum, -ī (*n*), mud
lūx, lū́cis (*f*), light, daylight, dawn
62 **luxū́ria, -ae** (*f*), luxury
66 **lýmpha, -ae** (*f*), water
67 **lyrístēs, -ae** (*m*), lyre-player

M

67 **mádēns, -ntis,** wet, moist
68 **maéstus, -a, -um,** sad
mágis, more, rather
magistrā́tus, -ūs (*m*), magistrate, magistracy
59 **magnitū́dō, -inis** (*f*), magnitude, size
magnópere, greatly
mágnus, -a, -um, great, big, large, loud (voice)
maíor, -ṓris, greater, bigger
58 **maledíctum, -ī** (*n*), insult, taunt
66 **malleā́tor, -ṓris** (*m*), hammerer, beater
mā́lō, -lle (*irreg.*), **-luī,** to prefer
málus, -a, -um, bad, evil
mále (*adverb*), badly
mandā́tum, -ī (*n*), order, instruction

mā́ne, early in the day, in the morning
máneō, -ḗre (2), **-sī, -sum**, to remain, stay
65 **maniféstus, -a, -um**, clear, evident
55 **manucíolum, -ī** (*n*), handful, small bundle
56 **manūmíttō, -míttere** (3), **-mī́sī, -míssum**, to manumit, set (a slave) free
mánus, -ūs (*f*), hand, band (of men)
66 **márculus, -ī** (*m*), small hammer, mallet
máre, -is (*n*), sea
54 **margarī́tum, -ī** (*n*), pearl
62 **marítimus, -a, -um**, belonging to the sea, maritime
marī́tus, -ī (*m*), husband
66 **mássa, -ae** (*f*), mass, heap
55 **matélla, -ae** (*f*), vessel, chamber pot
mā́ter, -tris (*f*), mother
61 **mātéria, -ae** (*f*), timber, matter
54 **māxílla, -ae** (*f*), jaw
máximus, -a, -um, very great, greatest, very large
médius, -a, -um, mid-, middle of
Mehércule! or **Mehérculēs!** By Hercules! Indeed!
mélior, meliṓris, better
54 **méminī, -isse** (perfect with present meaning) (+ *gen.* or *acc.*), to remember
61 **mémor, -oris** (+ *gen.*), remembering, mindful of
memória, -ae (*f*), memory
54 **mēns, -tis** (*f*), mind, heart, reason, sanity
mḗnsa, -ae (*f*), table
mḗnsis, -is (*m*), month
54 **méntior, -ī́rī** (4), **-ī́tus sum**, to lie
60 **méreō** (2) (sometimes deponent), to deserve, earn
67 **merīdiā́nus, -a, -um**, of noon, midday
63 **méritō**, deservedly
55 **mérus, -a, -um**, pure, undiluted, nothing but
66 **merx, -cis** (*f*), merchandise, goods
60 **métuō, -ere** (3), **-ī, metū́tum**, to fear, be afraid of
métus, -ūs (*m*), fear
méus, -a, -um, my, mine
mícō, -ā́re (1), **-uī**, to move quickly to and fro, flash; to play morra
mī́les, -itis (*m*), soldier
62 **mīlitā́ris, -is, -e**, military
mī́lle, a thousand
55 **mílvus, -ī** (*m*), kite (a bird of prey)
59 **mínimē**, least, not at all, by no means, no
64 **miníster, -trī** (*m*), subordinate official, attendant
64 **ministérium, -ī** (*n*), service, employment
65 **minístra, -ae** (*f*), attendant
58 **minitābúndus, -a, -um**, menacing
65 **mínor, -ā́rī** (1), **-ā́tus sum**, to threaten
mínor, -ṓris, smaller
54 **minū́tus, -a, -um**, small, little
mī́rus, -a, -um, wonderful, marvelous, strange
55 **miscix** (spelling and meaning uncertain), mixed, diluted, wishy-washy
54 **misellus, -a, -um** (diminutive of **míser**), poor little
míser, -era, -erum, unhappy, miserable, wretched
54 **miséreor, -ḗrī** (2), **-itus sum** (+ *gen.*), to pity, take pity on
63 **míseret (mē)** (impersonal + *gen.*), I pity
68 **miséria, -ae** (*f*), affliction, trouble
míttō, -ere (3), **mī́sī, míssum**, to send, let go
61 **mōbílitās, -ā́tis** (*f*), quickness, mobility, maneuverability
63 **moderā́tiō, -ṓnis** (*f*), moderation, restraint
60 **modéstē**, with restraint, under control
módo, only, only recently, just now
59 **nōn módo . . . sed étiam**, not only . . . but also
55 **módo . . . módo**, now . . . now, sometimes . . . sometimes
módus, -ī (*m*), way, method
64 **eiúsmodī**, of this kind, this sort of
60 **nū́llō módō**, in no way, not at all
66 **móllis, -is, -e**, soft, gentle
61 **mōméntum, -ī** (*n*), a short period of time, a (short) distance
móneō (2), to advise, warn
mōns, -tis (*m*), mountain, hill
monuméntum, -ī (*n*), monument, tomb, reminder, token
54 **mórdeō, -dḗre** (2), **momórdī, -sum**, to bite
mórior, -ī (3), **-tuus sum**, to die
móror, -ā́rī (1), **-ā́tus sum**, to delay, remain, stay
mors, -tis (*f*), death
63 **mortā́lis, -is, -e**, mortal, human
mórtuus, -a, -um, dead
mōs, mṓris (*m*), custom, (*pl*) habits, ways, character (of a person)
68 **mṓtor, -ṓris** (*m*), one who moves, shakes, rocks
móveō, -ḗre (2), **mṓvī, mṓtum**, to move, remove, shake
mox, soon, presently
múlier, -eris (*f*), woman
multitū́dō, -inis (*f*), crowd, mob
múltus, -a, -um, much, (*pl*) many
múltum (*adverb*), much, greatly, very

63 **múndus, -ī** (*m*), world, universe
58 **mūnicípium, -ī** (*n*), town
64 **mūnítiō, -ṓnis** (*f*), construction, repair
mū́nus, -eris (*n*), duty, gift, (gladiatorial) show
mū́rus, -ī (*m*), wall
mūs, mū́ris (*m*), mouse
61 **mū́sculus, -ī** (*m*), covered gallery used in siege warfare

N

nam, for
61 **nancī́scor, -ī** (3), **náctus sum,** to gain possession of, acquire, get
55 **nánnus, -ī** (*m*), dwarf
nā́rrō (1), to tell (a story)
nā́scor, -ī (3), **nā́tus sum,** to be born
nátō (1), to swim
nātū́ra, -ae (*f*), nature
56 **naúfragō** (1), to be wrecked
66 **naúfragus, -ī** (*m*), a shipwrecked person
61 **naúta, -ae** (*m*), sailor
66 **nāvícula, -ae** (*f*), small ship, boat
nā́vigō (1), to sail
56 **nā́vis, -is** (*f*), ship
-ne, (indicates a question)
nē (+ *subjunctive*), in order to prevent, not to
nec, and . . . not
  nec . . . nec . . . , neither . . . nor
64 **necessā́riō** (*adverb*), necessarily, unavoidably
62 **necessā́rius, -a, -um,** necessary
necésse, necessary
67 **necéssitās, -ā́tis** (*f*), necessity, necessary duty, obligation
68 **necessitū́dō, -inis** (*f*), (personal) connection, relative
nécō (1), to kill
59 **négō** (1), to say that . . . not, deny, refuse, decline
56 **negōtiā́tiō, -ṓnis** (*f*), business
56 **negṓtior, -ā́rī** (1), **-ā́tus sum,** to do business, be a businessman
nḗmō, -inis (*m*), no one
66 **némus, -oris** (*n*), wooded pasture, grove
neque, and . . . not
55 **nérvia, -ṓrum** (*n pl*), sinews, tendons
nésciō (4), to be ignorant, not know
54 **nésciō quid,** something or other
níger, -gra, -grum, black
68 **nigréscō, -ḗscere** (3), **-uī,** to grow black
níhil, nothing
nímis, too much, too
62 **nímius, -a, -um,** excessive, too much
nísi, unless, if . . . not, except
66 **nítēns, -ntis,** shining, glittering
63 **nōbíliter,** with distinction, splendidly
nóceō (2) (+ *dat.*), to harm
noctúrnus, -a, -um, occurring at night
55 **noctúrnae, -ā́rum** (*f pl*), Nocturnal Ones, witches
nṓlō, -lle, -luī, to be unwilling, not wish, refuse
nṓmen, -inis (*n*), name
61 **nōminā́tim** (*adverb*), by name
nṓminō (1), to name, mention by name, speak of
nōn, not
nṓndum, not yet
nṓnus, -a, -um, ninth
nōs, we, us
nóster, -tra, -trum, our
nṓtus, -a, -um, known, well-known
66 **novā́cula, -ae** (*f*), razor
nox, -ctis (*f*), night
67 **nóxius, -a, -um,** harmful, dangerous, rapacious
nū́bō, -bere (3), **-psī, -ptum** (+ *dat.*), to marry
54 **nū́dus, -a, -um,** naked, bare
56 **nū́gae, -ā́rum** (*f pl*), trifles, jokes
nū́llus, -a, -um, no, none
Num . . . ? Surely . . . not . . . ? (introduces a question that expects the answer "no")
65 **nū́men, -inis** (*n*), divine power, divinity, god
númerō (1), to count
númerus, -ī (*m*), number
66 **nummulā́rius, -ī** (*m*), money-changer
54 **númmus, -ī** (*m*) (*irreg. gen. pl.* **númmūm**), coin, money
númquam, never
nunc, now
nū́per, recently
67 **nū́ptiae, -ā́rum** (*f pl*), wedding
63 **nū́tus, -ūs** (*m*), nod, divine will

O

54 **Ō!** Oh! (expressing a wish)
63 **ob** (+ *acc.*), because of, on account of
63 **óbeō, -īre** (*irreg.*), **-iī, -itum,** to meet (death), die
62 **obíciō, -ícere** (3), **-iḗcī, -iéctum,** to throw in one's face, taunt
56 **oblīvī́scor, -vī́scī** (3), **-tus sum** (+ *gen.*), to forget
58 **obscḗnus, -a, -um,** obscene
óbsecrō (1), to beseech, beg
obsérvō (1), to watch, pay attention to, comply with

65 **obstinā́tiō, -ṓnis** (*f*), obstinacy, stubbornness

59 **óbstō, -ā́re** (1), **-itī** (+ *dat.*), to stand against, oppose

65 **obstríngō, -ngere** (3), **-nxī, -ctum,** to bind up, tie to

68 **obvérsor, -ā́rī** (1), **-ā́tus sum,** to appear before (in thought or imagination)

67 **occā́siō, -ṓnis** (*f*), opportunity

occī́dō, -dere (3), **-dī, -sum,** to kill

óccupō (1), to seize, occupy, take over

occúrrō, -rrere (3), **-rrī, -rsum** (+ *dat.*), to meet

54 **óculus, -ī** (*m*), eye

64 **ódor, odṓris** (*m*), scent, odor

offícium, -ī (*n*), duty, job

67 **ṓlla, -ae** (*f*), pot

ómnis, -is, -e, all, the whole, every, each

56 **ónerō** (1), to load

57 **ópera, -ae** (*f*), effort, work, (political) henchman, ruffian

57 **óperam dáre,** to give attention to, work hard

opériō, -īre (4), **-uī, -tum,** to hide, cover

opórtet, -ḗre (2), **-uit** (+ *infin.*), it is proper, right, one must

óppidum, -ī (*n*), town

ópprimō, -ímere (3), **-éssī, -éssum,** to overwhelm

61 **oppugnā́tiō, -ṓnis** (*f*), attack, assault

62 **oppúgnō** (1), to attack, assault

60 **óps, ópis** (*f*), aid, help

57 **optimā́tēs, -ā́tium** (*m pl*), the "best men," the senatorial party at Rome

óptimus, -a, -um, best, very good, excellent

óptimē, best, very well, very carefully

óptō (1), to wish

ópus, -eris (*n*), work, effort, (penal) labor

57 **ópus est,** it is necessary, there is need of

58 **ōrā́tiō, -ṓnis** (*f*), speech, oration

ōrā́tor, -ṓris (*m*), orator, speaker

63 **órbis, -is** (*m*), circle

63 **órbis terrā́rum,** the world

68 **órbus, -a, -um,** bereaved

59 **ṓrdō, -inis** (*m*), order, rank, class

órior, -ī́rī (4), **-tus sum,** to rise, arise, begin

ṓrō (1), to beg, entreat

ōs, -ṓris (*n*), mouth, face, expression

os, óssis (*n*), bone

osténdō, -dere (3), **-dī, -tum,** to show, point out

54 **ṓstium, -ī** (*n*), door

64 **ōtiṓsus, -a, -um,** at leisure, idle, free from public duty, not working

67 **ṓtium, -ī** (*n*), leisure

P

paedagṓgus, -ī (*m*), tutor

paéne, almost

65 **paeniténtia, -ae** (*f*), regret, repentance

63 **paénitet, -ḗre** (2), **-uit,** it causes one (*acc.*) to regret something (*gen.*), one regrets

57 **pálam,** openly, publicly

60 **pálma, -ae** (*f*), palm branch of victory

66 **pálmes, -itis** (*m*), vine-branch, vine

62 **palūdāméntum, -ī** (*n*), cloak worn by high-ranking military officers

66 **pálux, -ucis** (*f*), gold dust

pā́nis, -is (*m*), bread, food

54 **pánnus, -ī** (*m*), cloth, rag, garment

57 **pār, páris,** equal

párcō, -cere (3), **pepércī** (+ *dat.*), to spare

párēns, -ntis (*m/f*), parent, father, mother

pā́reō (2) (+ *dat.*), to obey

55 **páriō, -ere** (3), **péperī, -tum,** to bear, give birth to

pars, -tis (*f*), part, (political) party

67 **párvulus, -a, -um,** small, little, baby

párvus, -a, -um, small

pā́scō, -cere (3), **pā́vī, pā́stum,** to feed

54 **pássus, -a, -um,** dishevelled

páter, -tris (*m*), father

pátior, -tī (3), **-ssus sum,** to suffer, endure, permit

62 **pátiēns, -ntis,** (long-)suffering, patient

55 **pátria, -ae** (*f*), native land, home-town, town

57 **patrícius, -ī** (*m*), patrician, aristocrat

54 **patrimṓnium, -ī** (*n*), patrimony

66 **pátrius, -a, -um,** belonging to a father, father's

patrṓnus, -ī (*m*), patron, former master of a freed slave

paúcī, -ae, -a, few

59 **paucíssimī, -ae, -a,** a very few

paulā́tim, gradually, little by little

58 **paúlō,** (by) a little

paúper, -eris, poor

68 **páveō, -ḗre** (2), **pávī,** to be frightened or terrified at

pāx, pā́cis (*f*), peace

pecū́nia, -ae (*f*), money

peíor, -ṓris, worse

68 **penā́tēs, -ium** (*m pl*), household gods, home

68 **pénes** (+ *acc.*), in the possession of

65 **péragō, -ágere** (3), **-ḗgī, -ā́ctum,** to carry through, complete

55 **pérdō, -ere** (3), **-idī, -itum,** to destroy, lose

56 **perdū́co, -cere** (3), **-xī, -ctum,** to lead to, bring to

55 **péreō, -ī́re** (*irreg.*), **-iī, -itum,** to perish, die
pérferō, -rre (*irreg.*), **pértulī, perlā́tum,** to bring to (a destination), deliver, report
61 **perfíciō, -ícere** (3), **-ḗcī, -éctum,** to complete, finish
62 **pérfruor, -ī** (3), **-ū́ctus sum,** to enjoy
62 **perfúngor, -gī** (3), **-ctus sum,** to perform (a task), finish
67 **pergrā́tus, -a, -um,** very pleasing, very popular
perīculṓsus, -a, -um, dangerous
perī́culum, -ī (*n*), danger
68 **permíttō, -íttere** (3), **-ī́sī, -íssum,** to permit, allow
67 **permū́tō** (1), to change, modify
58 **perṓrō** (1), to complete a speech
58 **perpétuus, -a, -um,** continuous, complete, entire
54 **pérsequor, -quī** (3), **-cū́tus sum,** to pursue, chase
54 **persevḗrō** (1), to persevere, continue, persist, last
persuā́deō, -dḗre (2), **-sī, -sum** (+ *dat.*), to persuade
62 **pertérreō, -ḗre** (2), **-uī, -itum,** to frighten, terrify
65 **pertinā́cia, -ae** (*f*), stubbornness
54 **pertíneō, -ḗre** (2), **-uī,** to pertain to, relate to, reach to, lie near
pervéniō, -enī́re (4), **-ḗnī, -éntum,** to come through to, arrive at, reach
pēs, pédis (*m*), foot
péssimus, -a, -um, worst, very bad
59 **péstis, -is** (*f*), plague, disease
péto, -ere (3), **-ī́vī, -ī́tum,** to seek, aim at, attack
56 **philósophus, -ī** (*m*), philosopher
63 **píetās, -ā́tis** (*f*), devotion (to duty)
67 **píger, -gra, -grum,** lazy, indolent
66 **pī́la, -ae** (*f*), pillar, column
54 **pílō** (1), to remove the hair from
54 **pílus, -ī** (*m*), a hair
56 **píngō, -ngere** (3), **-nxī, -ctum,** to paint, depict
54 **píper, -ris** (*n*), pepper
pīrā́ta, -ae (*m*), pirate
66 **píscor, -ā́rī** (1), **-ā́tus sum,** to fish
pístor, -ṓris (*m*), miller, baker
56 **píus, -a, -um,** devoted to duty, loyal
pláceō, -ḗre (2), **-uī** (+ *dat.*), to please
63 **plácidus, -a, -um,** kindly, indulgent, calm
54 **plā́nē,** wholly, absolutely, nothing but
54 **plángō, -gere** (3), **-xī, -ctum,** to beat, strike, mourn for
55 **plaúdō, -dere** (3), **-sī, -sum,** to applaud, clap the hands
57 **plēbs, -ḗbis** (*f*), plebeians, common people
plḗnus, -a, -um, full
62 **plērúsque, -aque, -úmque,** most of, (*pl.*) very many
56 **plṓrō** (1), to weep
plúit, -úere (3), **plúit,** it is raining
plū́rimus, -a, -um, most, very much
plūs, plū́ris, more
55 **plússcius, -a, -um,** knowing more than others, skilled (in witchcraft)
poéna, -ae (*f*), punishment, penalty
poḗta, -ae (*m*), poet
56 **pṓmum, -ī** (*n*), fruit, fruit tree
68 **póndus, -eris** (*n*), weight, quantity
pṓnō, pṓnere (3), **pósuī, pósitum,** to put, place
pōns, -ntis (*m*), bridge
popī́na, -ae (*f*), eating house, bar, cookshop
pópulus, -ī (*m*), people
pórcus, -ī (*m*), pig
54 **pórrō,** then, furthermore
pórta, -ae (*f*), gate
59 **pórtus, -ūs** (*m*), harbor, haven
64 **posséssiō, -ṓnis** (*f*), possession
66 **possídeō, -idḗre** (2), **-ḗdī, -éssum,** to take possession of
póssum, pósse (*irreg.*), **pótuī,** to be able
post (+ *acc.*), after
pósteā, afterwards
pósterus, -a, -um, next, following
póstquam, after
postrḗmō, finally
postrḗmus, -a, -um, last
60 **potéstās, -ā́tis** (*f*), power, opportunity
62 **pótior, -ī́rī** (4), **-ī́tus sum** (+ *abl.*), to get possession of, obtain
pótius, rather, more (than)
61 **praecéptum, -ī** (*n*), command
55 **praecī́dō, -dere** (3), **-dī, -sum,** to cut off, cut through
66 **praecíngō, -gere** (3), **-xī, -ctum,** to gird, wrap around
praecípiō, -ípere (3), **-ḗpī, -éptum** (+ *dat.*), to instruct, order
praecipitā́re (sē), to hurl oneself, rush
praeclā́rus, -a, -um, distinguished, famous
60 **praédium, -ī** (*n*), landed property, estate
praédō, -ṓnis (*m*), robber
65 **praéeō, -ī́re** (*irreg.*), **-iī, -itum,** to go before, lead the way
praéferō, -férre (*irreg.*), **-tulī, -lā́tum,** to carry in front, give precedence to, prefer
62 **praefíciō, -ícere, -ḗcī, -éctum** (+ *dat.*), to put in charge of

61 **praefríngō, -íngere** (3), **-ḗgī, -áctum,** to break off in front
60 **praemíttō, -íttere** (3), **ī́sī, -íssum,** to send ahead
60 **praeséntia, -ae** (*f*), presence
62 **praesídium, -ī** (*n*), defense, protection
62 **praésum, -ésse** (*irreg.*), **-fuī** (+ *dat.*), to be in charge of
praetéreā, besides, moreover
praetéreō, -ī́re (*irreg.*), **-iī, -itum,** to go past
65 **in praetéritum,** in the past, formerly
praetextā́tus, -a, -um, wearing the **tóga praetéxta**
praétor, -ṓris (*m*), praetor
57 **praetū́ra, -ae** (*f*), praetorship, office of praetor
66 **prā́tum, -ī** (*n*), meadow, grass
65 **prā́vus, -a, -um,** depraved, perverse
63 **précor, -ā́rī** (1), **-ā́tus sum,** to pray, beg, request
68 **prex, -écis** (*f*), prayer, request
56 **prī́mus, -a, -um,** first
60 **in prī́mīs,** in particular
prī́mō, at first, first
prīmum (*adverb*), first, at first
quam prī́mum, as soon as possible
67 **ut prī́mum,** when first, as soon as
prī́nceps, -cipis (*m*), emperor, leader, leading citizen
60 **prístinus, -a, -um,** previous, former
63 **prīvā́tim,** privately, in private
59 **(in) prīvā́tō,** in private, privately
57 **prō** (+ *abl.*), in front of, before, on behalf of, for, in place of, equivalent to
57 **prō cṓnsule,** proconsul
64 **próbus, -a, -um,** honest, upright
64 **prōcṓnsul, -lis** (*m*), proconsul
61 **prōcúmbo, -mbere** (3), **-buī, -bitum,** to keel over
54 **prōcúrrō, -cúrrere** (3), **-cucúrrī, -cúrsum,** to run forth, rush out
57 **prṓdō, -ere** (3), **-idī, -itum,** to give rise to, produce, appoint
61 **proélium, -ī** (*n*), battle
59 **prōfíciō, -ícere** (3), **-ḗcī, -éctum,** to accomplish, gain
proficī́scor, -icī́scī (3), **-éctus sum,** to set out
57 **prōfúndō, -úndere** (3), **-ū́dī, -ū́sum,** to pour forth
65 **prohíbeō** (2), to prohibit, forbid, prevent
55 **prōíciō, -ícere** (3), **-iḗcī, -iéctum,** to throw forward or headlong
67 **proínde,** therefore
65 **prōmíscuus, -a, -um,** common, ordinary
60 **própérō** (1), to hurry, hasten
propínquus, -ī (*m*), relative
66 **própius** (*adverb*), nearer
65 **prōpṓnō, -ṓnere** (3), **-ósuī, -ósitum,** to put forth
própter (+ *acc.*), on account of
58 **prósperus, -a, -um,** prosperous, successful, favorable
61 **prōspíciō, -ícere** (3), **-éxī, -éctum,** to see before one, to look out over
60 **prṓsum, -désse** (*irreg.*), **-fuī** (+ *dat.*), to be useful, benefit, help
62 **prṓtinus,** immediately
61 **prōvídeō, -idḗre** (2), **-ī́dī, -ī́sum,** to foresee, expect
61 **prōvíncia, -ae** (*f*), province
58 **próximus, -a, -um,** nearest, next
56 **pū́blicō** (1), to publish, make public
pū́blicus, -a, -um, public
in pū́blicō, in public, publicly
63 **púdet, -ḗre** (2), **-itum,** it makes one (*acc.*) ashamed of something (*gen.*), one is ashamed
puélla, -ae (*f*), girl, girlfriend
púer, -erī (*m*), boy
púgna, -ae (*f*), battle, fight
púgnō (1), to fight
púlcher, -chra, -chrum, beautiful, handsome
pulchritū́dō, -inis (*f*), beauty
68 **púngō, -gere** (3), **púpugī, -ctum,** to prick
pū́niō (4), to punish
68 **pūpílla, -ae** (*f*), orphan
64 **purgā́tiō, -ṓnis** (*f*), a cleaning
pū́rus, -a, -um, pure, spotless, clean
pútō (1), to think, consider

Q

54 **quācúmque,** wherever
55 **quadringentī, -ae, -a,** four hundred
quaérō, -rere (3), **-sī́vī, -sī́tum,** to seek, look for, ask (for)
65 **quāliscúmque, -iscúmque, -ecúmque,** of whatever kind
Quam . . . ! How . . . !
quam, than
quam (+ *superlative*), as . . . as possible
63 **quam tardíssimē,** as late as possible
quámquam, although
65 **quámvīs,** although
quándō, when
61 **sī quándō,** whenever
quántus, -a, -um, how big, how much
64 **quántum** (*adverb*), to what extent, to the extent to which
54 **Quā́rē . . . ?** For what reason . . . ? Why . . . ?
quā́rtus, -a, -um, fourth
quási, as if
66 **quátiō, -tere** (3), **-ssum,** to shake

quáttuor, four
56 **quemadmodum**, in what way, as
59 **quéror, -rī** (3), **-stus sum**, to moan, whine, complain
quī, quae, quod, who, which, that
Quī . . . ? Quae . . . ? Quod . . . ? What . . . ? Which . . . ?
54 **quía**, because, that
56 **quīcúmque, quaecúmque, quodcúmque**, whoever, whatever
quī́dam, quaédam, quóddam, a certain, (*pl*) some
quídem, indeed
nē . . . quídem, not even
quiḗscō, -ere (3), **quiḗvī, quiḗtum**, to rest
62 **quiḗtus, -a, -um**, at rest, inactive
60 **quīn**, (but) that, who . . . not
quī́nque, five
Quis . . . ? Quid . . . ? Who . . . ? What . . . ? Which . . . ?
67 (**sī**) **quis**: see **áliquis**
55 **quísquam, quícquam**, anyone, anything
61 **quísque, quaéque, quídque**, each
56 **quísquis, quícquid**, whoever, whatever
quō, there, to that place
Quō . . . ? Where . . . to?
55 **quod**, because, that
quóniam, since
quóque, also
quot, as many as
Quot . . . ? How many . . . ?
66 **quótiēns**, as often as, whenever
Quótus, -a, -um . . . ? Which (in numerical order) . . . ?

R

raéda, -ae (*f*), traveling carriage, coach
56 **rā́na, -ae** (*f*), frog
68 **rā́rus, -a, -um**, rare
63 **rátiō, -ṓnis** (*f*), reason
67 **raúcus, -a, -um**, hoarse
68 **recḗdō, -dere** (3), **-ssī, -ssum**, to withdraw, retire
62 **récēns, -ntis**, recent, fresh, untired
récitō (1), to read aloud, recite
60 **recognṓscō, -ṓscere** (3), **-ṓvī, -itum**, to recognize
63 **reconcíliō** (1), to reconcile, bring into harmony
67 **recordā́tiō, -ṓnis** (*f*), recollection
rḗctus, -a, -um, right, proper, upright, honest, straight
60 **rḗctē ésse**, to be all right
réddō, -ere (3), **-idī, -itum**, to give back, return
rédeō, -ī́re (*irreg.*), **-iī, -itum**, to return, go back
redū́cō, -cere (3), **-xī, -ctum**, to lead back, take back, bring back
réferō, -rre (*irreg.*), **réttulī, relā́tum**, to bring back
57 **reférre ad senā́tum**, to put a motion before the senate
62 **refúgiō, -úgere** (3), **-ū́gī**, to turn and run away, flee for safety
65 **rḗgnō** (1), to rule as king, reign
rḗgnum, -ī (*n*), kingdom
regrédior, -dī (3), **-ssus sum**, to go back, return
54 **religiṓsus, -a, -um**, religious
61 **réligō** (1), to hold in place, make fast, secure
relínquō, -ínquere (3), **-ī́quī, -íctum**, to leave, leave behind
60 **relíquus, -a, -um**, the rest of, the remaining
60 **relíquum est**, it remains (to do something)
61 **remáneō, -ḗre** (2), **-sī**, to remain
65 **remíttō, -íttere** (3), **-ī́sī, -íssum**, to send back
repéllō, -ere (3), **réppulī, repúlsum**, to drive off, drive back, beat back
61 **repentī́nus, -a, -um**, sudden
répetō, -ere (3), **-ī́vī, -ī́tum**, to seek again, return to
67 **repṓnō, -ṓnere** (3), **-ósuī, -ósitum**, to put back, repay
67 **réputō** (1), to think over, bear in mind, consider
68 **réquiēs, -ḗtis** (*f*), rest
56 **requiḗscō, -ḗscere** (3), **-ḗvī, -ḗtum**, to rest
67 **requī́rō, -rere** (3), **-sī́vī, -sī́tum**, to ask, inquire
rēs, réī (*f*), thing, matter, affair, situation
56 **rēs géstae**, deeds, exploits, history
57 **rēs pū́blica**, republic, state
rē vḗrā, really, actually
54 **resalū́tō** (1), to greet in return, return a greeting
55 **résecō, -cā́re** (1), **-cuī, -ctum**, to cut off, clip
resístō, -ístere (3), **-titī** (+ *dat.*), to resist, stand up to
56 **respíciō, -ícere** (3), **-éxī, -éctum**, to look round at
respóndeō, -dḗre (2), **-dī, -sum**, to answer, reply
55 **réstis, -is** (*f*), rope
57 **restítuō, -úere** (3), **-uī, -ū́tum**, to restore, reinstate
59 **retíneō, -ḗre** (2), **-uī, reténtum**, to hold back, keep
67 **retráctō** (1), to rework, revise

54 **rétrahō, -here** (3), **-xī, -ctum,** to pull back, bring back, restore
54 **retrōvérsus** (*adverb*), backwards
58 **revértor, -tī** (3), **-sus sum,** to turn back, return, come home
révocō (1), to recall, call back
rēx, rēgis (*m*), king
56 **ríguus, -a, -um,** watering, irrigating
rīma, -ae (*f*), crack
rīsus, -ūs (*m*), laughter, laugh, smile
ríxa, -ae (*f*), quarrel, brawl
57 **rogā́tor, -ṓris** (*m*), beggar
rógō (1), to ask
56 **rosā́rium, -ī** (*n*), rose garden, rose plantation
51 **róstrum, -ī** (*n*), beak, a ship's rammingbeak
58 **róstra, -ṓrum** (*n pl*), speaker's platform in the Forum, adorned with the beaks of captured enemy ships
ruī́na, -ae (*f*), ruin, collapse
57 **rū́mor, -ṓris** (*m*), rumor
58 **rúmpia, -ae** (*f*), pike, spear
rúmpō, rúmpere (3), **rūpī, rúptum,** to burst, break
rúrsus, again
58 **rūs, rū́ris** (*n*), country (as opposed to city)
rū́sticus, -a, -um, of or belonging to the country or farm
rū́sticus, -ī (*m*), peasant, farmer

S

56 **sácculus, -ī** (*m*), little sack, bag
65 **sacrāméntum, -ī** (*n*), oath
63 **saéculum, -ī** (*n*), reign, age
saépe, often
quam saepíssimē, as often as possible
62 **sagittā́rius, -ī** (*m*), archer, bowman
60 **sálūs, -ū́tis** (*f*), greetings, safety
salū́tō (1), to greet, welcome
sálvus, -a, -um, undamaged, all right, safe
59 **sánctitās, -ā́tis** (*f*), holiness, sanctity
63 **sā́nctus, -a, -um,** hallowed, august
64 **sápiēns, -ntis,** wise
59 **satélles, -itis** (*m*), follower, henchman, accomplice
sátis, enough
58 **saúcius, -a, -um,** wounded
61 **sáxum, -ī** (*n*), rock, stone
sceléstus, -a, -um, wicked
scélus, -eris (*n*), crime
54 **schḗma, -atis** (*n*) (Greek), figure of speech
55 **scī́licet,** obviously, of course, no doubt (sometimes ironic)
scíō (4), to know
58 **scrī́ba, -ae** (*m*), scribe, clerk
scrī́bō, -bere (3), **-psī, -ptum,** to write
56 **scúlpō, -pere** (3), **-psī, -ptum,** to sculpt, carve
sē, himself, herself, oneself, itself, themselves
67 **sēcḗdō, -dere** (3), **-ssī, -ssum,** to withdraw, retire
55 **sécō, -ā́re** (1), **-uī, -tum,** to cut, beat, flog
56 **secúndum** (+ *acc.*), beside, next to, according to
sed, but
sédeō, -ḗre (2), **sḗdī, séssum,** to sit
59 **sḗdēs, -is** (*f*), site, abode
57 **sḗdō** (1), to settle, calm
61 **sḗmis, -íssis** (*m*), a half
66 **sḗmita, -ae** (*f*), path
sémper, always
55 **sempitérnō,** forever
59 **sēmúncia, -ae** (*f*), one twenty-fourth
senā́tor, -ṓris (*m*), senator
senā́tus, -ūs (*m*), senate
57 **senā́tūs cōnsúltum,** decree of the senate
sénex, -is (*m*), old man
57 **senténtia, -ae** (*f*), motion, feeling, opinion
séntiō, -tī́re (4), **-sī, -sum,** to feel, notice, realize
sepéliō, -elī́re (4), **-elī́vī, -últum,** to bury
séptimus, -a, -um, seventh
sepúlc(h)rum, -ī (*n*), tomb
séquor, -quī (3), **-cū́tus sum,** to follow
serḗnus, -a, -um, clear, bright
64 **sḗrius** (*adverb*), too late
sérmō, -ṓnis (*m*), conversation, talk
sérvō (1), to save, keep, protect, take care of
sérvus, -ī (*m*), slave
55 **sēstertiā́rius, -a, -um,** worth one **sēstértius,** i.e., worthless
55 **sēstértius, -ī** (*m*) (*gen pl,* **sēstértiūm**), sestertius, coin worth four **ássēs**
64 **sevḗrus, -a, -um,** severe, harsh, heartless
56 **sḗvir, -irī** (*m*), member of a board of six
56 **sḗvir Augustā́lis,** a priest in charge of the worship of the emperor in provincial towns
56 **sēvirā́tus, -ūs** (*m*), the office of **sḗvir**
sī, if
sīc, thus, in this way
54 **síccitās, -ā́tis** (*f*), dryness, drought
63 **sī́dus, -eris** (*n*), star
59 **sígnifer, -erī** (*m*), standard-bearer, leader
67 **sígnō** (1), to affix a seal to, attest by affixing a seal to
sígnum, -ī (*n*), signal, sign
60 **síleō** (2), to be silent

símilis, -is, -e (+ *dat.*), like, similar (to)

68 **simplícitās, -ā́tis** (*f*), frankness, honesty

símul, together, at the same time

61 **simulā́crum, -ī** (*n*), image, statue

60 **sīn** (**sī + -ne**), but if, on the other hand

síne (+ *abl.*), without

60 **singulā́ris, -is, -e,** extraordinary, unique

54 **síngulī, -ae, -a,** single, individual, each and every one

siníster, -tra, -trum, left

66 **sínus, -ūs** (*m*), curve, bay

65 **sístō, -ere** (3), **stítī, státum,** to set up, establish

58 **sī́ve,** or rather

66 **sócculus, -ī** (*m*), low-heeled shoe worn by comic actors

59 **sócius, -ī** (*m*), ally

sōl, sṓlis (*m*), sun

58 **sōlā́cium, -ī** (*n*), comfort, consolation, relief

sóleō, -ḗre (2), **-itus sum,** to be accustomed, in the habit

sōlitū́dō, -inis (*f*), loneliness, solitude

57 **sṓlum** (*adverb*), only

57 **nōn sṓlum . . . sed étiam,** not only . . . but also

sṓlus, -a, -um, alone

63 **sólvō, -vere** (3), **-vī, -ū́tum,** to release, set free

sómnus, -ī (*m*), sleep

sórdidus, -a, -um, dirty

66 **spatiṓsus, -a, -um,** spacious

62 **spátium, -ī** (*n*), space

65 **spéciēs, -ḗī** (*f*), appearance, kind, type

59 **spectā́culum, -ī** (*n*), sight, spectacle

spectā́tor, -ṓris (*m*), spectator, onlooker

spēlúnca, -ae (*f*), cave

spḗrō (1), to hope

61 **spēs, -éī** (*f*), hope

59 **spī́rō** (**1**), to breathe, be alive

67 **spónda, -ae** (*f*), bed, couch

spōnsā́lia, -ium (*n pl*), betrothal

státim, immediately

státua, -ae (*f*), statue

64 **státuō, -úere** (3), **-uī, -ū́tum,** to lay down a rule, establish

57 **státus, -ūs** (*m*), state, condition, situation

stō, stā́re (1), **stétī, státum,** to stand

54 **stolā́ta, -ae** (*f*), woman dressed in a **stóla** (long robe)

55 **strāmentī́cius, -a, -um,** of straw

55 **strāméntum, -ī** (*n*), straw

55 **strā́tum, -ī** (*n*), blanket, saddlecloth, saddle

strépitus, -ūs (*m*), noise, din

54 **strī́deō, -ḗre** (2), **-ī,** to shriek, howl

54 **strī́dor, -ṓris** (*m*), a shrieking, howling

54 **strī́ga, -ae** (*f*), witch

stríngō, -ngere (3), **-nxī, -ctum,** to draw (a sword)

67 **strúēs, -is** (*f*), heap, pile

stúdeō (2) (+ *dat.*), to study, favor, support

63 **stultítia, -ae** (*f*), foolishness, folly

56 **suā́vis, -is, -e,** sweet, delightful

61 **subdū́cō, -cere** (3), **-xī, -ctum,** to pull from under, remove

58 **súbeō, -ī́re** (*irreg.*), **-iī, -itum,** to go under, undergo, endure, occur

súbitō, suddenly

55 **subolfáciō, -ere** (3), to perceive as if by smell, suspect

58 **subséllium, -ī** (*n*), bench

61 **súbsum, -ésse, súffuī** (+ *dat.*), to be under

62 **succḗdō, -dere** (3), **-ssī, -ssum** (+ *dat.*), to relieve, reinforce

57 **succíngō, -gere** (3), **-xī, -ctum,** to equip

61 **succúrrō, -rrere** (3), **-rrī, -rsum** (+ *dat.*), to help, aid

68 **sūdā́rium, ī** (*n*), towel

54 **sū́dō** (1), to sweat

68 **súfferō, súfferre** (*irreg.*), **sústulī, sublā́tum,** to take up

55 **súfflō** (1), to blow on, breathe on

68 **suffrā́gium, -ī** (*n*), vote, influence exerted on behalf of a candidate

66 **sulpurā́tus, -a, -um,** sulfured

sum, ésse (*irreg.*), **fúī,** to be

65 **súmma, -ae** (*f*), sum, total, full extent

55 **ad súmmam,** in sum, in short

57 **súmmē,** in the highest degree, very vigorously

62 **summōveō, -ovḗre** (2), **-ṓvī, -ṓtum,** to drive off, remove

súmmus, -a, -um, very great, the greatest, the top of . . .

sū́mō, -mere (3), **-mpsī, -mptum,** to take

56 **súper** (+ *acc.*), over, above

supérbus, -a, -um, proud, arrogant, magnificent

61 **supérior, -or, -us,** higher, more advanced (in age)

63 **súperō** (1), to overcome, defeat

65 **superstítiō, -ṓnis** (*f*), superstition

64 **supérsum, -ésse** (*irreg.*), **-fuī,** to remain, be left, survive

66 **supī́nus, -a, -um,** low-lying

61 **súpplex, -icis** (*m/f*), suppliant

65 **supplícium, -ī** (*n*), punishment

65 **súpplicō** (1), to offer worship to

55 **suppṓnō, -ṓnere** (3), **-ósuī, -ósitum,** to put in place of, substitute

67 **suprḗmus, -a, -um,** last, final, highest

súrgō, -rgere (3), **-rrḗxī, -rrḗctum,** to get up, rise

55 **súrsum** (*adverb*), up, high
63 **suscípiō, -ípere** (3), **-ḗpī, -éptum,** to accept, begin, undertake
65 **suspéctus, -a, -um,** suspect, suspected
64 **(in) suspḗnsō,** undecided, in suspense
68 **suspī́rium, -ī** (*n*), sigh
59 **sustíneō** (2), to withstand, check, support
súus, -a, -um, his, hers, one's, its, their (-own)

T

tabellā́rius, -ī (*m*), courier
tabérna, -ae (*f*), shop, tavern
56 **tábula, -ae** (*f*), board, tablet, gameboard
táceō (2), to be quiet, say nothing
63 **taédet, -ḗre** (2), **-sum est,** it makes one (*acc.*) tired of something (*gen.*)
66 **taédium, -ī** (*n*), weariness, boredom, annoyance
tā́lis, -is, -e, such, of this kind
tam, so
támen, however, nevertheless
54 **támquam,** like, as if, as
tándem, at last, at length
54 **tángō, -ere** (3), **tétigī, tā́ctum,** to touch
tántus, -a, -um, so great, so much
tántum (*adverb*), to such an extent, so much, only
tárdus, -a, -um, slow, late in coming
63 **quam tardíssimē,** as late as possible
58 **tárdius** (*adverb*), more slowly
55 **taúrus, -ī** (*m*), bull
61 **tḗlum, -ī** (*n*), weapon
temerā́rius, -a, -um, rash, reckless, bold
63 **témperō** (1), to control, rule, abstain, refrain
témplum, -ī (*n*), temple
témpus, -oris (*n*), time
61 **téndō, -dere** (3), **teténdī, -tum,** to stretch, extend
54 **ténebrae, -ā́rum** (*f pl*), darkness
téneō, -ḗre (2), **-uī, -tum,** to hold
66 **ténuis, -is, -e,** slender, narrow
67 **ter,** three times, thrice
térgum, -ī (*n*), back, rear
62 **ā térgō,** (from) behind
62 **térga vértere,** to turn tail, flee
66 **térō, -ere** (3), **trī́vī, trī́tum,** to rub, wear away
térra, -ae (*f*), earth, land
térror, -ṓris (*m*), terror, fear
55 **tertiā́rius, -ī** (*m*), gladiator substituted for one who has been killed
tértius, -a, -um, third
65 **tértiō,** (for) the third time
testāméntum, -ī (*n*), testament, will

66 **téxtilis, -is, -e,** woven
tímeō (2), to fear
tímor, -ṓris (*m*), fear
68 **títulus, -ī** (*m*), inscription
tóga, -ae (*f*), toga; sometimes symbolic of life in peacetime as opposed to war, of civil as opposed to military life, or of a formal as opposed to an informal life style
tóga virī́lis, plain white toga worn by adult men; its assumption at puberty was celebrated by a coming-of-age ceremony
tóllō, -ere (3), **sústulī, sublā́tum,** to lift, raise, pick up
68 **tóndeō, -ḗre** (2), **totóndī, -sum,** to shave
66 **tṓnsor, -ṓris** (*m*), barber
61 **torméntum, -ī** (*n*), torment, torture; war-machine for hurling missiles
tot, so many
tṓtus, -a, -um, all, the whole
65 **tractā́tus, -ūs** (*m*), investigation
57 **tracto** (1), to discuss, handle
trā́dō, -ere (3), **-idī, -itum,** to hand over, pass on (information), report
66 **tragoédia, -ae** (*f*), tragedy
tráhō, -here (3), **-xī, -ctum,** to drag, pull, draw out, prolong
54 **trāíciō, -ícere** (3), **-iḗcī, -iéctum,** to stab through, pierce
63 **tranquíllus, -a, -um,** tranquil, peaceful
trā́ns (+ *acc.*), across
66 **trā́nseō, -íre** (*irreg.*), **-iī, -itum,** to go across, go past, pass
55 **trecéntiēs,** three hundred times
trēs, trēs, tría, three
56 **tribū́nal, -ā́lis** (*n*), tribunal, magistrate's raised platform
57 **tribū́nus, -ī** (*m*), tribune
57 **tribū́nus plḗbis,** magistrate elected to protect the interests of the lower classes at Rome
62 **tribū́nus mī́litum,** one of the six senior officers of a Roman legion
61 **tríbuō, -úere** (3), **-uī, -ū́tum,** to allot, grant
61 **tríbus, -ūs** (*f*), tribe
triclī́nium, -ī (*n*), dining room
55 **tríduum, -ī** (*n*), three-day period
65 **triénnium, -ī** (*n*), three-year period
68 **tríēns, -ntis** (*m*), drinking cup holding one-third of a sextarius, or about five ounces
62 **tríplex, -icis,** triple
61 **trirḗmis, -is, -e,** having three oars to a bench
54 **trīstimṓnium, -ī** (*n*), sadness, sorrow
trī́stis, -is, -e, sad, gloomy, harsh

55 **trū́dō, -dere** (3), **-sī, -sum,** to push, shove (along)
66 **trúncus, -ī** (*m*), trunk (of the body), body
tū, you (sing.)
54 **túba, -ae** (*f*), trumpet
túbicen, -inis (*m*), trumpeter
62 **túeor, tuḗrī** (2), **túitus sum,** to look out for, protect
54 **tum,** at that moment, then
63 **túmeō** (2), to swell with anger
tumúltus, -ūs (*m*), uproar, din, commotion
54 **tunc,** then, at that time, in those days
túrba, -ae (*f*), crowd, mob
62 **túrma, -ae** (*f*), cavalry squadron of thirty men
62 **turmā́tim,** in squadrons
61 **túrris, -is** (*f*), tower, siege tower, dovecote
65 **tūs, tū́ris** (*n*), incense
57 **tū́tus, -a, -um,** safe
60 **tū́tō,** safely
túus, -a, -um, your (sing.)

U

56 **ūbértim,** abundantly, copiously
úbi, where, when
55 **ubī́que,** everywhere
54 **ū́dus, -a, -um,** wet, soaked
59 **ulcī́scor, -cī́scī, -tus sum,** to take revenge on, punish
64 **ū́llus, -a, -um,** any
últimus, -a, -um, last, least, most wretched
58 **últrā** (+ *acc.*), beyond
úmbra, -ae (*f*), shadow, shade
58 **úmerus, -ī** (*m*), upper arm
úmquam, ever
Únde . . . ? Where . . . from?
úndique, on all sides, from all sides
unguéntum, -ī (*n*), ointment, perfume, oil
55 **únguis, -is** (*m*), nail (of the hand or foot), claw
únguō, -guere (3), **-xī, -ctum,** to anoint, smear with oil
59 **ūnivérsus, -a, -um,** whole, entire
64 **in ūnivérsum,** in general
ū́nus, -a, -um, one
urbs, -bis (*f*), city
54 **urceā́tim,** by the pitcher, in buckets
58 **úrgeō, -ḗre** (2), **úrsī,** to press, insist
56 **úrna, -ae** (*f*), urn
56 **ū́rō, -ere** (3), **ússī, ústum,** to burn
59 **úsquam,** anywhere
63 **úsque,** up to, as far as
59 **ū́stor, -ṓris** (*m*), corpse burner
62 **ū́sus, -ūs** (*m*), use, need, requirement
ut (+ *indicative*), when, as
ut (+ *subjunctive*), so that, that, to
utérque, útraque, utrúmque, each (of two), both
59 **útinam,** would that, I wish that
55 **útique,** at any rate, at least
60 **ū́tor, -ī** (3), **ū́sus sum** (+ *abl.*), to use, take advantage of
úxor, -ṓris (*f*), wife

V

63 **vácō** (1), to be empty, free, have time
68 **vácuus, -a, -um,** empty
váldē, very, very much
váleō (2), to be strong, be well
62 **vállum, -ī** (*n*), palisade, stockade of wooden stakes
55 **várius, -a, -um,** particolored, spotted
55 **vávatō, -ṓnis** (*m*), doll
61 **véctis, -is** (*m*), lever, crowbar
veheménter, violently, vigorously, immensely, greatly
vehículum, -ī (*n*), (wheeled) vehicle
58 **véhō, -here** (3), **-xī, -ctum,** to carry, convey
63 **vḗlōx, -ṓcis,** swift, rapid
55 **vḗlum, -ī** (*n*), sail
véndō, -ere (3), **-idī, -itum,** to sell
59 **vḗneō, -ī́re** (4), **-iī, -itum,** to be sold
63 **venerā́tiō, -ṓnis** (*f*), veneration, homage
65 **véneror, -ā́rī** (1), **-ā́tus sum,** to venerate, worship
65 **vénia, -ae** (*f*), pardon
véniō, venī́re (4), **vḗnī, véntum,** to come
67 **vēr, -ris** (*n*), spring (the season)
vérberō (1), to beat
véreor, -ḗrī (2), **-itus sum,** to be afraid, fear
62 **vérsor, -ā́ri** (1), **-ā́tus sum,** to stay
vérsus, -ūs (*m*), verse, line (of poetry)
60 **vértō, -tere** (3), **-tī, -sum,** to turn
vḗrus, -a, -um, true
vḗrō, truly, indeed
rē vḗrā, really, actually
véscor, -ī (3) (+ *abl.*), to feed (on)
véster, -tra, -trum, your (pl.)
véstis, -is (*f*), clothing, garment
vétō, -ā́re (1), **-uī, -itum,** to forbid, prohibit
vétus, -eris, old
64 **vetústus, -a, -um,** of long standing
véxō (1), to annoy, harass
vía, -ae (*f*), road, street
viā́tor, -ṓris (*m*), traveler
63 **více** (*abl., irreg.*), place, role, duty
vīcī́nus, -a, -um, neighboring, nearby

63 **vicíssim,** in turn, in exchange
58 **vicissitū́dō, -inis** (*f*), change, vicissitude
victṓria, -ae (*f*), victory
64 **vī́cus, -ī** (*m*), side street, alley
vídeō, vidḗre (2), **vī́dī, vī́sum,** to see
víduus, -a, -um, deprived, widowed
68 **vígil, -ilis,** awake, sleepless
vígilō (1), to be watchful, stay awake
vīgíntī, twenty
67 **vī́lica, -ae** (*f*), overseer's wife
vī́licus, -ī (*m*), overseer, farm manager
vī́lla, -ae (*f*), farmhouse, country house, villa
61 **vī́men, -inis** (*n*), wicker, reed
víncō, -ere (3), **vīcī, víctum,** to win, conquer, overcome
vī́nea, -ae (*f*), vines, vineyard, movable shelter for siege-workers
vīnum, -ī (*n*), wine
víolō (1), to harm, violate
vir, vírī (*m*), man, grown man
66 **víreō** (2), to be green, flourish
vírgō, -inis (*f*), maiden
virī́lis, -is, -e, a man's, of a man
tóga virī́lis: see **tóga**
59 **vírtūs, -ū́tis** (*f*), courage, determination, strength
vīs, vim (*acc.*), **vī** (*abl.*) (*f*), force, (*pl*) strength

68 **vī́sō, -ere** (3), **-ī,** to go to see, visit
vī́ta, -ae (*f*), life
63 **vítium, -ī** (*n*), fault, vice
vī́tō (1), to avoid
54 **vítulus, -ī** (*m*), calf
vī́vō, -vere (3), **-xī, -ctum,** to live
56 **vī́vus, -a, -um,** alive, living
vix, scarcely, with difficulty, only just
vócō (1), to call
55 **vólō** (1), to fly
vólō, vélle (*irreg.*), **vóluī,** to wish, want, be willing
58 **volúntās, -ā́tis** (*f*), will, willingness, consent
62 **volúptās, -ā́tis** (*f*), pleasure
vōs, you (pl.)
vōx, vṓcis (*f*), voice
65 **vṓtum, -ī** (*n*), vow
58 **vúlgus, -ī** (*n*), the common people, mob, rabble
vúlnerō (1), to wound
vúlnus, -eris (*n*), wound
54 **vúlpēs, -is** (*f*), fox

X

66 **xýstum, -ī** (*n*), (Greek word) shaded walkway

PROPER NAMES

Alcínous, -ī (*m*), legendary king encountered by Odysseus (*Od.* VI–VIII) (66C:10)
Anícius Máximus, Roman governor of Bithynia before Pliny (64:5)
Antónius, M. (Marc Antony), member of second Triumvirate and paramour of Cleopatra (Ex. 62c)
(Vía) Áppia, Rome's first great highway, built by Appius Claudius Caecus (312 B.C.), from Rome to the end of the Italian peninsula at Brundisium (58 *passim*)
Apūlia, modern Puglia, province of SE Italy, just above the "heel" of the Italian "boot" (60:25)
Arícia, town 16 miles S. of Rome on the Appian Way (58:3)
Asc(u)lānus, -ī (*m*), a resident of Asculum (61, p. 70)
Ásia, Asia Minor, modern Turkey (54:7)
Átticus, T. Pompōnius, close friend and correspondent of Cicero (60:12)
Augústus, first emperor of Rome (27 B.C.–A.D. 14) (63)
Avītus, Iūnius, young friend of Pliny (68B:2)
Bāiānus, -a, -um, belonging to the resort town of Baiae near Naples (66D:2)
Básilus, L. Minúcius, officer under Caesar in Gaul and one of his assassins (Ex. 62d)
Bíbulus, M., Caesar's colleague in the consulship of 59 B.C., proposer of Pompey's sole consulship in 52 B.C. (57:23)
Bílbilis, home town of the poet Martial in NE Spain (67C:3)
Bírria, -ae (*m*), a gladiator and henchman of Milo (58:10)
Bīthȳnus, -ī (*m*), a Bithynian, inhabitant of Bithynia in Asia Minor (64:2)
Bonōnia, modern Bologna, city in Italy (61, p. 71)
Bōtérdum, an unsophisticated village in NE Spain (67C:5)
Bovíllae, -ārum (*f pl*), a town S. of Rome on the Appian Way (58:3)
Bovillānus, -a, -um, of or belonging to Bovillae (58:14)
Brundísium, modern Brindisi, town in the "heel" of the Italian peninsula, port of embarkation to Greece (60:29)
Brūtus, D. Iūnius, one of Caesar's officers in Gaul (61:22)
Caésar, -aris, used generically of "the Emperor" (56S:4)
Caésar, C. Iūlius (100–44 B.C.), general, statesman, author of commentaries on the Gallic and civil wars, cos. 59 B.C. (62 *passim*)
Caesariānus, -ī (*m*), a soldier or supporter of C. Iulius Caesar (Ex. 62c)
Camíllus, a friend of Cicero (60:12)
Cáppadox, -ocis (*m*), a Cappadocian, inhabitant of Cappadocia in Asia Minor (54S:5)
Céltibēr, -rī (*m*), inhabitant of Celtiberia (region of NE Spain) (67C:5)
Charidēmus, Greek freedman, **paedagōgus** to the poet Martial (68C:1)
Chíus, -a, -um, Chian, of Chios (island off coast of Asia Minor), famous for luxurious living (54S:2)
Cícerō, M. Túllius (106–43 B.C.), statesman, orator, author of philosophical and rhetorical works and over 900 letters, cos. 63 B.C. (Part II *passim*)
Clōdia, sister of P. Clodius and mistress of the poet Catullus (58S:9)
Clōdiānus, -ī (*m*), a supporter of P. Clodius (58S:9)
Clōdius (P. Clōdius Púlcher), political strongman for the Caesarian faction, brother of the notorious Clodia; as tribune of the plebs in 58 B.C., responsible for Cicero's exile (Part II *passim*)
Clōdius, Sex., agent of P. Clodius, probably his freedman (58:29)
Dācius, -ī (*m*), inhabitant of Dacia (modern Rumania) (Ex.63c)
Dolābélla, P. Cornēlius, a Caesarian, Cicero's son-in-law (60:6)
Échion, -ōnis (*m*), a rag dealer, one of Trimalchio's guests (55:1)
Eudāmus, a gladiator and henchman of Milo (58:9)
Faústa, wife of Milo (58:7)
Fortūnáta, a freedwoman, wife of Trimalchio (56:21)
Fūfius, M., a friend of Milo (58:8)
Fúlvia, wife of Clodius (58:23)

Ganymḗdēs, -is (*m*), one of Trimalchio's guests in the *Cena* (54:1)
Germā́nicus, a surname of (among others) the emperor Domitian (66A:3)
Glýcō, -ṓnis (*m*), a deceived husband, gossiped about by Trimalchio's guests (55:14)
Habínnas, -ae (*m*), a stonemason, one of Trimalchio's guests (56:8)
Hermógenēs, -is (*m*), father-in-law of Glyco (55:17)
Hispā́nia, -ae (*f*), Spain (61:1)
Hispā́nus, -a, -um, Spanish (66B:7)
Hypsaéus, P. Plaútius, candidate for consul, 53 B.C. (57:1)
Iā́nus, -ī (*m*), patron god of gates, doors, and the month of January (66C:4)
Ī́sis, -idis (*f*), Egyptian goddess worshiped in the Greco-Roman world (64, p. 95)
Iúppiter, Ióvis (*m*), king of the gods (54:25)
Labiḗnus, T., principal lieutenant of Caesar in Gaul (Ex. 62c)
Lānúvium, Milo's home town, about 20 miles S. of Rome (58:1)
Lārī́sa, town in N. Greece near Pharsalus (62:34)
Lā́rius (lácus), modern Lake Como in N. Italy (66D:1)
Laurentī́num, -ī (*n*), a country estate near Laurentum (67D:2)
Mammaéa, -ae (*m*), popular small-town politician discussed in the *Cena* (55:19)
Mā́nēs, -ium (*m pl*), the deified spirits of the dead (68D:1)
Marcélla, a Spanish woman, friend and patron of the poet Martial (66C:8)
Marcéllus, M. Claúdius, cos. 51 B.C., a prominent Optimate (58S:1)
Martialis, M. Valerius, Roman writer of epigrams, from Spain (A.D. 40–104) (Ex. 66b)
Massília, modern Marseilles, on the Mediterranean coast of France (59S:5)
Massiliénsis, -is (*m/f*), a Massiliote, resident of Massilia (61:14)
Mílō, T. Ánnius, political strongman for the Optimates, rival and murderer of the Caesarian Clodius (Part II *passim*)
Nausícaā, daughter of King Alcinous (66C:9)
Nerōniā́nus, -a, -um, belonging to Nero, Roman emperor A.D. 54–68 (66B:6)
Nérva, Roman emperor A.D. 96–98 (Ex. 63e)
Nīcaéa, city in Bithynia (in Asia Minor) (64:17)
Nīcomḗdia, capital of Bithynia (in Asia Minor) (64:17)
Norbā́nus, unpopular small-town politician discussed in the *Cena* (55:20)
Ōrcīniā́nus, -a, -um, belonging to Orcus (the underworld), pertaining to death (67A:7)
Paéstum, town on the Italian coast south of Naples (66C:3)
Petraítēs, -is (*m*), a famous gladiator of the 1st century A.D. (56:11)
Pharsā́lus, -ī (*f*), town in N. Greece, site of the final defeat of Pompey by Caesar in 48 B.C. (Ex. 62b)
Pláncus, T. Munā́tius, tribune of the plebs 53 B.C., a partisan of Pompey (57:12)
Plátea, an unsophisticated village in NE Spain (67C:5)
Plínius (C. Plínius Caecílius Secúndus), lawyer, statesman, and writer of the Imperial period (A.D. 62–114) (Part IV *passim*)
Pompēiā́nus, -ī (*m*), a Pompeian, partisan of Pompey the Great (Ex. 60c)
Pompḗius (C. Pompḗius Mágnus), general and statesman of the late Republic, Caesar's most powerful rival (57 *passim* and Part III *passim*)
Pompṓnius (60:12), (see Atticus)
Pónticus, -ī (*m*), an inhabitant of Pontus in Asia Minor (64:2)
(Basílica) Pórcia, Rome's oldest basilica, built by the censor M. Porcius Cato in 184 B.C. (58:31)
Safínius, a small-town politician mentioned in the *Cena* (54:7)
Scīpiō, Q. Metéllus, candidate for consul in 53 B.C., father-in-law of Pompey (57:1)
Spársus, a wealthy friend of Martial (66B:1)
Súlla, L. Cornḗlius, dictator 81–79 B.C., an extreme Optimate and father-in-law of Milo (58:7)
Sulpícius, Sérvius, interrex who appointed Pompey sole consul in 52 (57:24)
Teídius, Sex., Roman senator who brought Clodius's corpse back to Rome (58:19)
Teréntia, wife of Cicero (60:1)
Thraex (Thrax), -cis (*m*), Thracian, inhabitant of Thrace in N. Greece; also a gladiator with Thracian-style equipment (62:20; 55:25)
Títus, aedile of the town where the *Cena* takes place (55:8)
Trāiā́nus, M. Úlpius, Roman emperor A.D. 98–117 (Part IV *passim*)

Trebónius, C., Caesar's lieutenant (later one of his assassins) who conducted the siege of Massilia in 49 B.C. (61:1)

Trimálchiō (C. Pompéius Trimálchiō Maecēnātiā́nus), nouveau-riche freedman, host of the banquet described in the *Cena Trimalchionis* (56:1)

Tullíola (diminutive of Tullia), daughter of Cicero (60:1)

Týrius, -a, -um, pertaining to Tyre, center of the purple-dye industry; hence, purple, luxurious, extravagant (68C:11)

Vāriā́nus, -a, -um, pertaining to P. Quintilius Varus, Roman general who suffered a disastrous defeat in Germany in A.D. 9 (61s, p. 71)

ACKNOWLEDGMENTS

The authors and publisher are grateful to the following for permission to reproduce photographs: Alinari/Art Resource, New York, for pages 23, 47, 55a, 82, 91, 112; The Bettman Archive, New York, for page 55c; the Trustees of the British Museum for pages 15, 79, 86; the Vindolanda Trust, the Chesterholm Museum for page 123a; Frederick Lewis, New York, for page 83; Ron Palma for page 55b; the Romisch-Germanisches Museum, Cologne, for page 123c; the Royal Commission on Historical Monuments, London, for page 123b.

The drawings that appear on pages 6, 63, 70, 71, 75, and 118 of this book were done by Claudia Karabaic Sargent.

For literary extracts we would like to credit the following individuals and/or sources:

pages 33, 41, and 54: Professor James S. Ruebel, Iowa State University; page 36: Casson, "And Never Say No—Politics as usual in Ancient Rome," Smithsonian, Oct. 1984; page 79: Workman, *They Saw It Happen in Classical Times*, Basil Blackwell, Oxford, 1965; page 80: Warner, *Fall of the Roman Republic: Plutarch's Life of Pompey*, Penguin, Baltimore, 1964; page 81: Lewis and Reinhold, *Roman Civilization, Sourcebook II: The Empire*, Harper & Row, 1966; pages 83 and 101: Radice, *Pliny, Letters and Panegyricus*, Harvard University Press, Cambridge, 1975.